A translation with photographic images of
the premier anthology of Japanese poetry

Man'yō Luster

Ian Hideo Levy
Hakudo Inoue
Kazuya Takaoka

Man'yō Luster

Photographs copyright © 2002 Hakudo Inoue
English Text copyright © 2002 Ian Hideo Levy
Text copyright © 2002 Susumu Nakanishi
Book and cover design © 2002 Kazuya Takaoka
Published by PIE BOOKS

All rights reserved. No part of this publication
may be reproduced in any form or by any means,
graphic, electronic or mechanical, including
photocopying and recording by an information
storage and retrieval system, without permission
in writing from the publisher.

PIE BOOKS
2-32-4, Minami-Otsuka, Toshima-ku,
Tokyo 170-0005 JAPAN
Tel: +81-3-5395-4811 Fax: +81-3-5395-4812
http://www.piebooks.com
e-mail: editor@piebooks.com
e-mail: sales@piebooks.com

ISBN4-89444-186-1 C0072
Printed in Japan

万葉集

リービ英雄　井上博道　高岡一弥

The *Man'yōshu* is Japan's first anthology of poetry. It is possibly the greatest single collection of lyric poetry in classical world literature. As its name, literally "The Collection of Ten Thousand Leaves" suggests, this work is the summation, the totality of poetic expression from the first golden age of Japanese culture. Shortly after the turn of the eighth century A.D., Japan saw the rise of a sophisticated and cosmopolitan urban center, the great capital of Nara. And yet the sensibility of the courtiers who lived among the temples and palaces which lined Nara's broad avenues was informed by a legacy of animism, a sense that nature itself, in all its details, was somehow magically alive.

The *Man'yōshu* includes the works of hundreds of poets, from emperors to beggars. The range of expression is extremely broad. There are ritual poems in celebration of the emperor and stately public "laments" on imperial demise. Alongside these are intensely private expressions of love and erotic longing; poems of travel in which the courtier leaves behind the "firmly pillared" capital for the wilderness; poems of urban wit and sophistication; and poems in which the animistic richness of nature is transformed into verbal landscapes of breathtaking power and beauty. Many of the poems display rich visual imagery, a dynamic, at times almost kinetic, use of natural phenomena as the material of expression. All of

nature was a source of visual metaphor. This makes these ancient works eminently translatable — the core of sensibility seems "contemporary." There is a luster to these thirteen-hundred year old Japanese poems which makes its appear as if they had been written yesterday.

Here is a selection of the best of the *Man'yōshu*, combined with images by Japan's most eminent living photographer of the landscape which inspired "the ten thousand leaves." *Man'yō Luster* is a fusion of words and images, a double rendering of an archaic vision for the contemporary world.

Ian Hideo Levy

万葉の艶

　日本文学の書き手になる前に、ぼくは日本文学の読み手だった。二十年近く、日本とアメリカの間を行ったり来たりして、その間に日本文学を読みつづけた。二十世紀の詩と小説から始まって、それから古典文学も、すこしずつ、読めるようになった。日本語の引力によって古い方へ古い方へとさかのぼり、いつの間にか万葉集にたどりついた。

　万葉集にたどりついたとき、逆にもう一つの「現代文学」に出合ったという不思議な感じがした。

　万葉集は、他の時代のどんな日本文学より、新鮮だった。日本語がはじめて書かれたときの、その日本語によって書かれた世界には、圧倒的な力と、スケールと、鮮やかさがあった。

　日本でつづられた最も古いことばが、新しい。千三百年が経って、あたかもきのう書かれたと錯覚させるように、新しい。

　万葉集を最初に読みだしたとき、ぼくは日本にいたのかアメリカにいたのかは、覚えていない。読みだしてからしばらくして、万葉集の文庫本をリュックに入れて奈良から、山の辺の道を経て、明日香までひとりで歩いた。そして、そのような旅を経験してからまたアメリカにもどり、プリンストン大学やスタンフォード大学の研究室で大和路の風景をじっくりと思いだした。その風景の中に生きた歌人たちが創った数々の比喩と対句と、枕詞、その風景を何百何千もの長歌と短歌に結晶

させた膨大なアンソロジーを、おどろきながら、読みつづけた。大和路から遠く離れた、ニュージャージ州、カリフォルニア州、北米大陸の異質な風景の中で、あるときから日本の古代のことばをアメリカの現代のことばに翻訳するようになった。

翻訳しても翻訳しても、おどろきは消えなかった。

そして、翻訳してみると、おそらくは多くの日本人が想像している以上に、万葉集は「外」のことばにも伝わる、ということが分かった。

あをによし寧楽の京都は咲く花の
　　　　　にほふがごとく今盛りなり

という日本語が

The capital at Nara,
beautiful in green earth,
flourishes now
like the luster
of the flowers in bloom.

となる。花が「にほふ」。花が輝く。花には艶がある。ことばの艶、ことばのlusterが千三百年が経っても消えない。

万葉の艶は、英語にも出る。英語に出たとき、万葉集は、人類の古代から受けつがれている最大の抒情詩集、というもう一つの像を結ぶ。

万葉集は、新しい。

　　　　　　　　　　　　　リービ英雄

Man'yō Luster

万葉集

Poem by Emperor Yūryaku

Girl with your basket,
   with your pretty basket,
with your shovel,
   with your pretty shovel,
gathering shoots on the hillside here,
I want to ask your home.
Tell me your name!
This land of Yamato,
   seen by the gods on high—
it is all my realm,
in all of it I am supreme.
I will tell you
my home and my name.

一

天皇の御製歌（雄略天皇）
おほみうた

籠もよ　み籠持ち　掘串もよ　み掘串持ち　この岳に　菜摘ま
こ　　　こ　　　　ふくし　　　ふくし　　　　　　をか　　なつ
す児　家聞かな　名告らさね　そらみつ　大和の国は　おしな
　　　　　　　の　　　　　　　　　　やまと
べて　われこそ居れ　しきなべて　われこそ座せ　われこそは
　　　　　　　を　　　　　　　　　　　　　ま
告らめ　家をも名をも
の

籠（かご）よ、美しい籠を持ち、篦（へら）よ、美しい篦を手に、この岡に菜を摘む娘よ。あなたはどこの家の娘か。名は何という。そらみつ大和の国は、すべてわたしが従えているのだ。すべてわたしが支配しているのだ。わたしこそ明かそう。家がらも、わが名も。

Poem by Emperor Jomei when he climbed Kagu Hill to view the land

Many are the mountains of Yamato,
but I climb heavenly Kagu Hill
    that is cloaked in foliage,
and stand on the summit
to view the land.
    On the plain of land,
smoke from the hearths rises, rises.
    On the plain of waters,
gulls rise one after another.
A splendid land
    is the dragonfly island,
the land of Yamato.

二

天皇の、香具山に登りて望国したまひし時の
御製歌（舒明天皇）

大和には　群山あれど　とりよろふ　天の香具山　登り立ち
国見をすれば　国原は　煙立つ立つ　海原は　鷗立つ立つ
まし国そ　蜻蛉島　大和の国は

大和には多くの山がある　とりわけてりっぱに
装（よそお）っている天
の香具山、その頂に登り
立って国見をすると、国
の国は。

土には炊煙がしきりに立
ち、海上には鷗が翔（か
け）りつづけている。
美しい国よ、蜻蛉島大和

Envoy to poem of the three hills by Nakatsu Ōe

This night,
when I have watched the sun
plunge through the long, furled
        banner of clouds
            into the sea,
let the moon shine clear!

一五
中大兄の三山の歌一首　に付随する反歌

わたつみの豊旗雲に入日射し今夜の月夜さやけかりこそ

海上豊かになびく雲に落日が輝き、今夜の月は清らかであってほしい。

Poem by Emperor Temmu

On Mimiga Peak
in beautiful Yoshino
snow was falling,
   unbounded by time,
rain was falling,
   without interval.
The road that I have come,
   deep in longing
   with every bend,
like the snow,
   unbounded by time,
like the rain,
   without interval -
O that mountain road!

二五
天皇の御製歌（天武天皇）

み吉野の　耳我の嶺に　時なくそ　雪は降りける　間なくそ
雨は零りける　その雪の　時なきが如　その雨の　間なきが如
隈もおちず　思ひつつぞ来し　その山道を

吉野連山の耳我の山には、絶え間ないように、道を時しれず雪が降りしきる　曲がるごとに物思いを重という。間断なく雨が降ねながら辿って来たことるという。その雪や雨のだ。その山道を。

*Poem by Emperor Temmu, at the time
of his procession to Yoshino*

The good ones of the past
found Yoshino good,
and often had a good look,
and spoke good of it.
Have a good look, my good one,
have a good look.

二七

天皇の、吉野の宮に幸しし時の御製歌(天武天皇)

よき人のよしとよく見てよしと言ひし吉野よく見よよき人よく見つ

りっぱな人がよい処としてよく見て「よし(の)」といった。この吉野を、よく見るがいい。りっぱな人も良く見たことだ。

from
*Poem written by Kakinomoto Hitomaro when
he passed the ruined capital at Ōmi*

Though I hear
this was the great palace,
though they tell me
here were the mighty halls,
now it is rank with spring grasses.
Mist rises, and the spring sun is dimmed.
Gazing on the ruins of the great palace,
its walls once thick with wood and stone,
I am filled with sorrow.

二九

近江の荒れたる都を過ぎし時に、
柿本朝臣人麿の作れる歌　より

大宮は　此処と聞けども　大殿は　此処と言へども　春草の
繁く生ひたる　霞立ち　春日の霧れる　ももしきの　大宮処
見れば悲しも

大宮はここだと聞くが、
また大殿はここだと人は
いうが、春草がいたずら
に生い繁り、たちこめて
春日の霞が煙っている、
百しきの大宮のあたりを
見ると悲しいことだ。

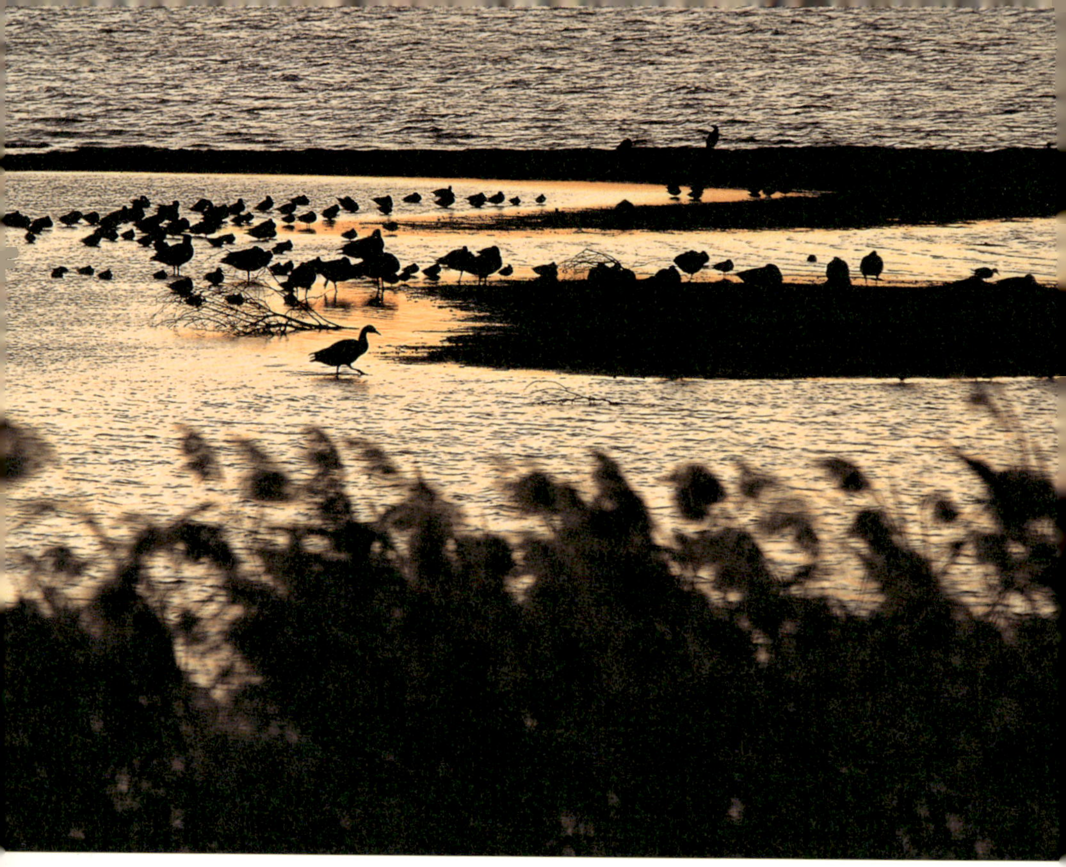

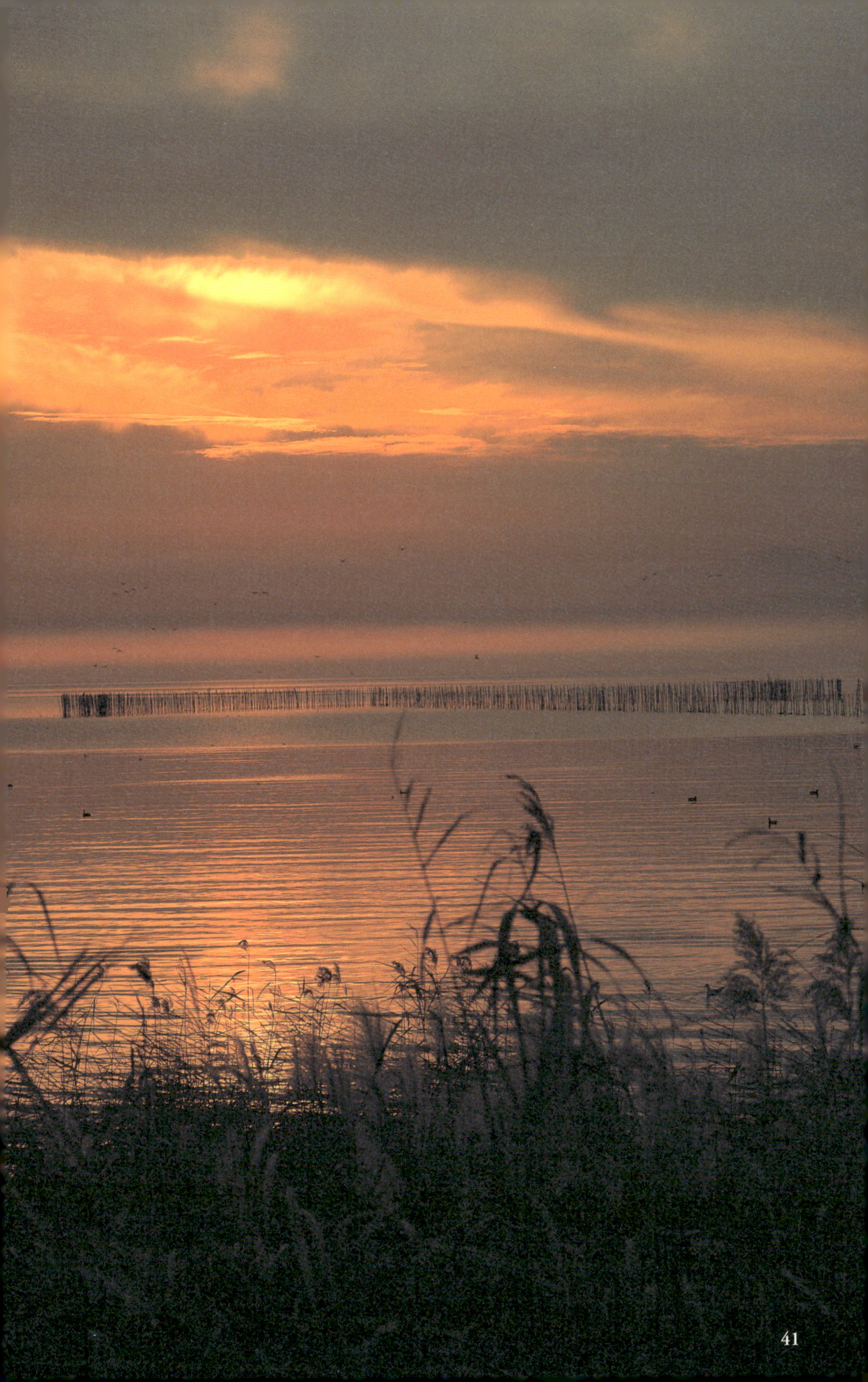

Poem written by Kakinomoto Hitomaro at the time of the imperial procession to the palace at Yoshino

Many are the lands under heaven
and the sway of our Lord,
sovereign of the earth's eight corners,
but among them her heart
finds Yoshino good
for its crystal riverland
among the mountains,
and on the blossom-strewn
fields of Akitsu
she drives the firm pillars of her palace.

And so the courtiers of the great palace,
its ramparts thick with stone,
line their boats

to cross the morning river,
race their boats
across the evening river.
Like this river
never ending,
like these mountains
commanding ever greater heights,
the palace by the surging rapids —
though I gaze on it, I do not tire.

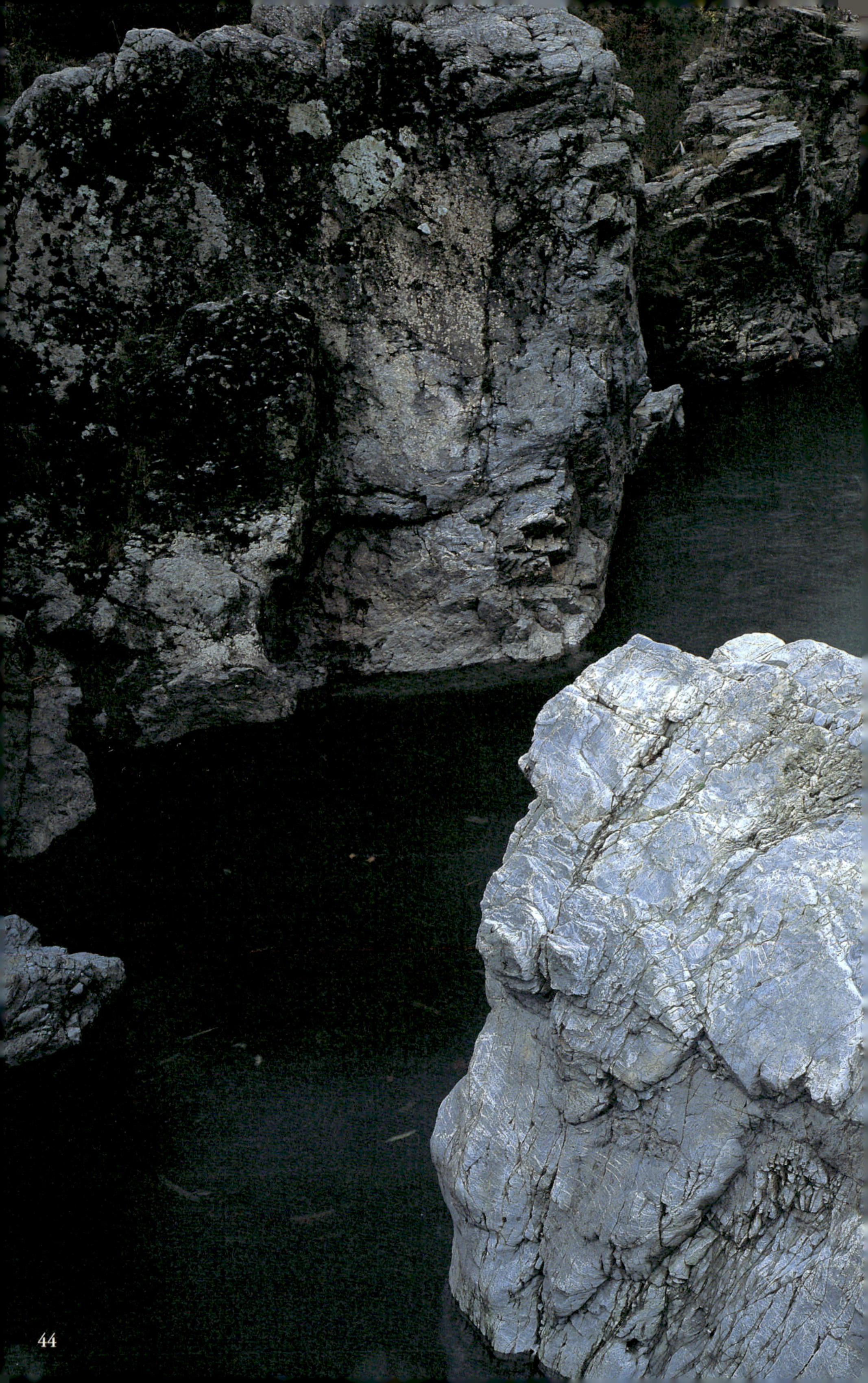

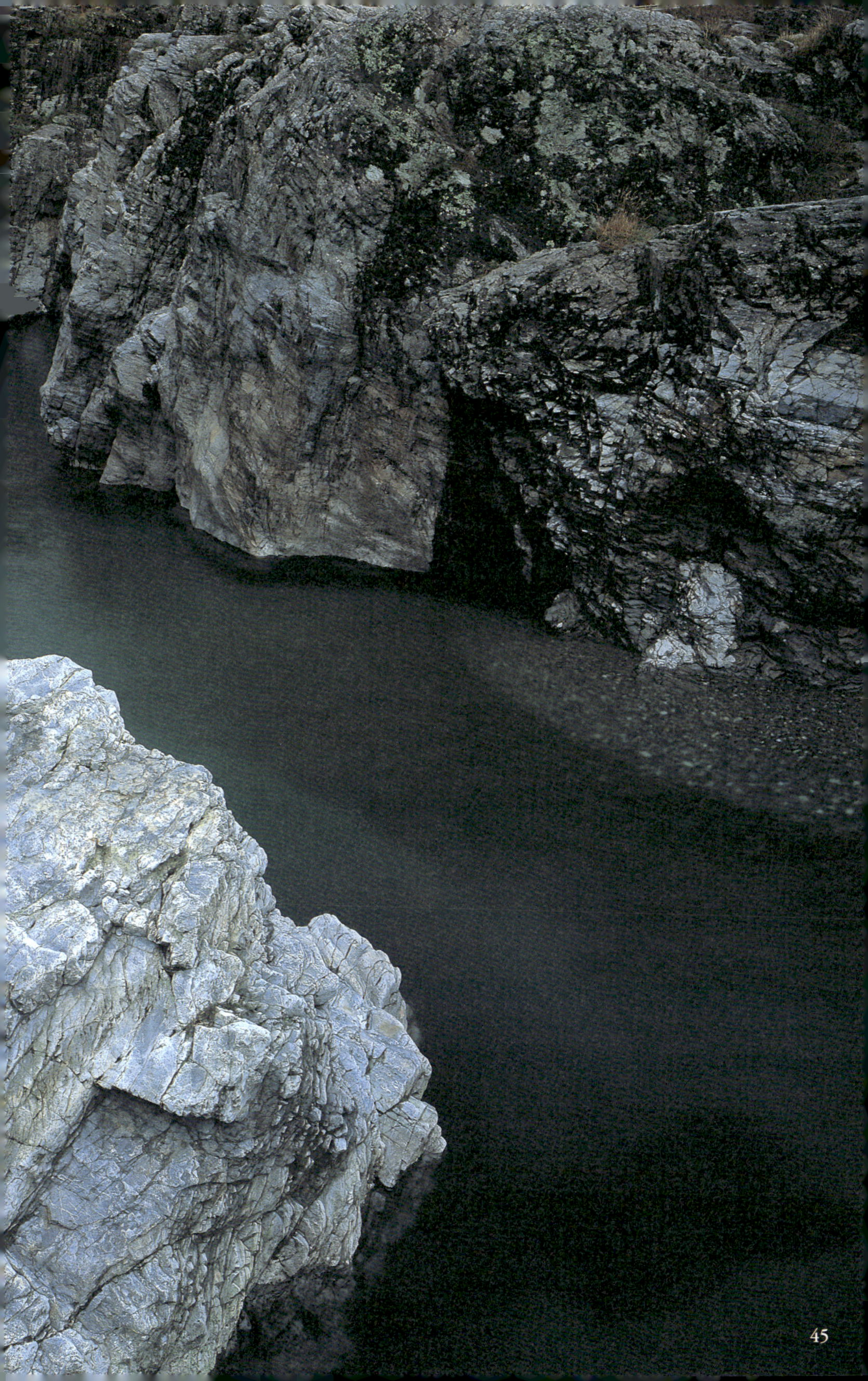

は　船並めて　朝川渡り　舟競ひ　夕河渡る　この川の　絶ゆることなく　この山の　いや高知らす　水激つ　滝の都は　見れど　飽かぬかも

あまねく国土を治めるわが天皇が統治なさる天下に、国々は多くあるけれども、山も川も清らかな河内として、御心をよしとなさる吉野の国の、花の散る秋津の野のほとりに、宮殿の柱も太く君臨なさると、百しきの大宮人は船を連ね競（きそ）い合って朝も夕も川を渡ってはなやぐ。この川の絶えることのないように、この山が高いように、ますます永遠に高々と統治なさる、この激流のほとばしる滝の宮居は、いつまでも見あきないことだ。

吉野の宮に幸しし時に、柿本朝臣人麿の作れる歌

やすみしし　わが大君の　聞し食す　天の下に　国はしも　多さはにあれども　山川の　清き河内と　御心を　吉野の国の　花散らふ　秋津の野辺に　宮柱　太敷きませば　百磯城の　大宮人

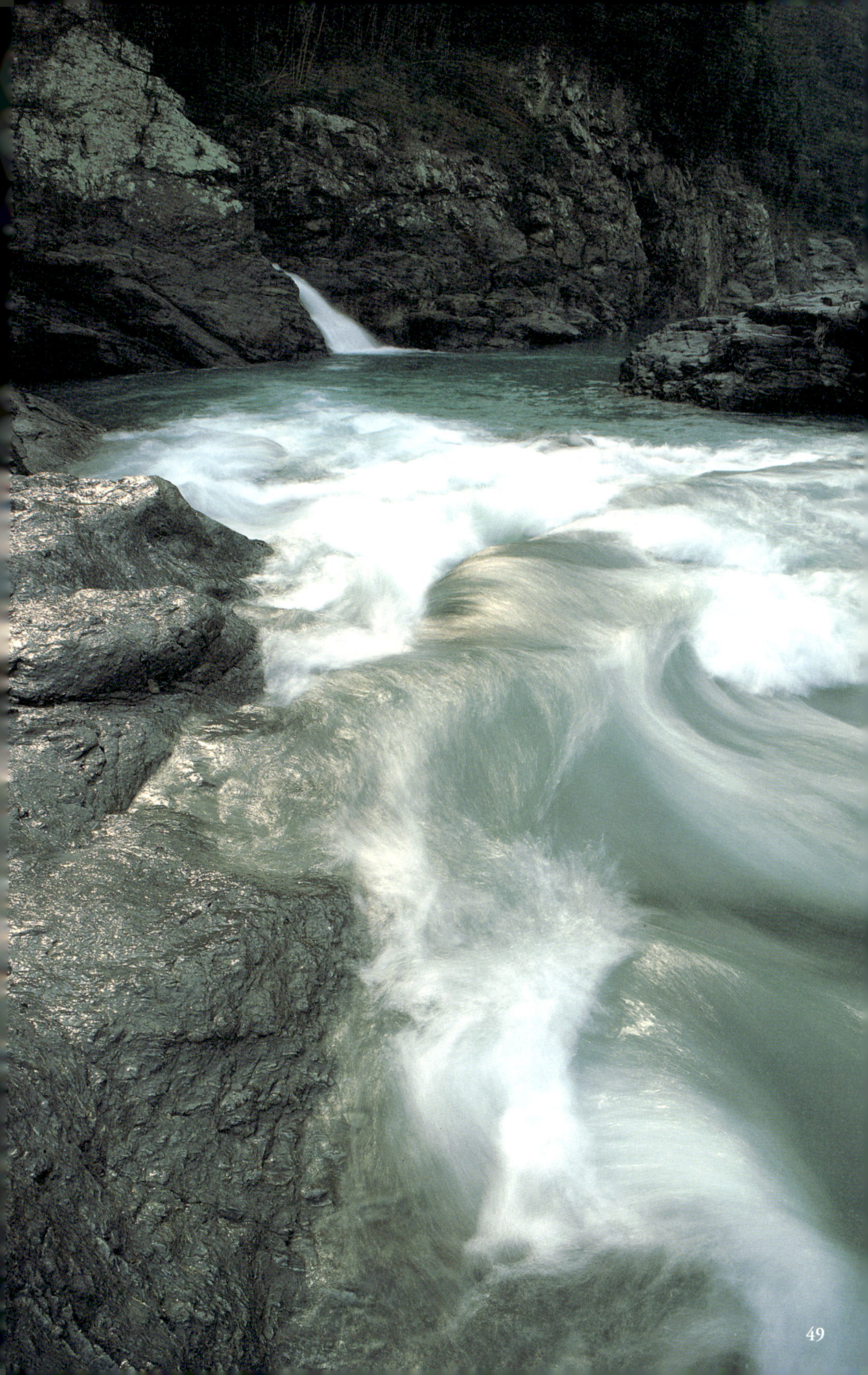

By Kakinomoto Hitomaro, when Crown Prince Karu sojourned on the fields of Aki

On the eastern fields
I can see the flames of morning rise.
Turning around,
I see the moon sink in the west.

48

四八

軽皇子の安騎(あき)の野に宿りましし時に、
柿本朝臣人麿の作れる歌　に付随する短歌

東(ひむがし)の野に炎(かぎろひ)の立つ見えてかへり見すれば月傾(かたぶ)きぬ

東方の野の果てに曙光がさしそめる。ふりかえると西の空に低く下弦の月が見える。

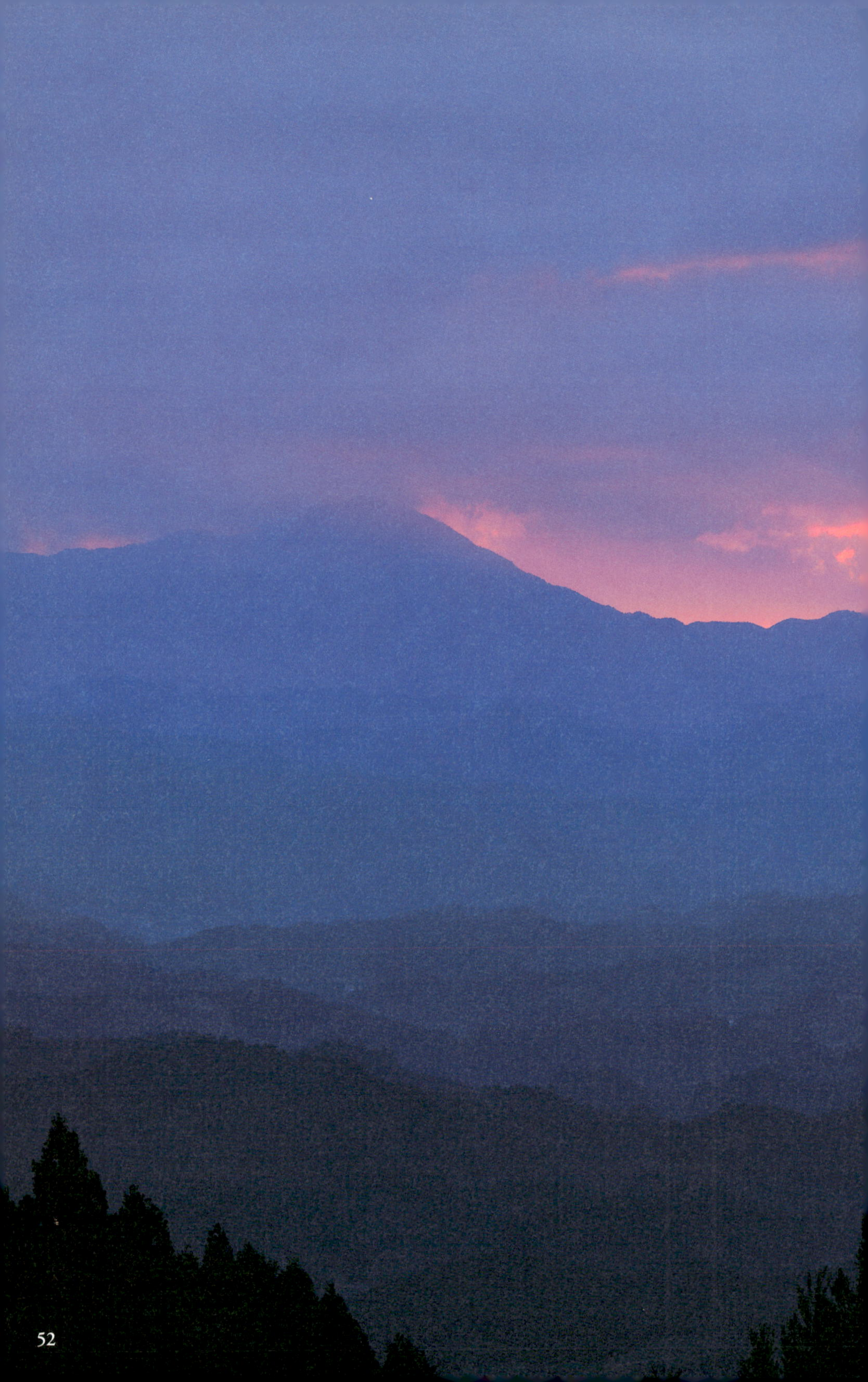

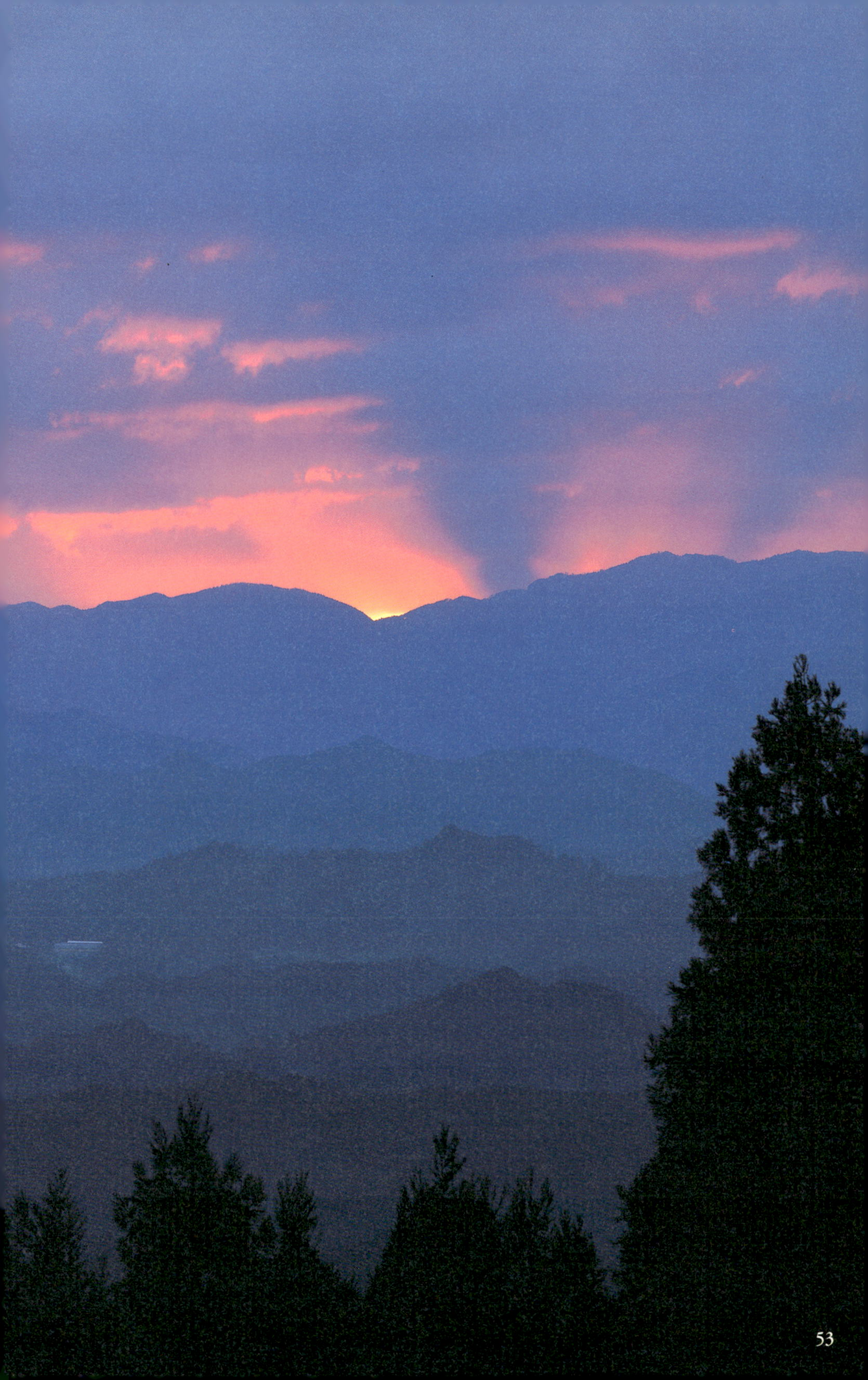

The time—
when the Crown Prince,
   Peer of the Sun,
lined his horses and set out
on the imperial hunt—
comes and faces me.

四九

日並(ひなみし)皇子の命(みこと)の馬並(な)めて御猟(みかり)立たしし時は来向かふ

日並皇子の命が馬を連ねて今しも出猟なさろうとした、あの払暁の時刻が今日もやがて来る。

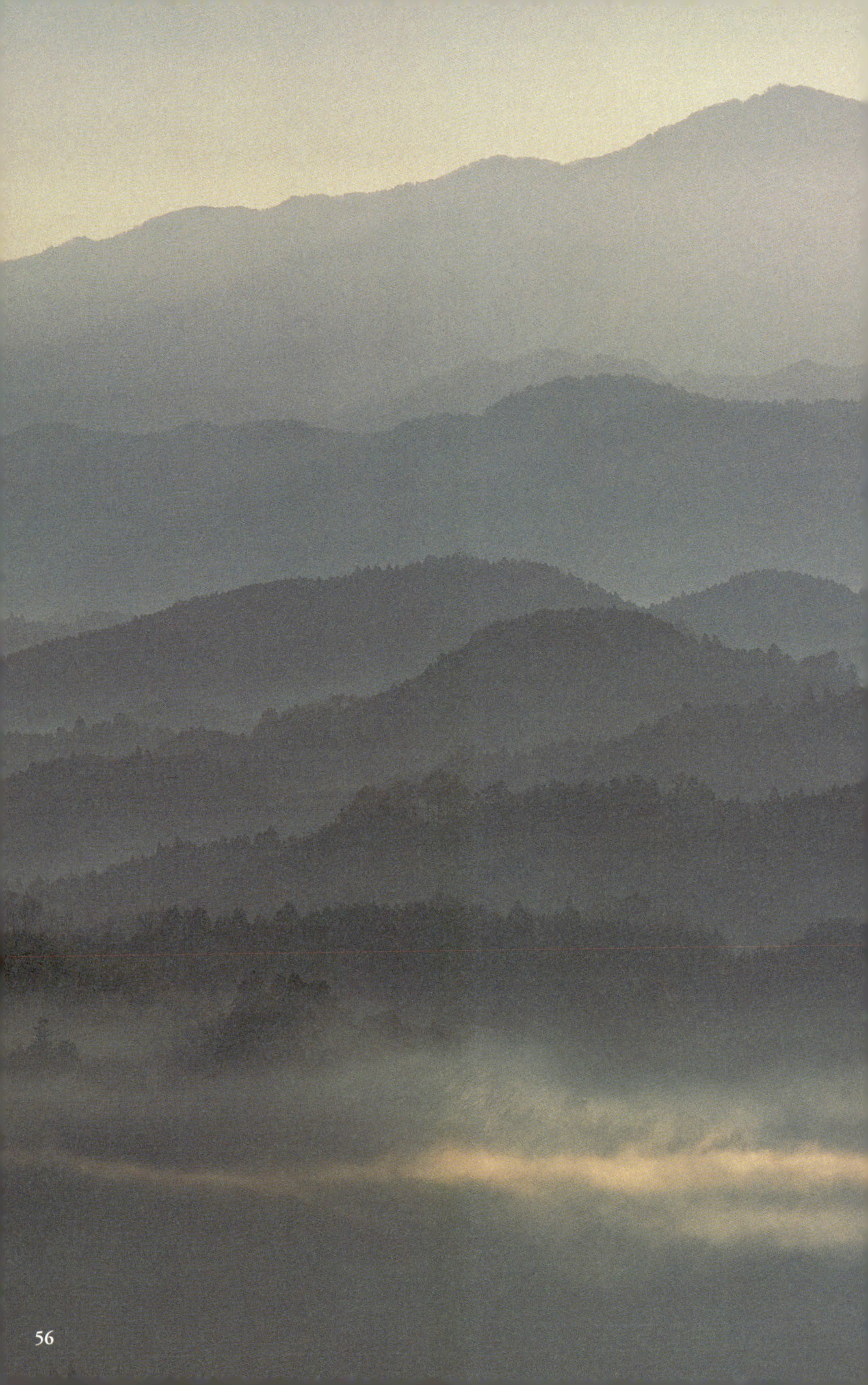

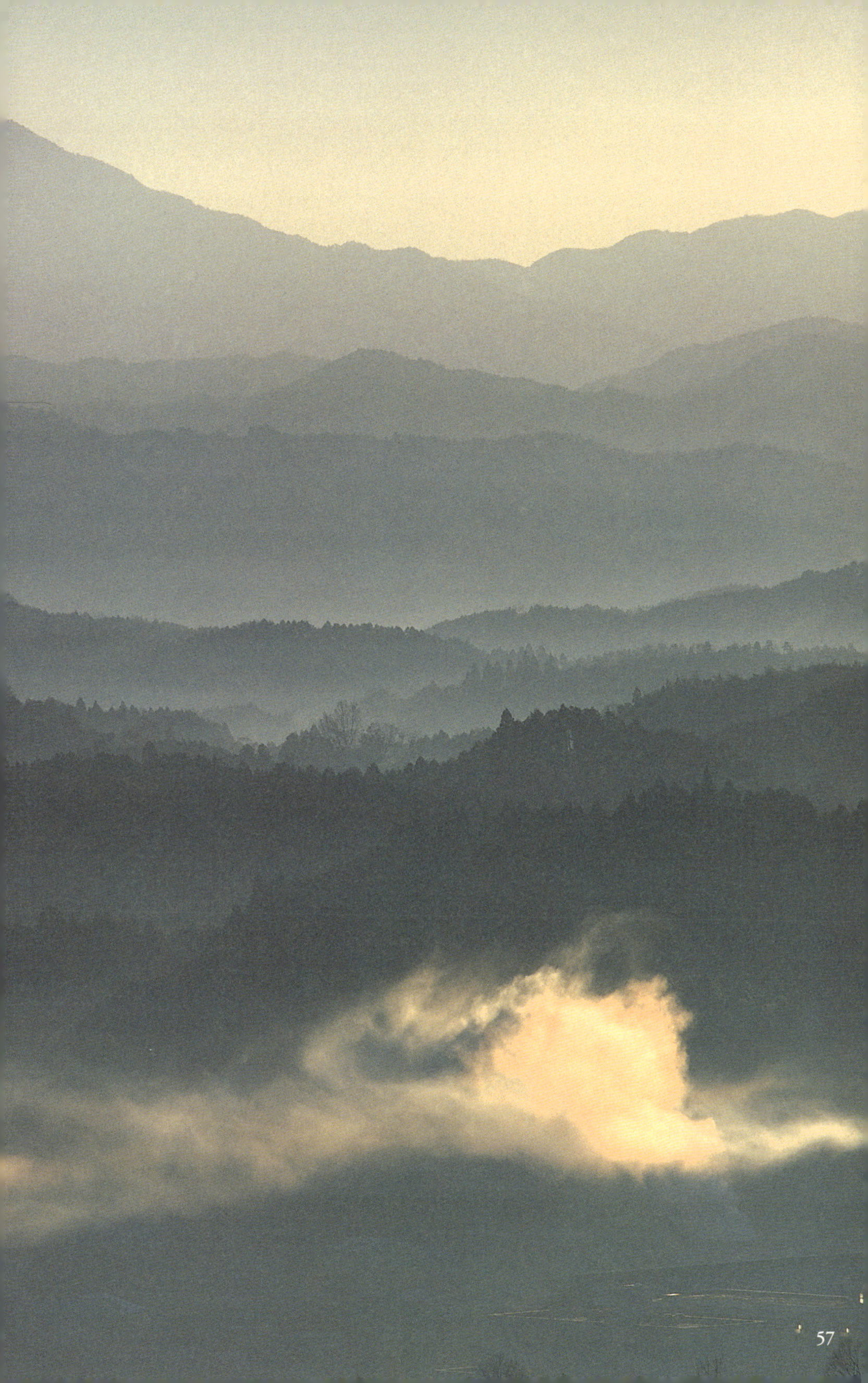

*Poem by Prince Shiki after the move from
the Asuka Palace to the Fujiwara Palace*

Asuka winds
furling back courtmaidens' sleeves:
the capital is far away,
and they blow in vain.

五一

明日香宮より藤原宮に遷居りし後に、
志貴皇子（しきのみこ）の作りませる御歌（うた）

采女（うねめ）の袖吹きかへす明日香風（あすかかぜ）都を遠みいたづらに吹く

采女の袖を吹きひるがえす明日香の風、今は都も遠く、空しく吹くことよ。

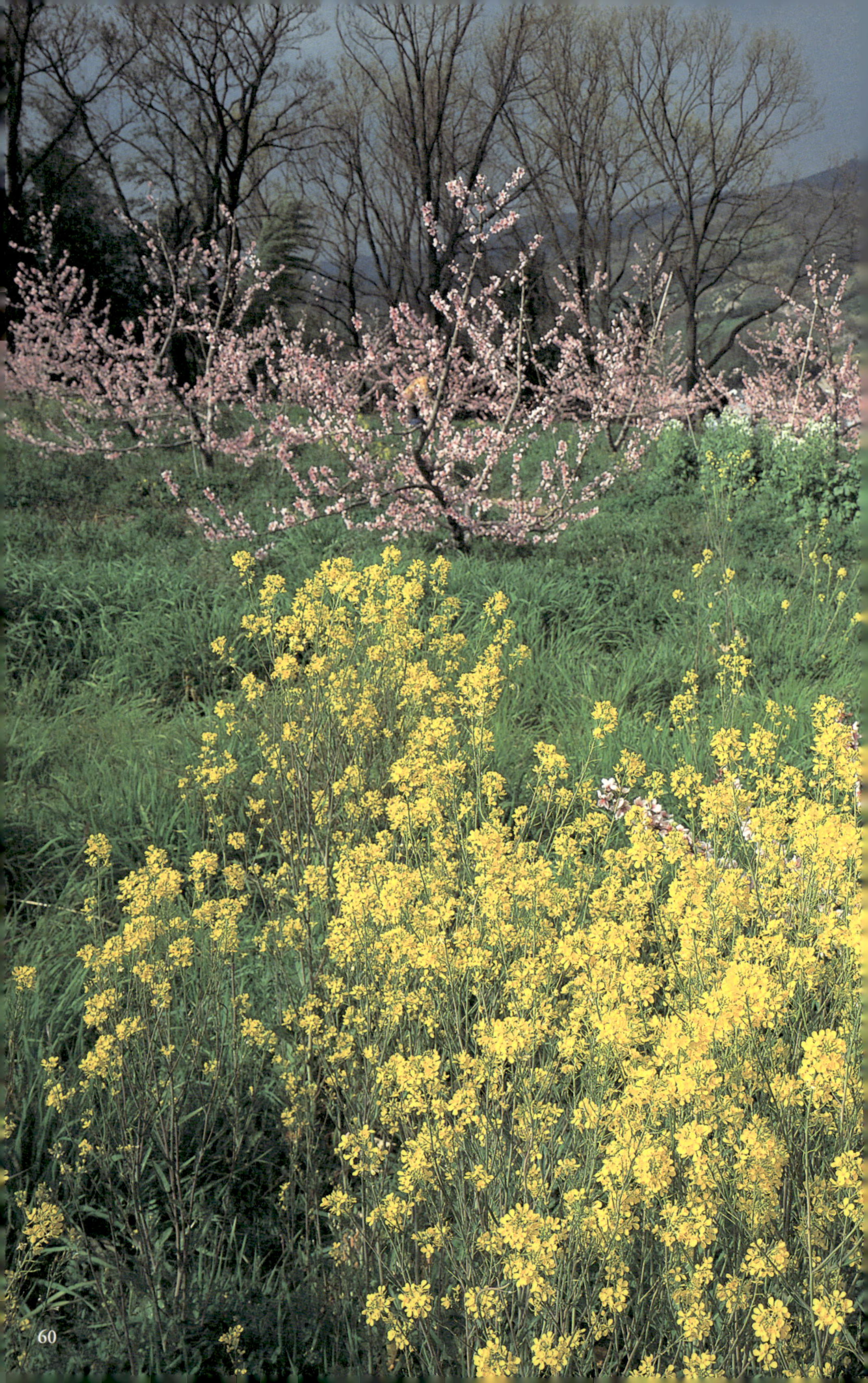

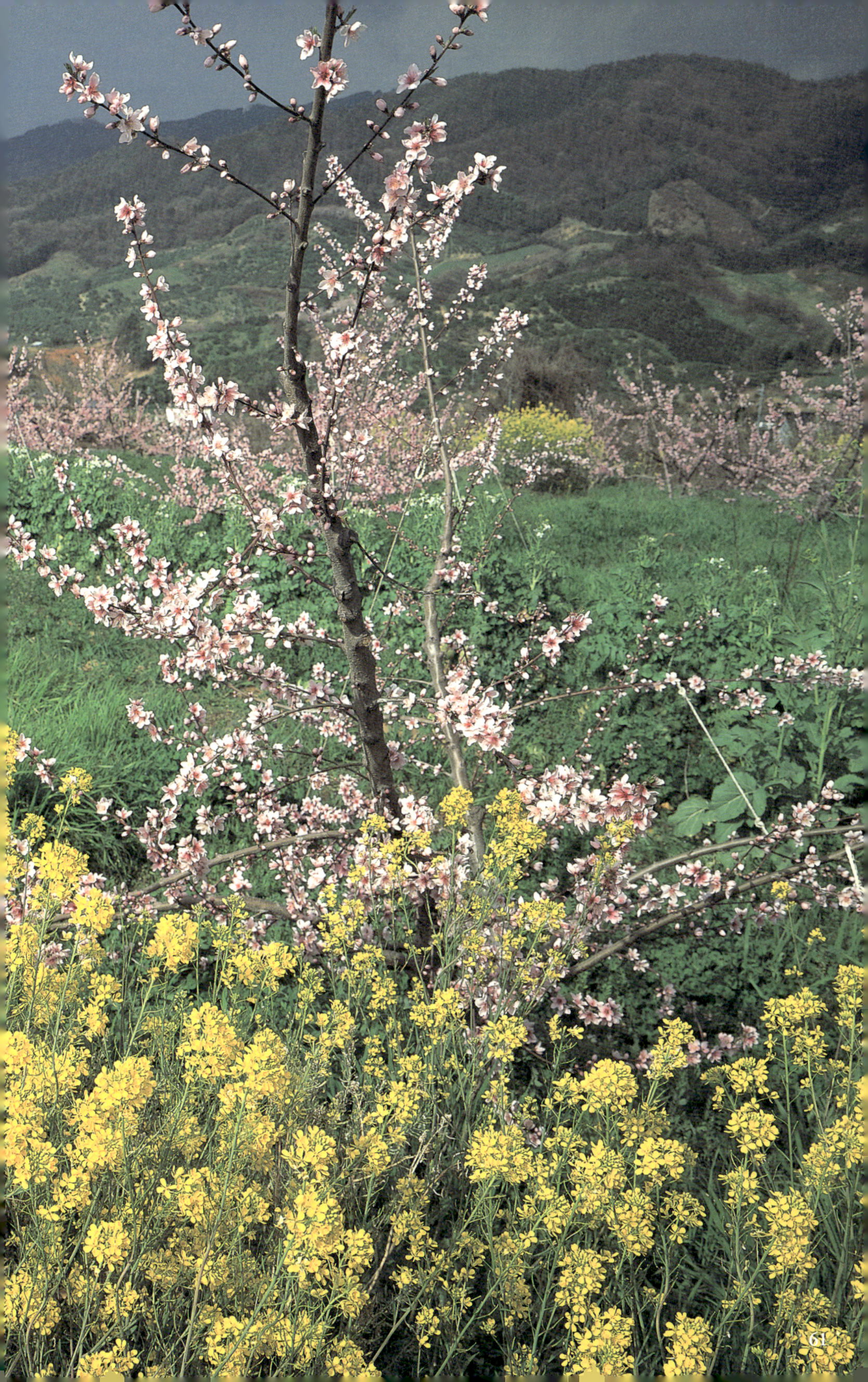

Tanka poem following
Poem of the Imperial Well at the Fujiwara Palace

Maidens born
into a line that serves
the great palace at Fujiwara—
how I envy them!

五三

藤原宮の御井（みゐ）の歌一首　に付随する短歌

藤原の大宮仕へ生（あ）れつぐや処女（をとめ）がともは羨（とも）しきろかも

藤原の大宮に仕えるべく
生まれつづく処女たちは
羨しいことだ。

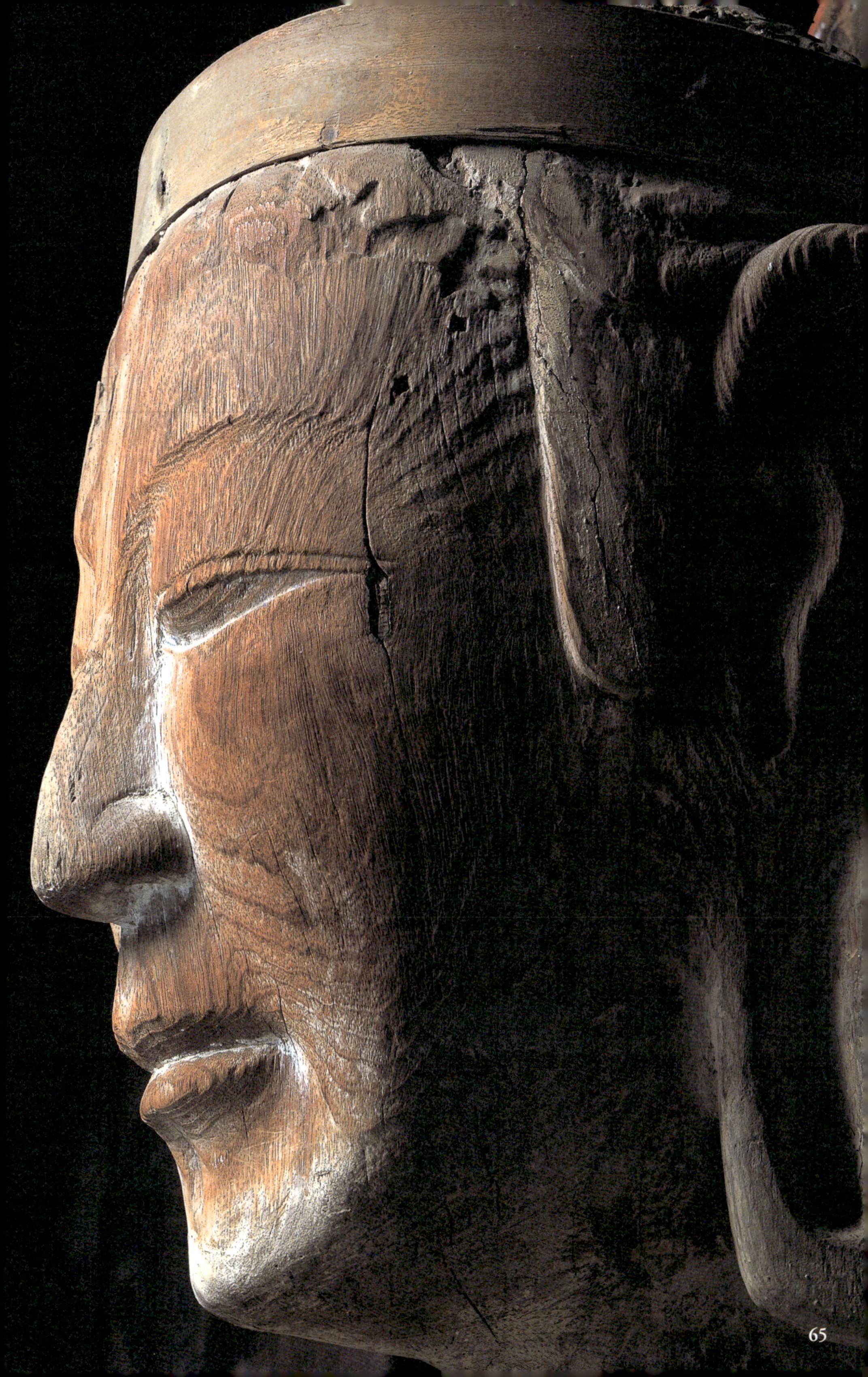

Poem by Prince Shiki at the time of the imperial procession to the palace at Naniwa in the third year of Keiun (706)

On the cold evening, when frost
glazes the pinioned wings of ducks
as they swim by the reedy shore,
it is of Yamato I think.

六四

慶雲三年丙午(へいご)に、難波の宮に幸しし時、
志貴皇子(しきのみこ)の作りませる御歌

葦辺(あしへ)行く鴨の羽(は)がひに霜降りて寒き夕へは大和し思ほゆ

葦べを泳ぐ鴨の背に霜が降り、寒さが身にしみる夕べは、大和が思われてならない。

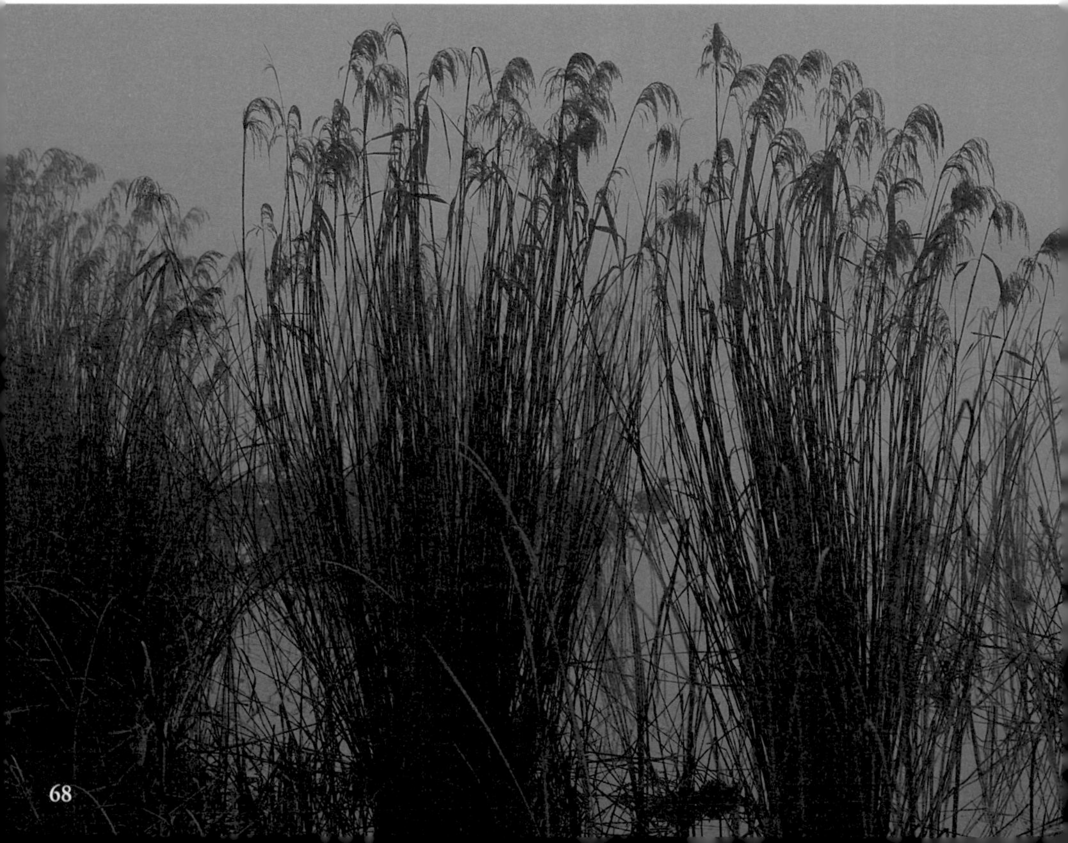

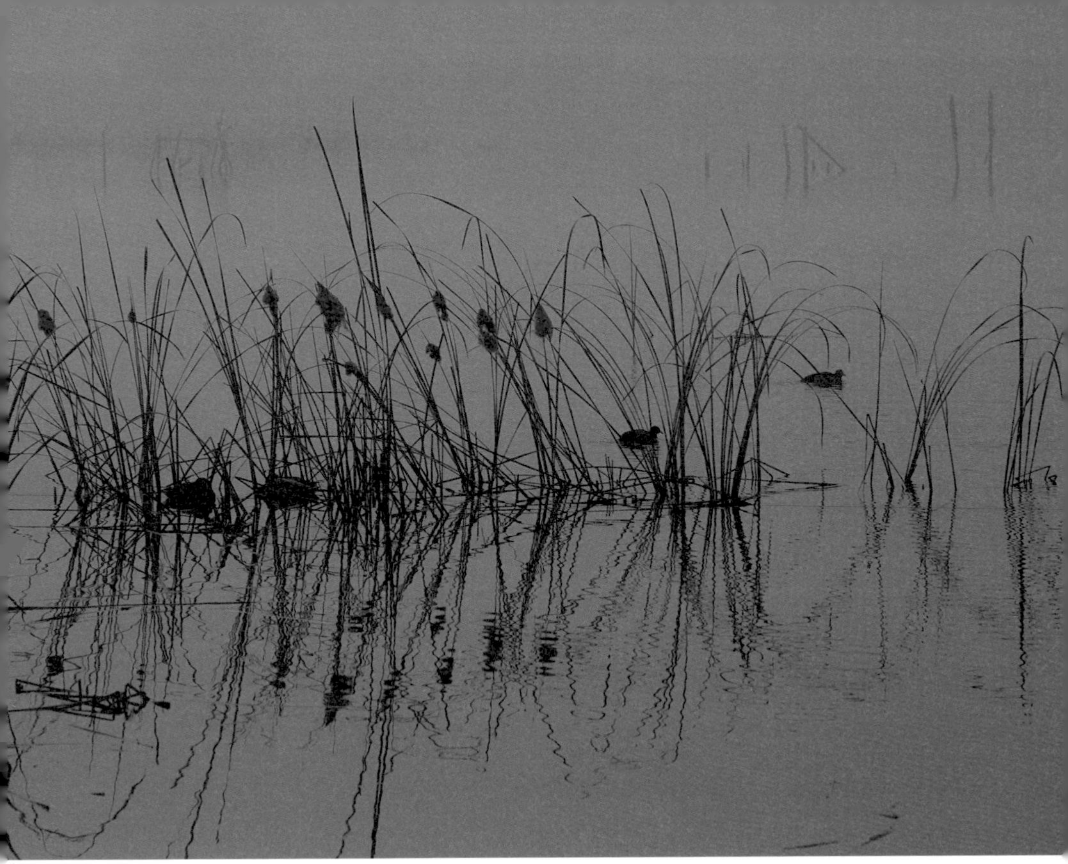

Poem at the time of the late Emperor Mommu's procession to the palace at Yoshino

Though chill is the storm
on beautiful Yoshino Mountain,
perhaps yet this night too
I may be sleeping alone.

七四
大行天皇の吉野の宮に幸しし時の歌

み吉野の山の嵐の寒けくにはたや今夜もわが独り寝む

み吉野の山の嵐は寒いことだのに、あるいは今夜も私は一人で寝るのだろうか。

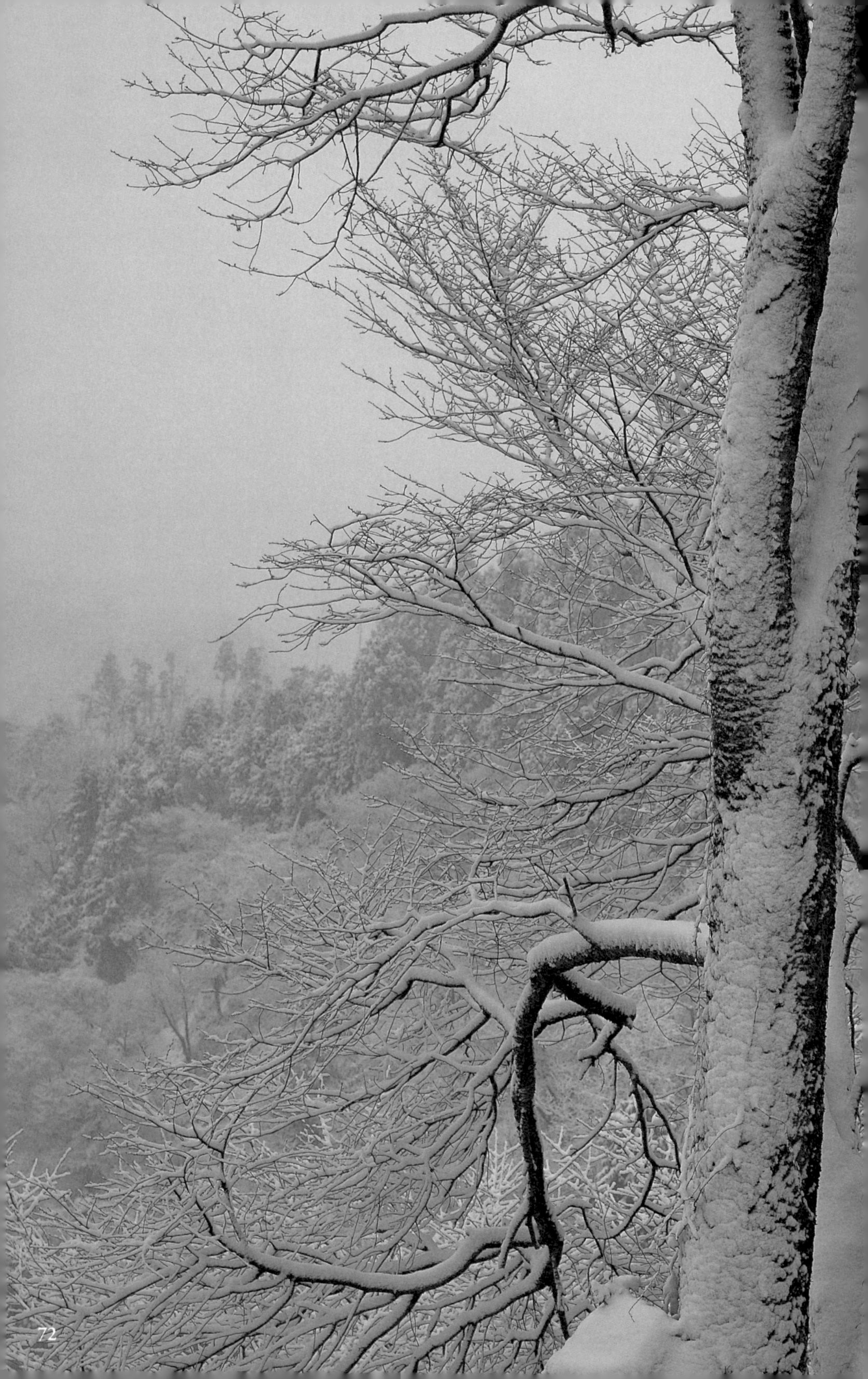

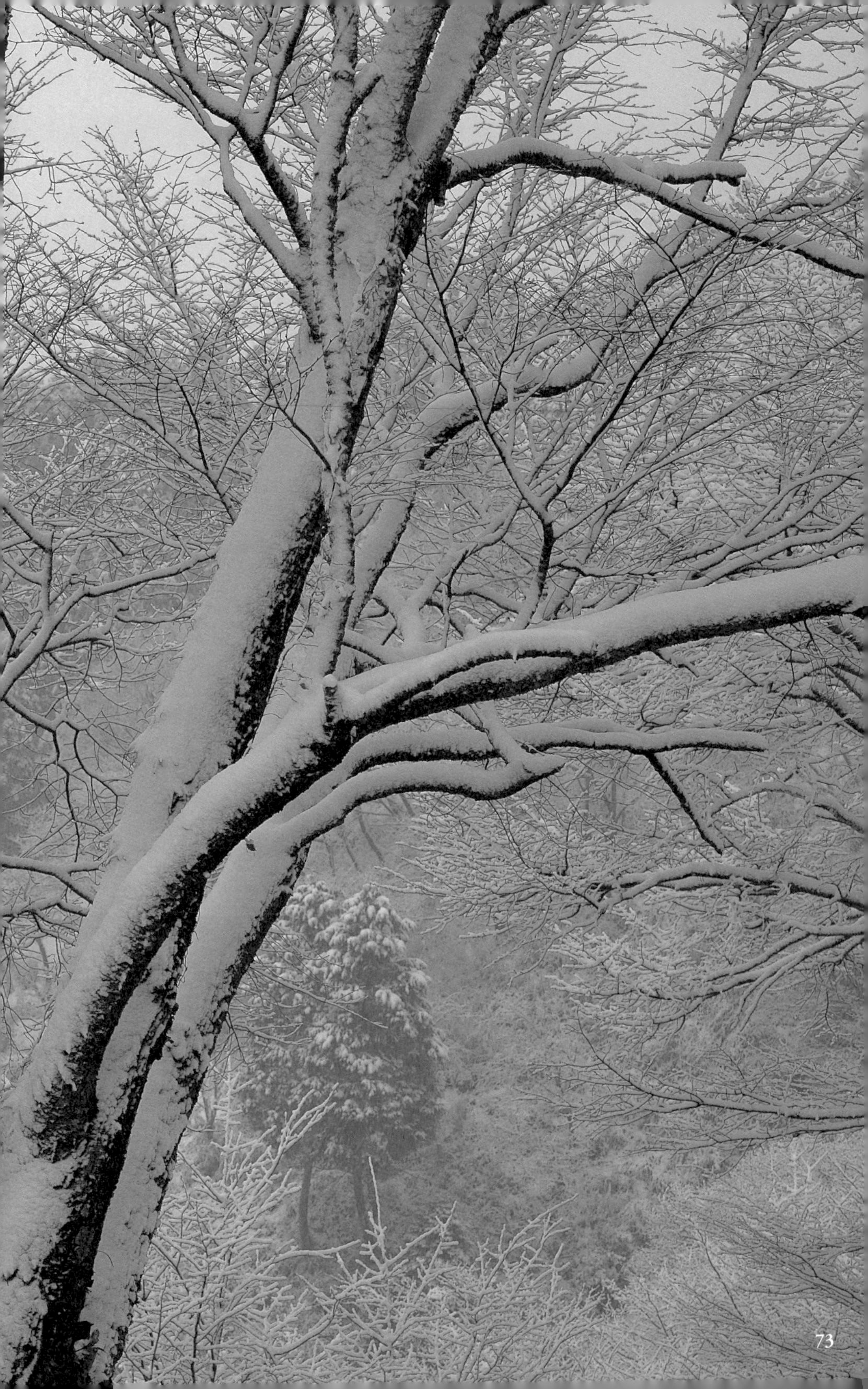

*Poem written when Prince Naga banqueted with
Prince Shiki at the Palace at Saki*

If autumn were here
these would be mountains
as we see them now,
where the deer cries
in longing for his wife —
on these high fields.

八四

長皇子の志貴皇子と佐紀宮に倶に宴せる歌

秋さらば今も見るごと妻恋ひに鹿鳴かむ山そ高野原の上

秋になると、ほらご覧のようにきまって妻恋いの鹿の声がひびく山なのですよ。この高野原の上は。

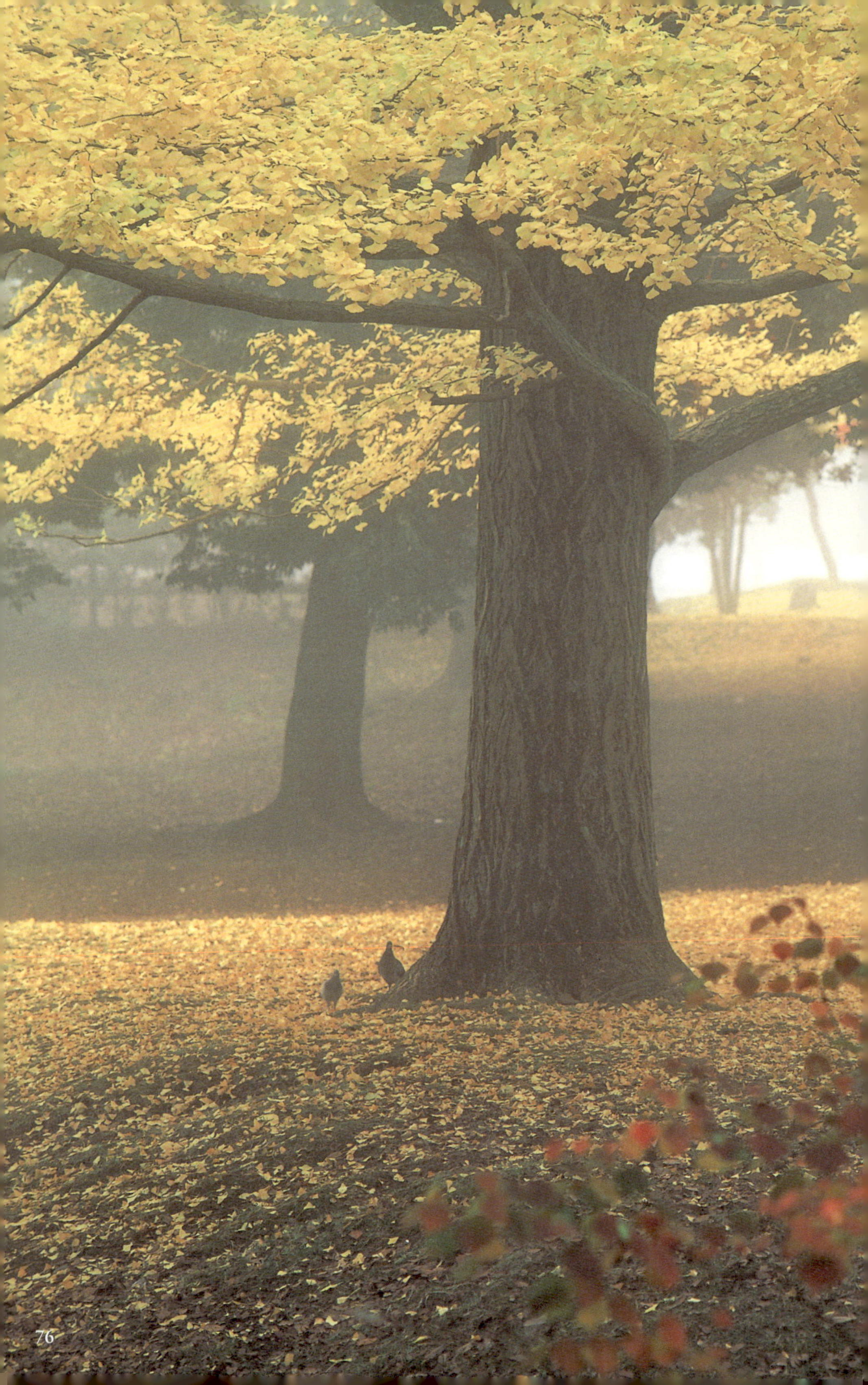

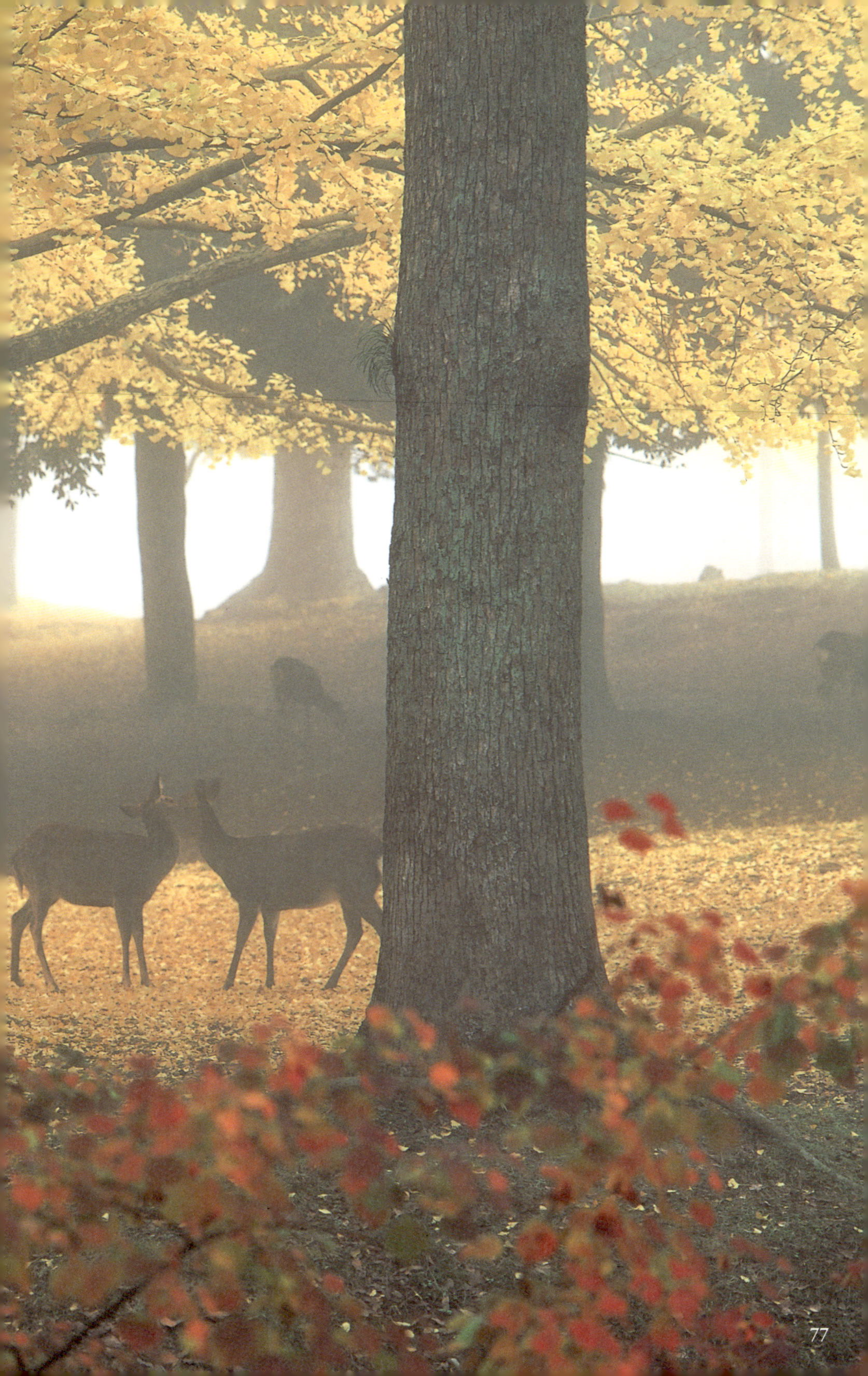

*By Empress Iwanohime, thinking of
Emperor Nintoku*

I shall wait for you
    like this
as long as I live,
until the frost
cakes my trailing black hair.

八七

磐姫皇后（いはのひめのおほきさき）の、天皇を思（しの）ひて作りませる御歌四首（その一首）

ありつつも君をば待たむ打ち靡くわが黒髪に霜の置くまでに

居つづけてあなたを待っていよう。
長く靡くこの黒髪に霜がおくようになるまででも。

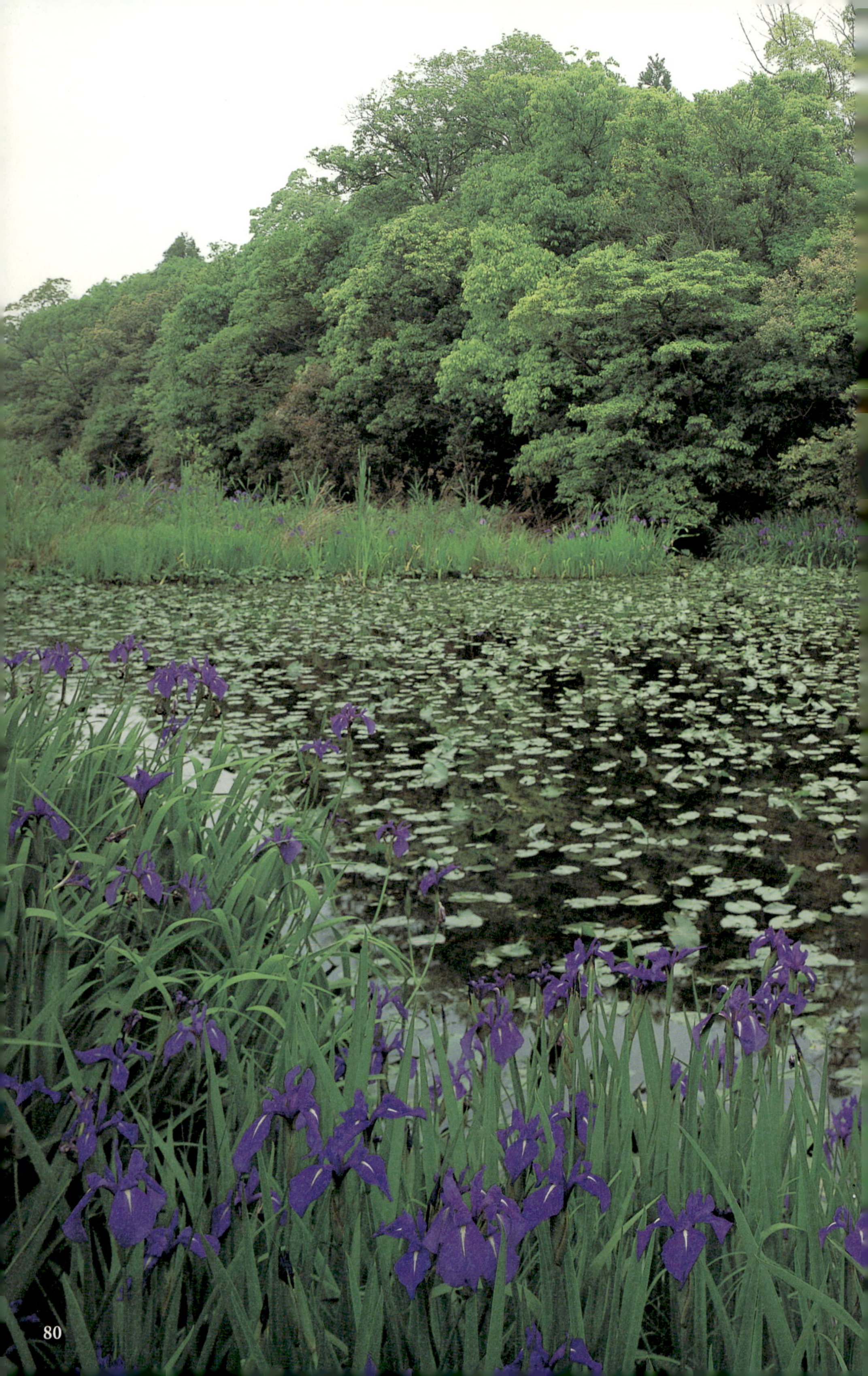

MIST GRAPH

井上博道「万葉集」ミストグラフ申込書

作品名	枚数	作品名	枚数
A. 幻想 (P.76)		D. 交響 (P.176)	
B. 記憶 (P.36)		E. 意匠 (P.244)	
C. 余韻 (P.124)		F. 幽宵 (P.309)	

申込者氏名：
申込者住所：〒　―　　　TEL.

お届け先氏名：
お届け先住所：〒　―　　　TEL.

キリトリ線

ミストグラフは従来の写真プリントと異なり、コンピューターによる最新画像処理技術と高精細印刷技術を融合させ版画用紙に画像を定着させる新しいプリント技法です。極細のインキ粒子が、カラーフィルムの階調と質感をリアルに再現します。また、耐光性にも優れ、室内で30年以上退色しません。その優れた品質から著名な作家の作品制作や、ミュージアムグッズへの採用などの支持を得ております。

今回は写真家自身が、「万葉集」の中から選んだ作品6点をミストグラフとして制作・頒布します。

各作品とも50部限定で、エディション・ナンバー及び作家直筆のサインが入ります。

- 商品の発送は入金確認後になりますので、お届けは約3週間後となります。
- お支払い方法は、銀行振込みでお願いいたします。
- エディション・ナンバーの指定は出来ません。
- 商品違い、不良品、破損品をお届けした場合は、お取り替えさせていただきますので8日以内に下記住所宛に送料着払いでご返送下さい。

UFJ銀行 大和高田支店 当座預金 No.3640
岡村印刷工業株式会社 アートプロデュース

制作・問い合わせ先
岡村印刷工業株式会社 アートプロデュース
〒558-0004 大阪市住吉区長居東3丁目4番17号
TEL.06-6697-6551　FAX.06-6690-2271

このハガキをFAXで送信していただいても、結構です。　FAX.03-5395-4812

Post Card

〒170-0005

東京都豊島区南大塚2-32-4

「ミスト・ブ・エピ」
ミストグラフス
係行

50円切手

井上博道
「ミストグラフ」万葉集セレクション
MistiGraph Selection

A. 幻想 (P.76)
B. 記憶 (P.36) 
C. 余韻 (P.124) 
D. 交響 (P.176) 
E. 意匠 (P.244) 
F. 幽昏 (P.309) 

各作品とも、50部限定

価格：¥50,000
絵柄サイズ：423×334mm　額サイズ：613×512mm

※価格は、額代、送料・消費税込みです。
※額は木目調アルミ・フレーム、グレーマット、アクリル仕様です。

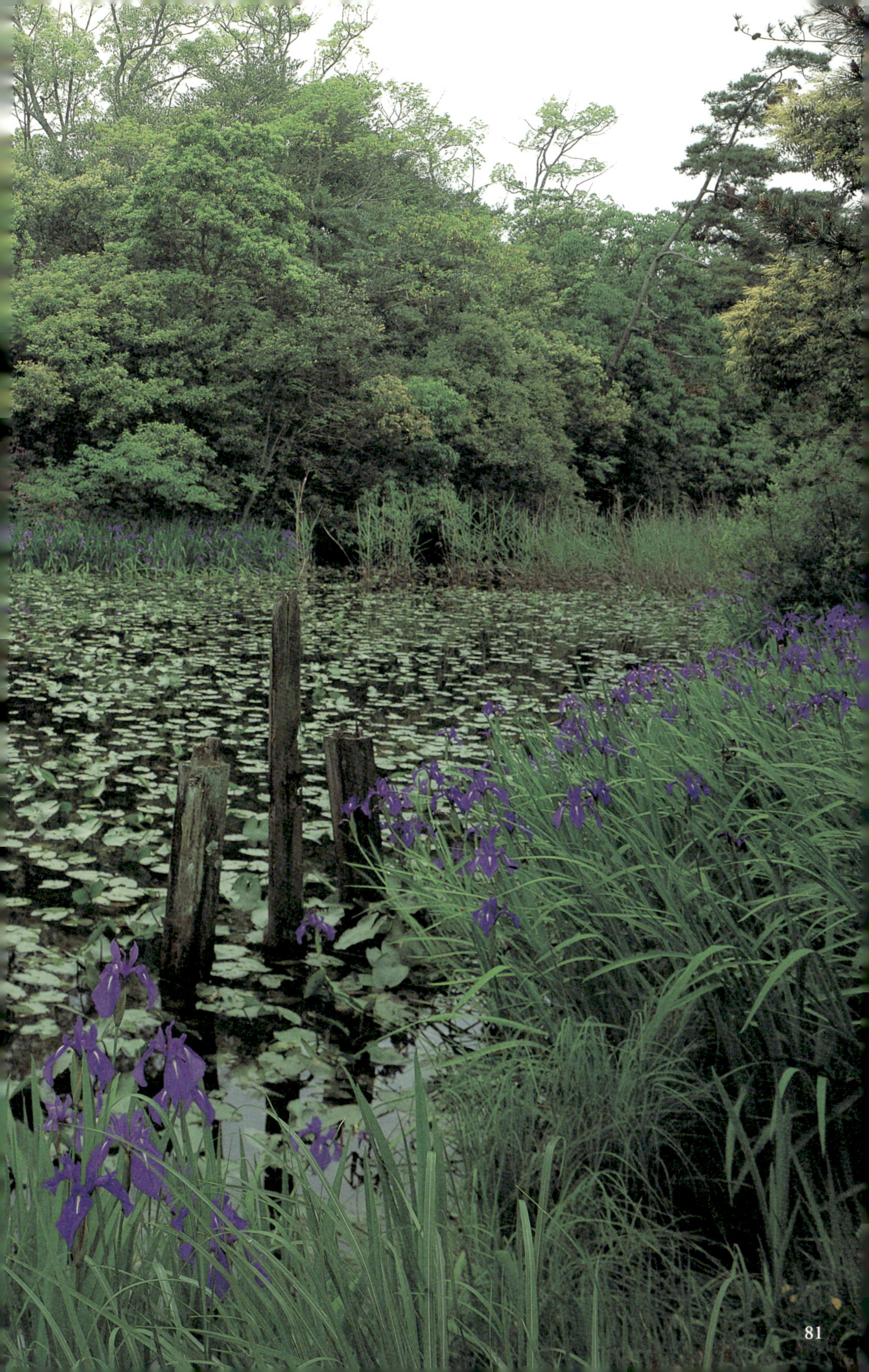

*When Lord Fujiwara, Great Minister of the Center,
asked Princess Kagami to wed him,
she sent him this poem.*

The jewelled box is easily opened,
and the night, opening into dawn,
    saw you leave.
What of your name
if this be known?
    My regrets are for my own.

九三

内大臣藤原卿の鏡王女を娉ひし時に、
鏡王女の内大臣に贈れる歌一首

玉くしげ覆ふを安み開けていなば君が名はあれどわが名し惜しも

玉くしげのように人目に
たっていないのをいいこ
とに夜も明けてからお帰
りになると、やがては人
に知られます。あなたの
お名前はともかく、私の
浮名の立つのは困ります。

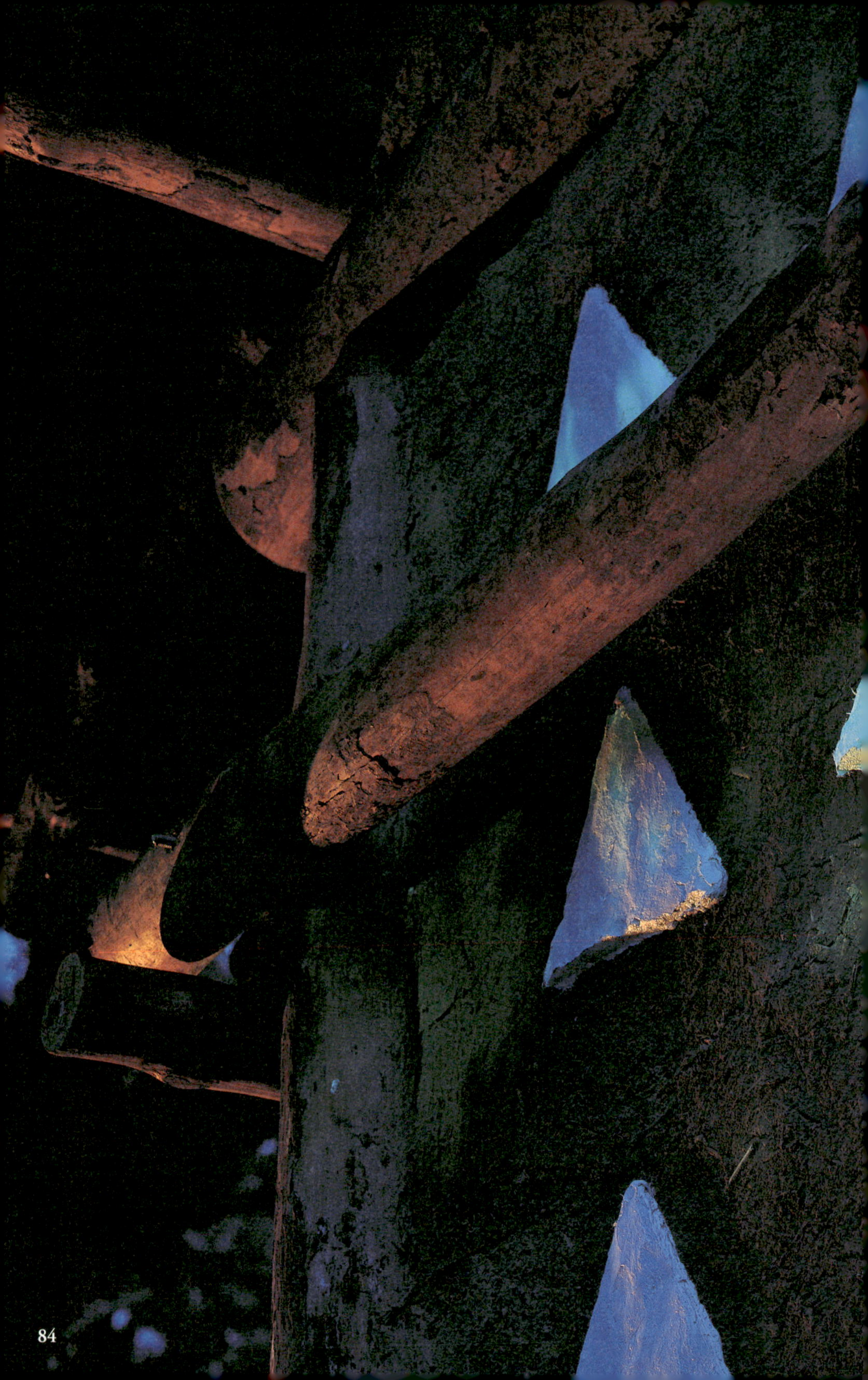

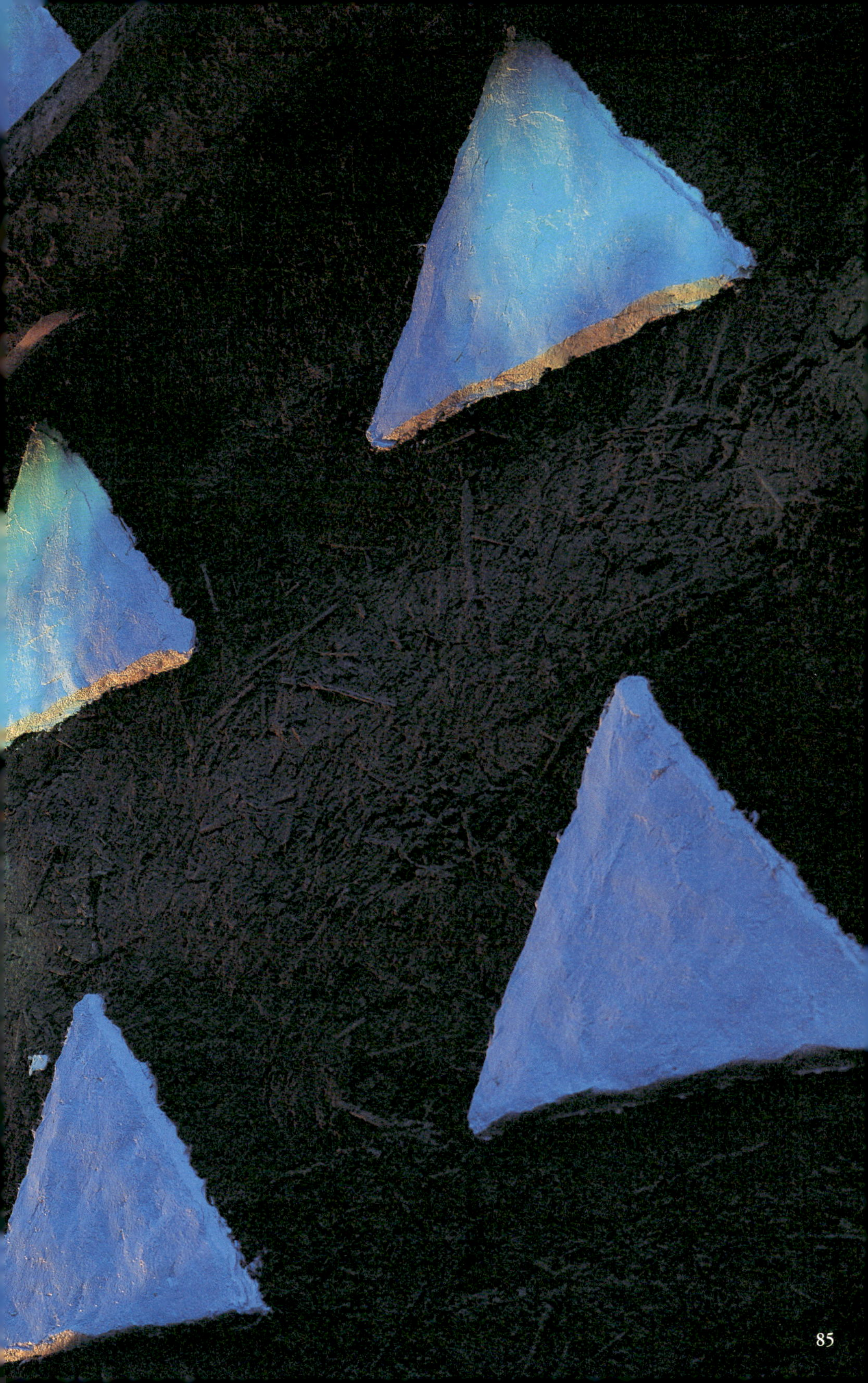

Poem by Princess Tajima when she was staying at Prince Takechi's palace thinking of Prince Hozumi

As the ears of rice
on the autumn fields
bend in one direction,
so with one mind would I bend to you,
painful though the gossip be.

一一四

但馬皇女の高市皇子の宮に在しし時に、穂積皇子を思ひて作りませる御歌一首

秋の田の穂向の寄れるかた寄りに君に寄りなな言痛くありとも

秋の田の稲穂の向きが風に靡くように、一方に心を靡かせてあなたに寄りたいことよ。いかに評判を立てられても。

89

By Prince Arima, written in his own sorrow as he tied the branches of a pine tree in a prayer for safety

I draw and tie together
    branches of the pine
        on the beach at Iwashiro.
If all goes well
I shall return to see them again.

郵 便 は が き

料金受取人払

170 - 8790

038

豊島局承認

6880

差出有効期間
平成17年5月
1日まで

東京都豊島区南大塚2-32-4
ピエ・ブックス 行

|ḷᵢḷ·ᵢḷᵢ··ᵢḷᵢḷᵢḷᵢ··ᵢ·ᵢḷᵢḷᵢḷᵢḷᵢḷᵢḷᵢḷᵢḷᵢḷᵢḷᵢḷ|

このたびは小社の本をお買い上げいただきありがとうございます。新刊案内の送付と今後の企画の参考とさせていただきますので、お手数ですが各欄にご記入の上お送り下さい。

万葉集

(フリガナ) お名前		年齢	性別 **男・女**

ご住所 〒	TEL ( )
e-mail	

ご職業	購入店名

● いままでに読者カードをお出しいただいたことが　　1.ある　2.ない

ご購入書籍名をご記入ください。

1. この本を何でお知りになりましたか
    1. 新聞・雑誌 (紙・誌名   )　2. チラシ・ポスター
    3. 友人、知人の話　　4. 店頭で見て　　5. プレゼントされた
    6. その他 (   )

2. この本についてのご意見、ご感想をお聞かせください。

   ……………………………………………………………………………
   ……………………………………………………………………………
   ……………………………………………………………………………
   ……………………………………………………………………………

3. よく購読されている雑誌名をお書き下さい。

●
   ……………………………………………………………………………
●
   ……………………………………………………………………………
●
   ……………………………………………………………………………

4. 今後、小社より出版をご希望の企画、テーマがありましたら、
   ぜひお聞かせください。

   ……………………………………………………………………………
   ……………………………………………………………………………
   ……………………………………………………………………………
   ……………………………………………………………………………

● アンケートにご協力いただきありがとうございました。　　　万葉集

一四一

有間皇子の自ら傷みて松が枝を結べる歌二首(その一首)

磐代の浜松が枝を引き結び真幸くあらばまた還り見む

磐代の浜松の枝を結びあわせて無事を祈るが、もし命あって帰路に通ることがあれば、また見られるだろうなあ。

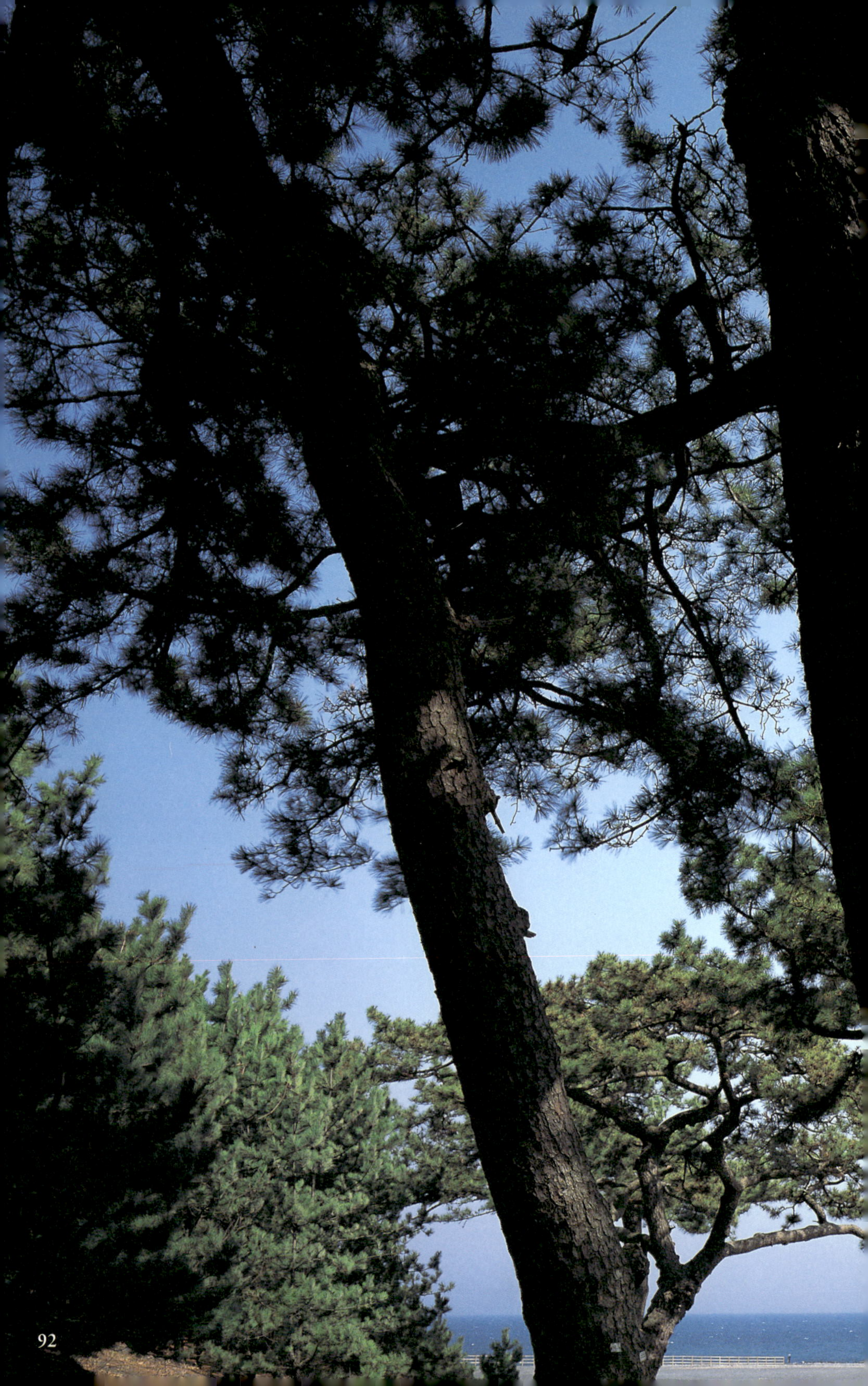

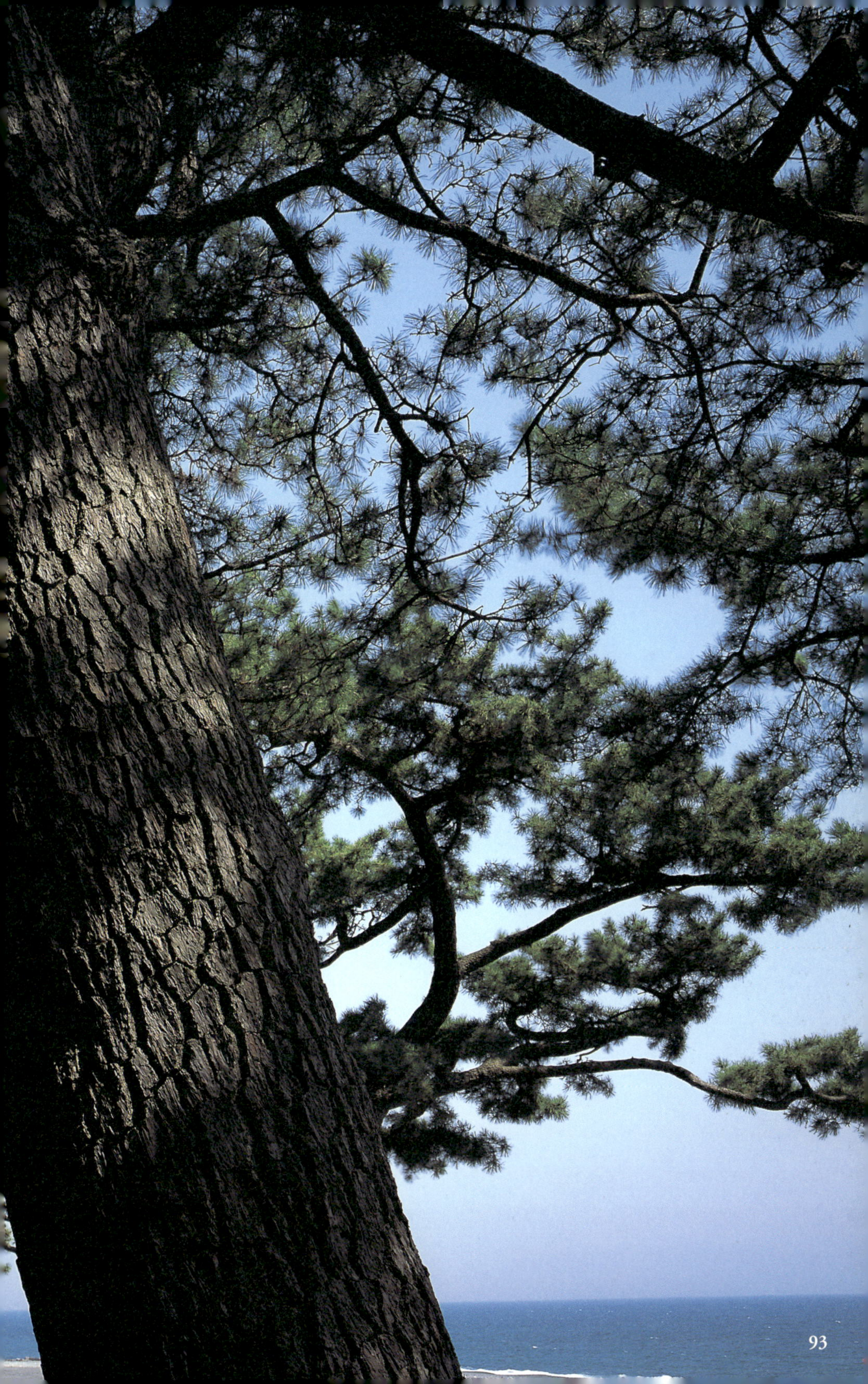

Poem by the Empress

Ships that come rowing
far on the offing,
ships that come rowing
close by the strand
on Ōmi's whale-hunted seas:
Oars on the offing,
do not splash so hard,
Oars by the strand,
do not splash so hard,
or the bird
   beloved of my husband,
who was gentle
   like the young grass,
will fly away.

一五三
大后の御歌一首

鯨魚取り　淡海の海を　沖放けて　漕ぎ来る船　辺附きて　漕
ぎ来る船　沖つ櫂　いたくな撥ねそ　辺つ櫂　いたくな撥ねそ
若草の　夫の　思ふ鳥立つ

鯨をとる海ともいうべき　てるな。岸船の櫂、ひど
淡海の海、その沖遠く漕　く波を立てるな。
ぎ来る船よ、岸近く漕ぎ　若草のようだった夫がい
来る船よ。　　　　　　　としんだ、あの鳥が飛び
沖船の櫂、ひどく波を立　去ってしまうものを。

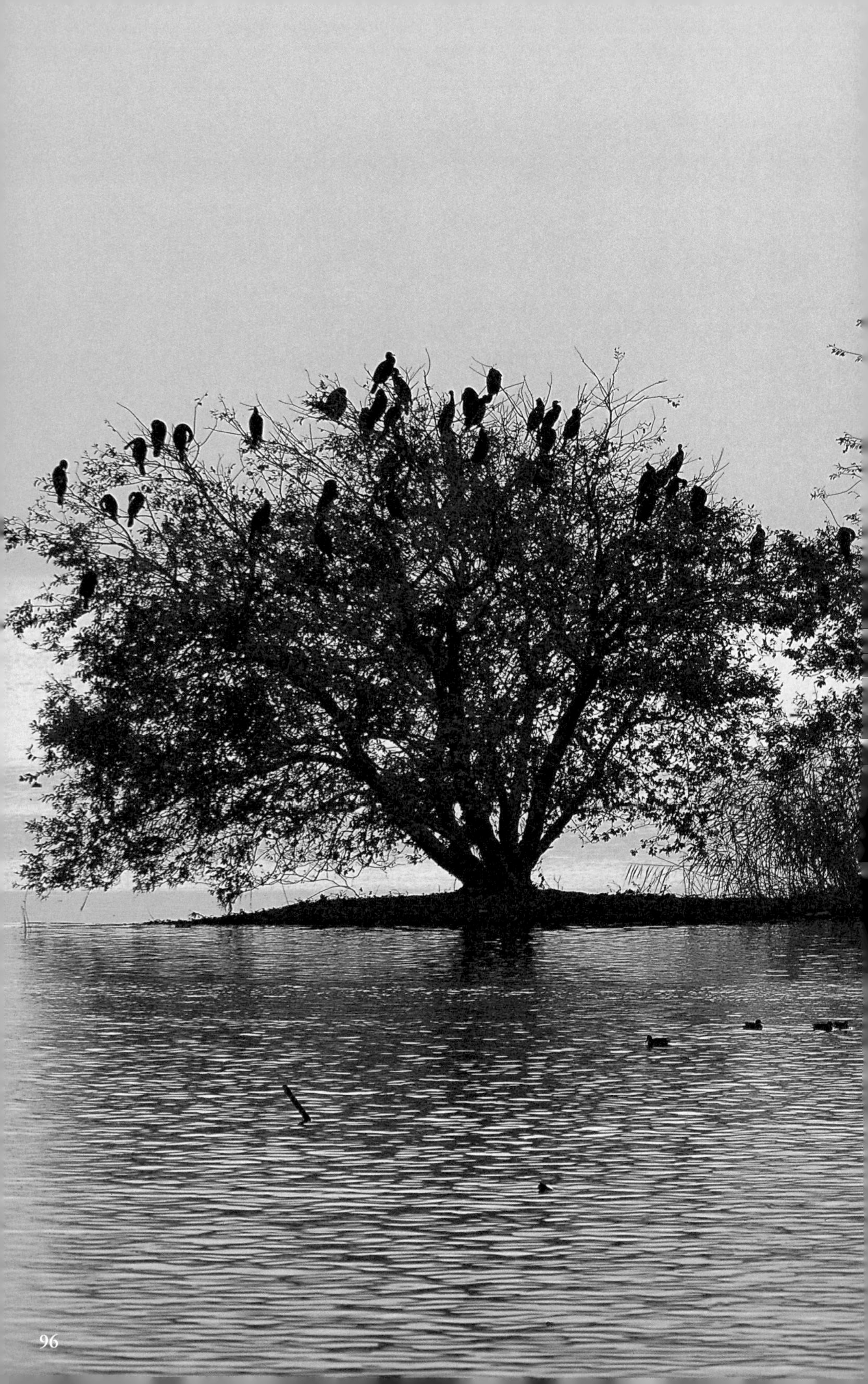

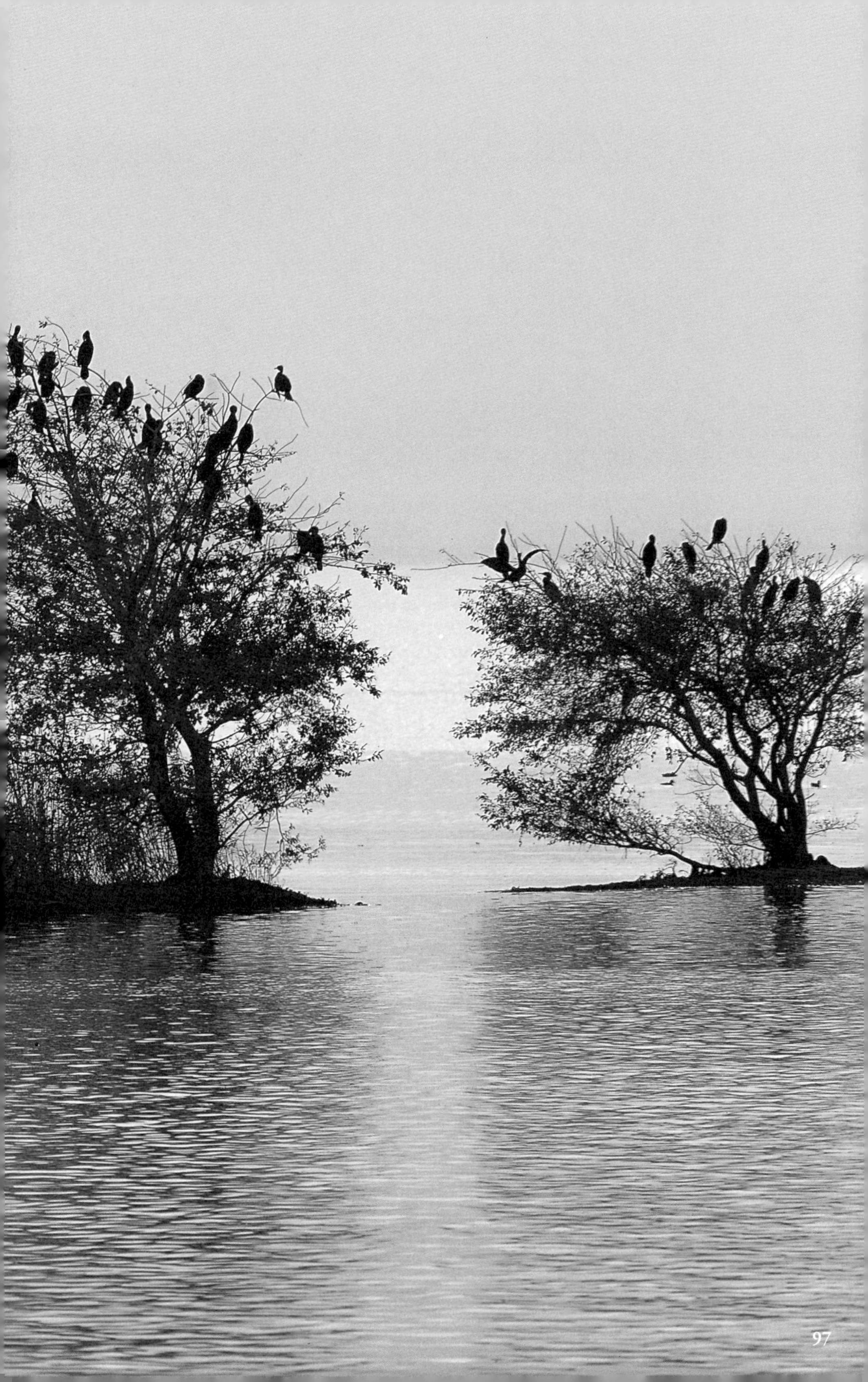

By the present Retired Empress
(at that time the Empress)
upon the death of Emperor Temmu

The clouds,
    the blue clouds
trailing on the northern mountain
tear away from the stars,
    tear from the moon.

一六一

一書に曰はく、天皇崩りましし時の太上天皇の御製歌二首（その一首）
（天皇＝天武天皇、太上天皇＝持統天皇）

神山（かむやま）にたなびく雲の青雲の星離れ行き月を離（はな）れて

神山にたなびく雲は、青雲の中の星からも離れ、月をも離れて去っていったことよ。

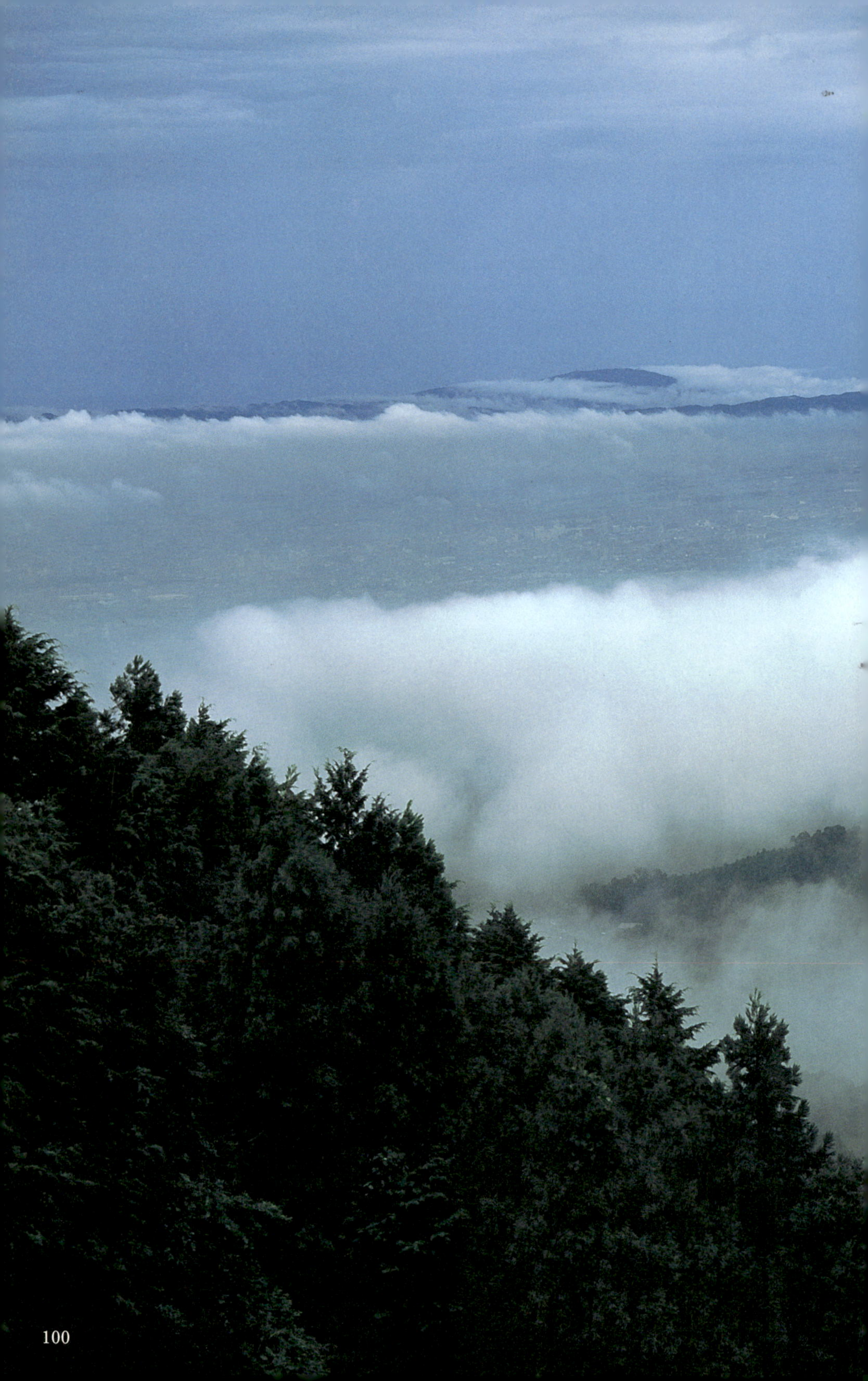

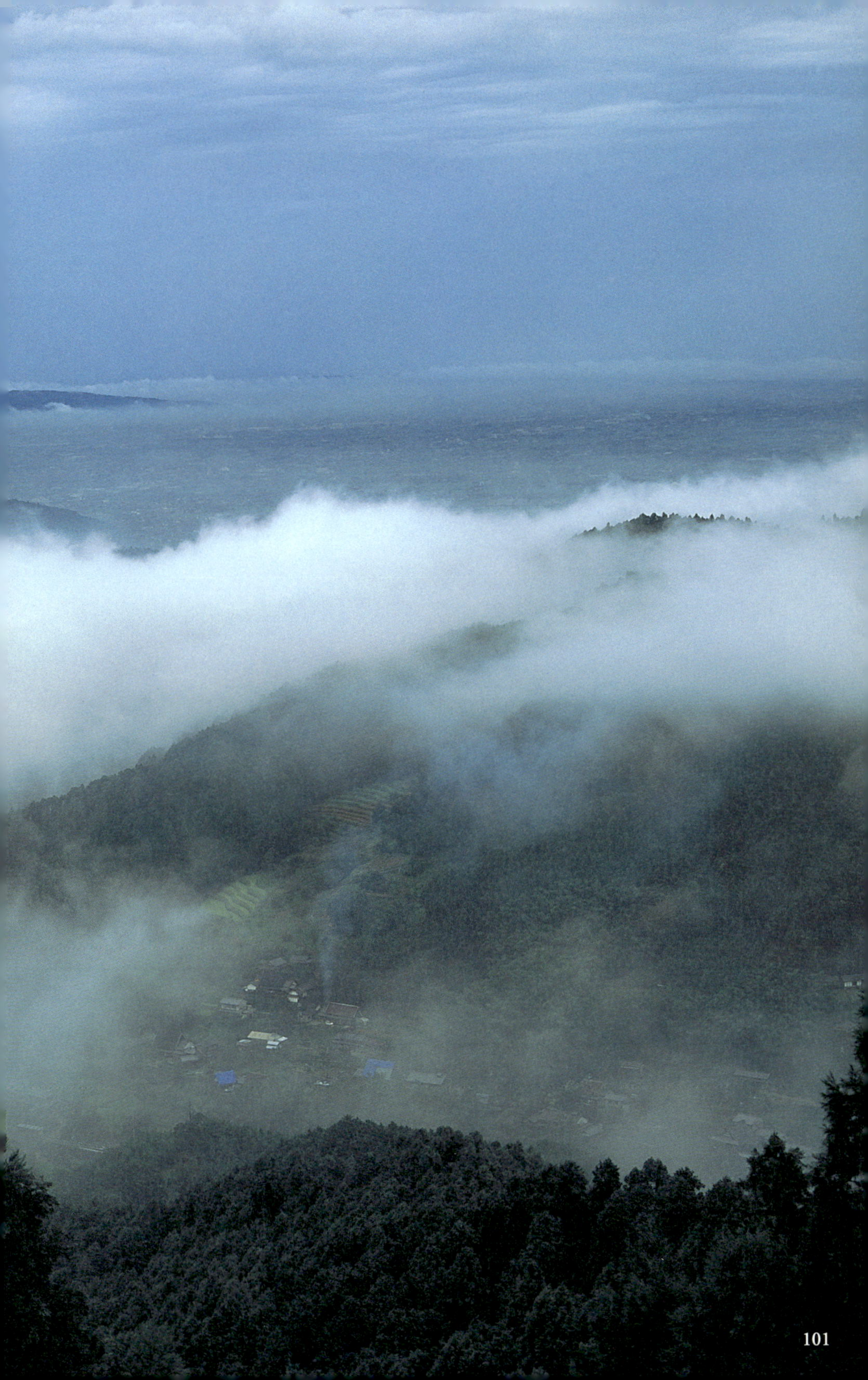

By Princess Ōku in sorrow when they removed the remains of Prince Ōtsu to Futakami Mountain in Katsuragi

I who stay among the living
shall, from tomorrow,
look on Futakami Mountain
　as you, my brother.

一六五

大津皇子の屍を葛城の二上山に移し葬りし時に、大来皇女の哀しび傷みて作りませる御歌二首(その一首)

うつそみの人にあるわれや明日よりは二上山を弟世とわが見む

現し身の人である私は、明日からは二上山をわが弟と見ようか。

*Two of twenty-three poems written by
the servingmen at the Palace of the Crown
Prince upon his demise*

When we looked
on the Garden where he stood,
our tears streamed down
   like sudden showers.
We could not hold them.

一七八

皇子尊の舎人らの慟しび傷みて作れる歌二十三首（その二首）

み立たしし島を見る時にはたづみ流るる涙止めそかねつる

お出ましを常とした庭園の島を見ると、大雨の溢れ出るような涙をとどめかねることだ。

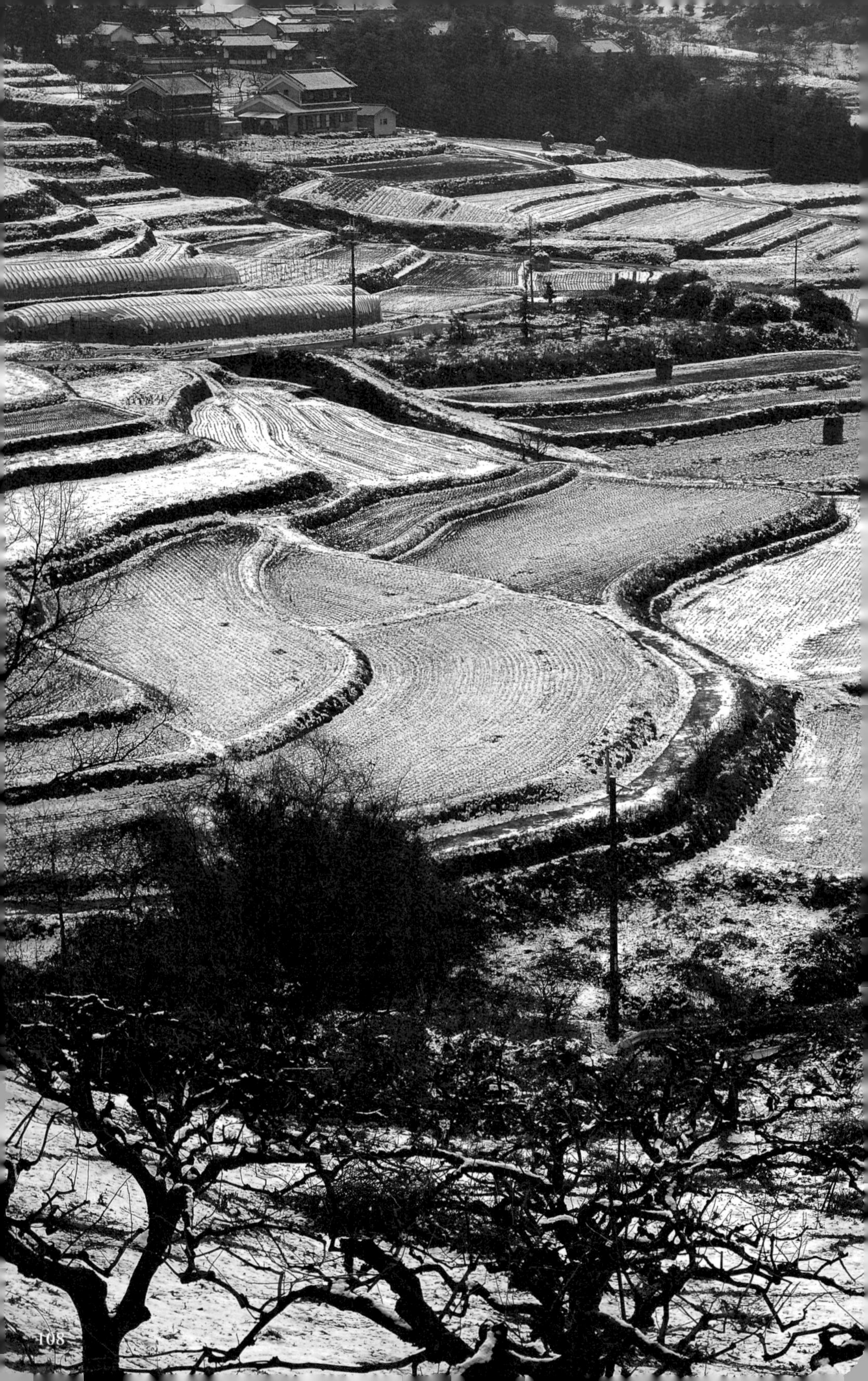

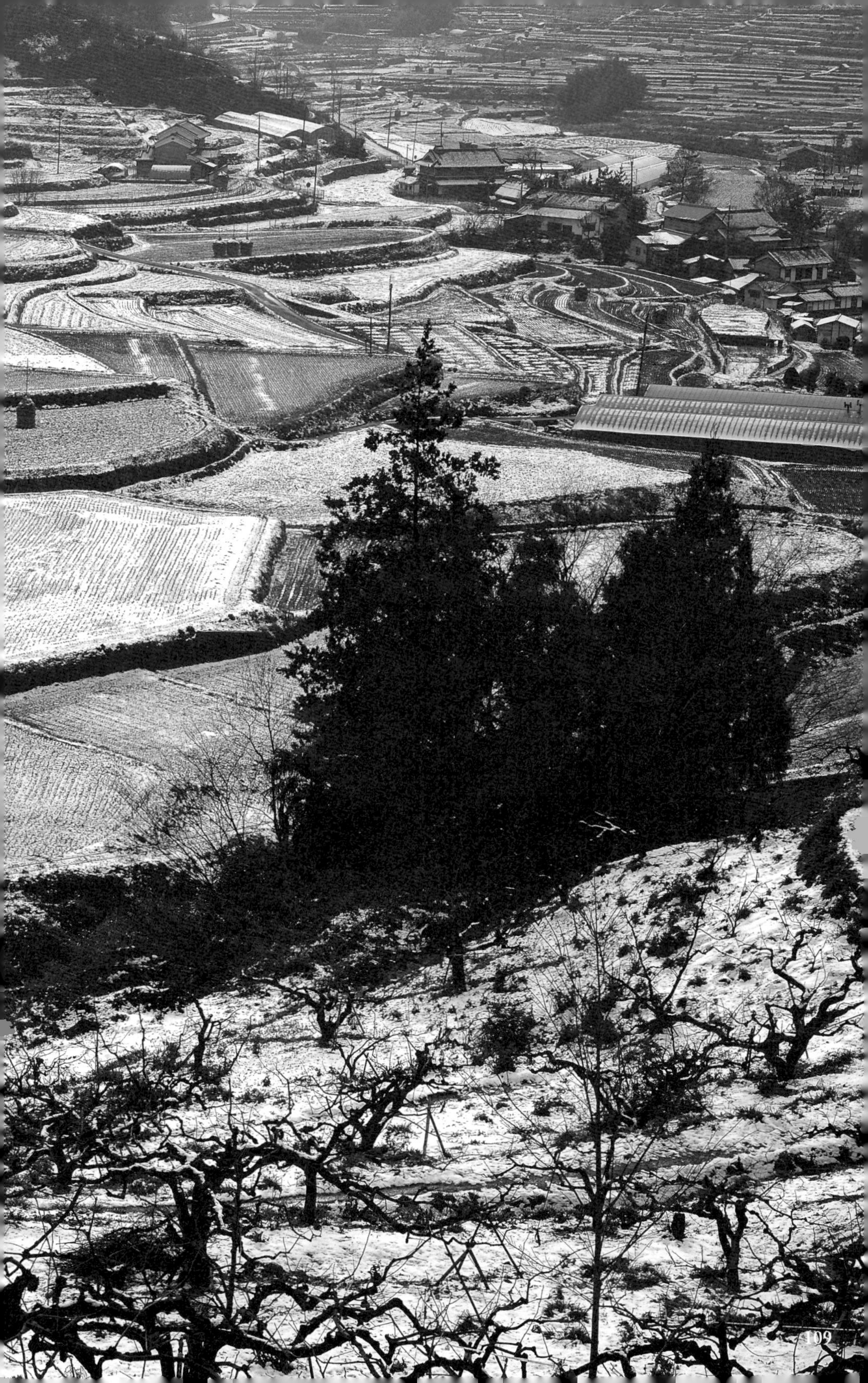

Will the great fields of Uda
    be remembered,
where he went on procession,
with stores of woolen clothes
for winter and for spring?

一九一

褻ころもを春冬片設けて幸しし宇陀の大野は思ほえむかも

いつもの衣を解き、時を待ちうけてお出ましになった宇陀の大野は、いつまでも思い出されるだろうなあ。

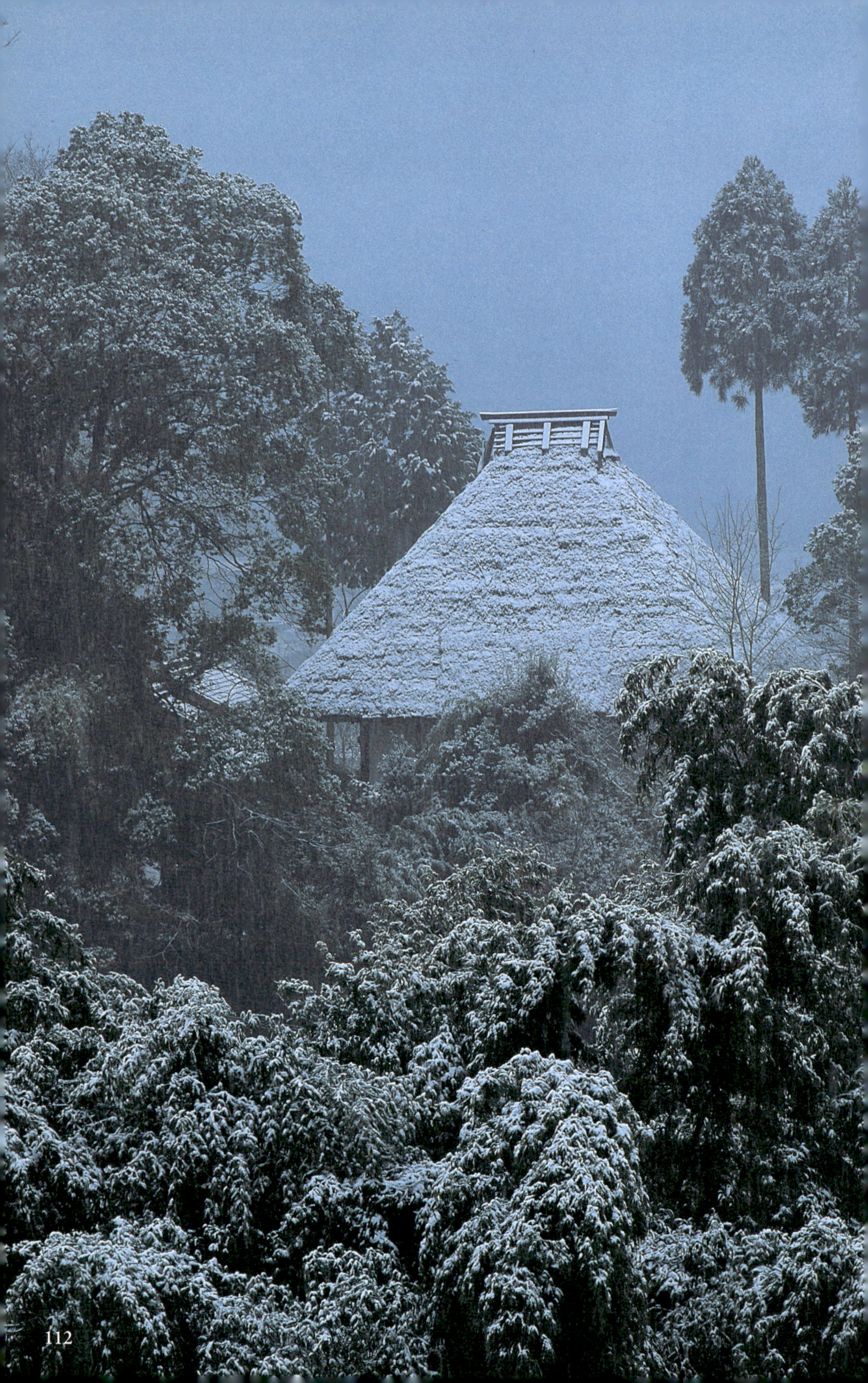

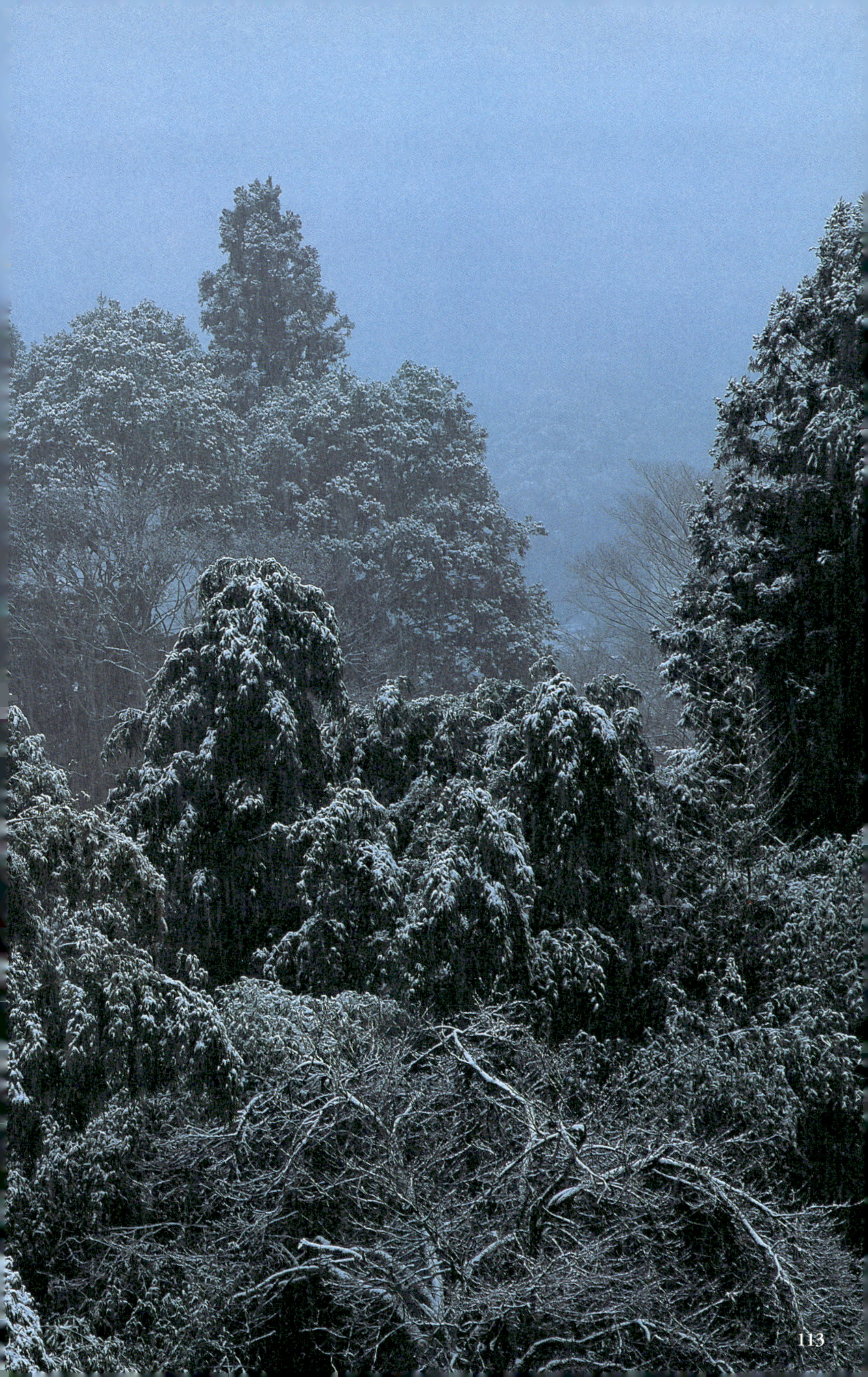

*Poem presented by Kakinomoto Hitomaro to
Princess Hatsusebe and Prince Osakabe*

Sleek seaweed streams
from where it grows
on the upper shallows of the Asuka,
            where the birds fly,
to touch and touch again
the lower shoals.
                    Asleep
without the folds of his wife's
soft skin,
        that once he kept beside him
            like his swords,
when she, like sleek seaweed,
bent toward him, swaying to and fro—
now desolate lies the bed

of his pitch-black nights.
So, inconsolate, yet hoping
she might meet him,
she sojourns,
             grass for pillow,
on the broad,
jewel-trailed fields of Ochi,
her pearly hems muddied
in morning dew,
her robe drenched in evening mist,
for the Prince she cannot meet again.

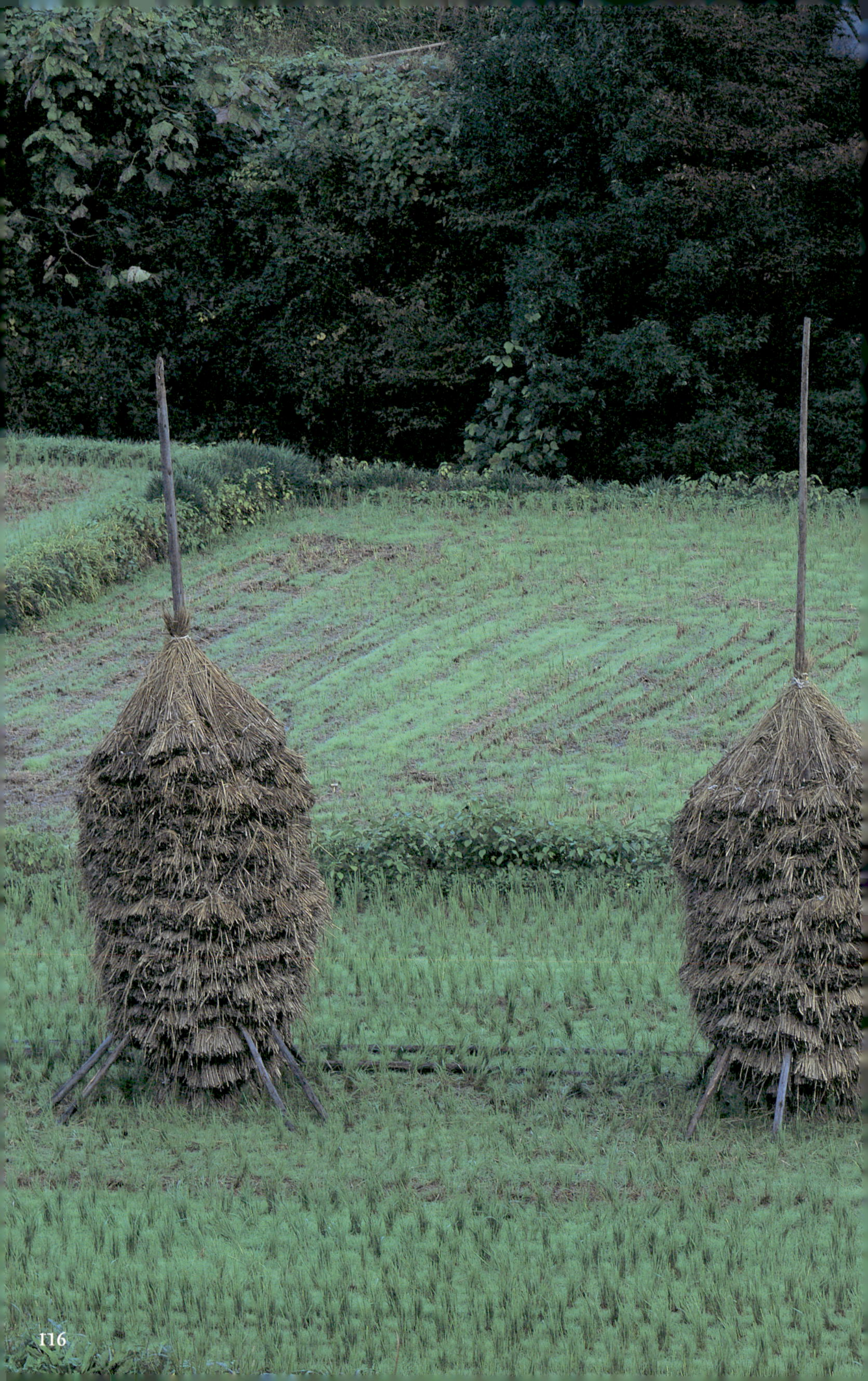

117

まの　夜床も荒るらむ　そこ故に　慰めかねて　けだしくも　逢ふやと思ひて　玉垂の　越智の大野の　朝露に　玉裳はひづち　夕霧に　衣は沾れて　草枕　旅宿かもする　逢はぬ君ゆゑ

飛ぶ鳥の明日香川の川上の美しい藻は川下に流れもつれあう。その藻のようにさまざまに寄りそいいるでしょう。闇の夜は、寝床も荒れているでしょう。闇の夜は、寝床も荒れて、私は草を枕の旅やどりをすることだ。そう思うと私の心は慰めかねてきっとお逢いできるだろうかと思って玉を貫く越智の大野の、朝の露に美しい裳裾（すそ）は濡れて、夕べの霧に衣は濡れて、私は草を枕の旅やどりをすることだ。もう生きて逢えないあなたゆゑに。

靡きあった夫のあなたは、重ね合ったやわらかな肌さえも、剣や大刀のよう

一九四 柿本朝臣人麿の泊瀬部皇女（はつせべのひめみこ）・忍坂部皇子（おさかべのみこ）に献（たてまつ）れる歌一首

飛鳥（とぶとり）の　明日香（あすか）の河の　上（かみ）つ瀬に　生（お）ふる玉藻は　下（しも）つ瀬に
流れ触（ふ）らばふ　玉藻なす　か寄りかく寄り　靡（なび）かひし　嬬（つま）の命（みこと）
のたたなづく　柔膚（にぎはだ）すらを　剣刀（つるぎたち）　身に副（そ）へ寝（ね）ねば　ぬばた

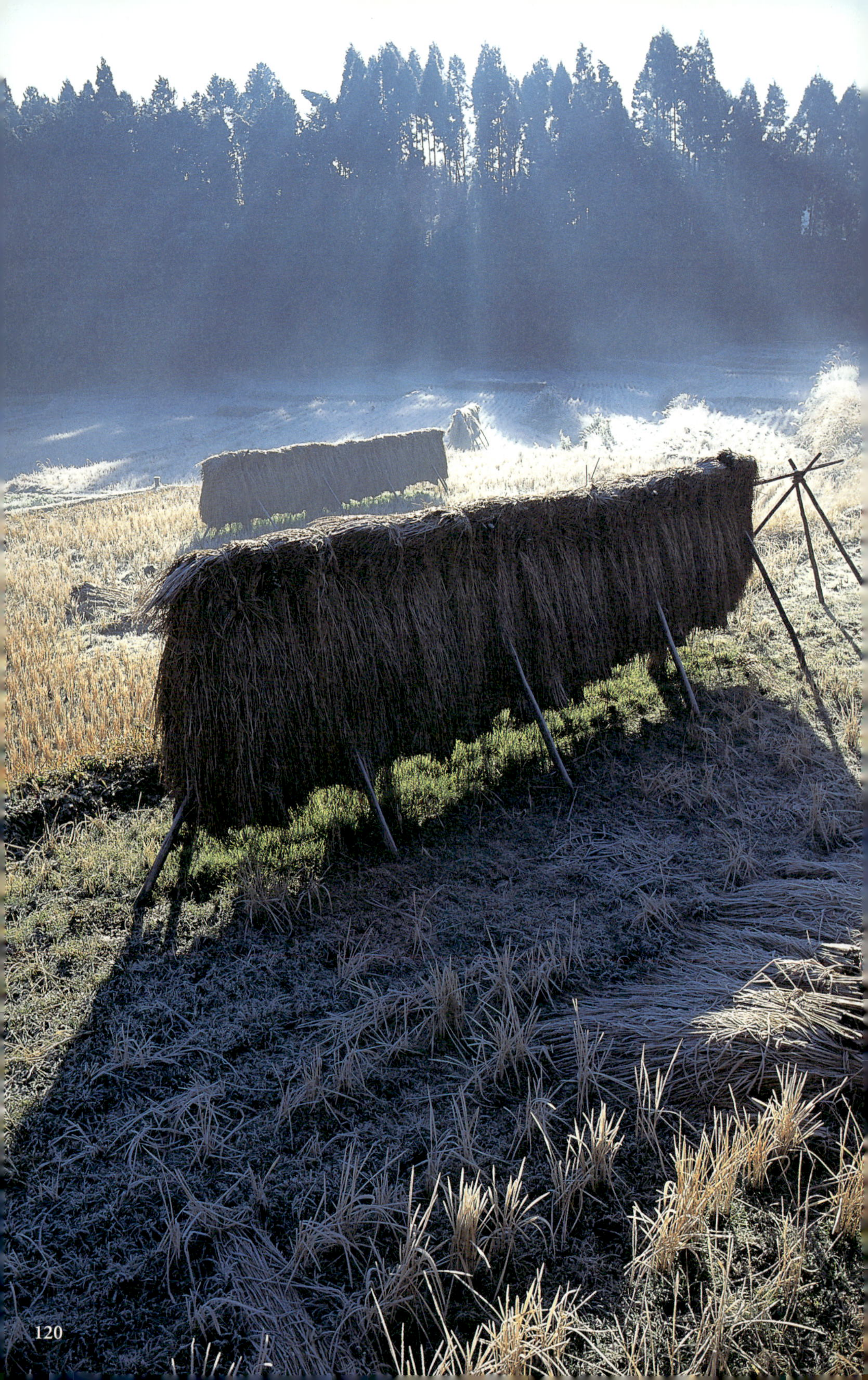

Envoys to two poems by Kakinomoto Hitomaro as he shed tears of blood in his grief following the death of his wife

Too dense the yellowed leaves
on the autumn mountain:
my wife is lost
and I do not know the path
to find her by.

二〇八

柿本朝臣人麿の妻死りし後に、泣血ち哀慟みて作れる歌二首　に付随する短歌二首

秋山の黄葉を茂み迷ひぬる妹を求めむ山道知らずも

秋山の黄葉が繁っているので道に迷ってしまった妻を探そうにも、山道を知らないことよ。

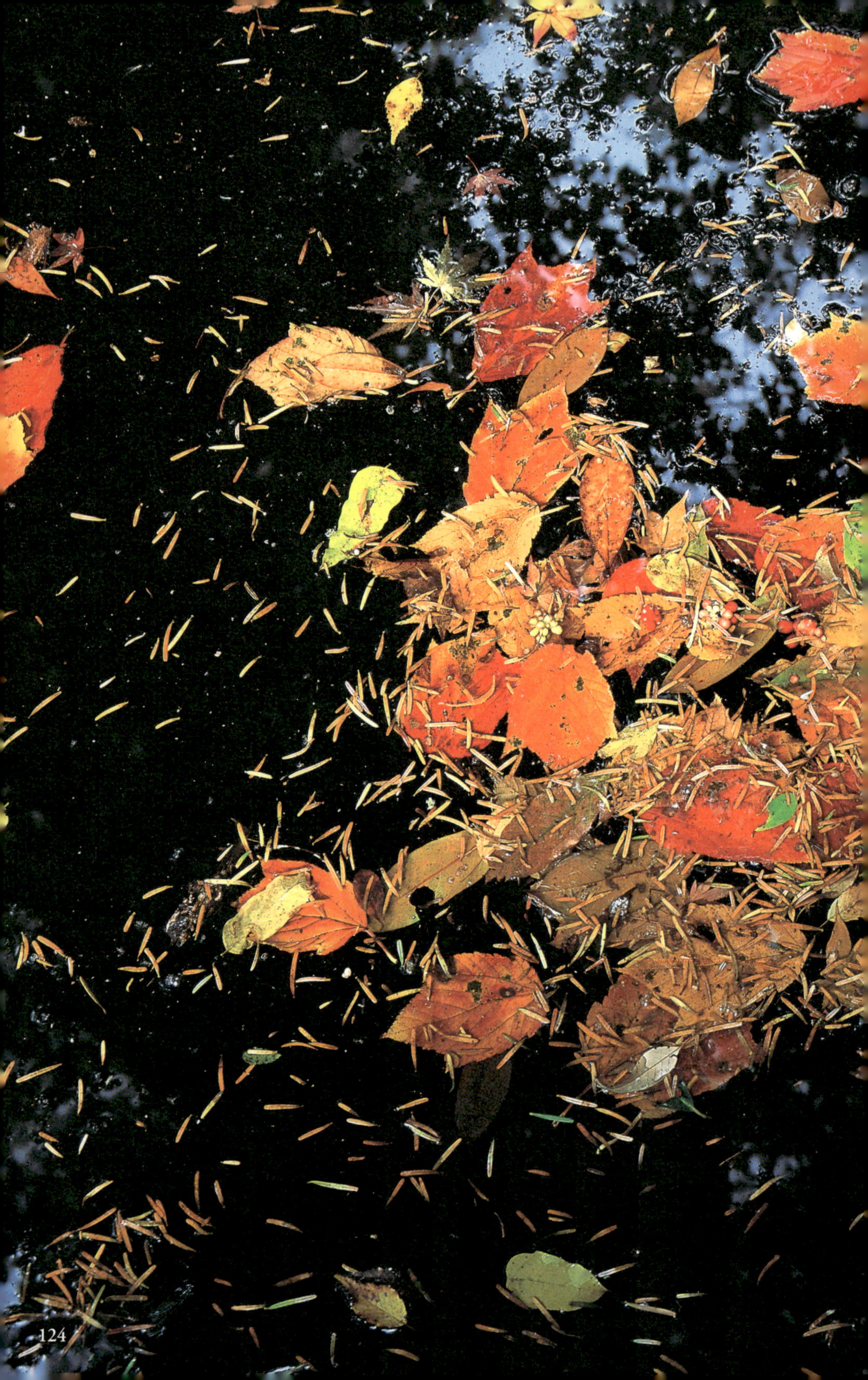

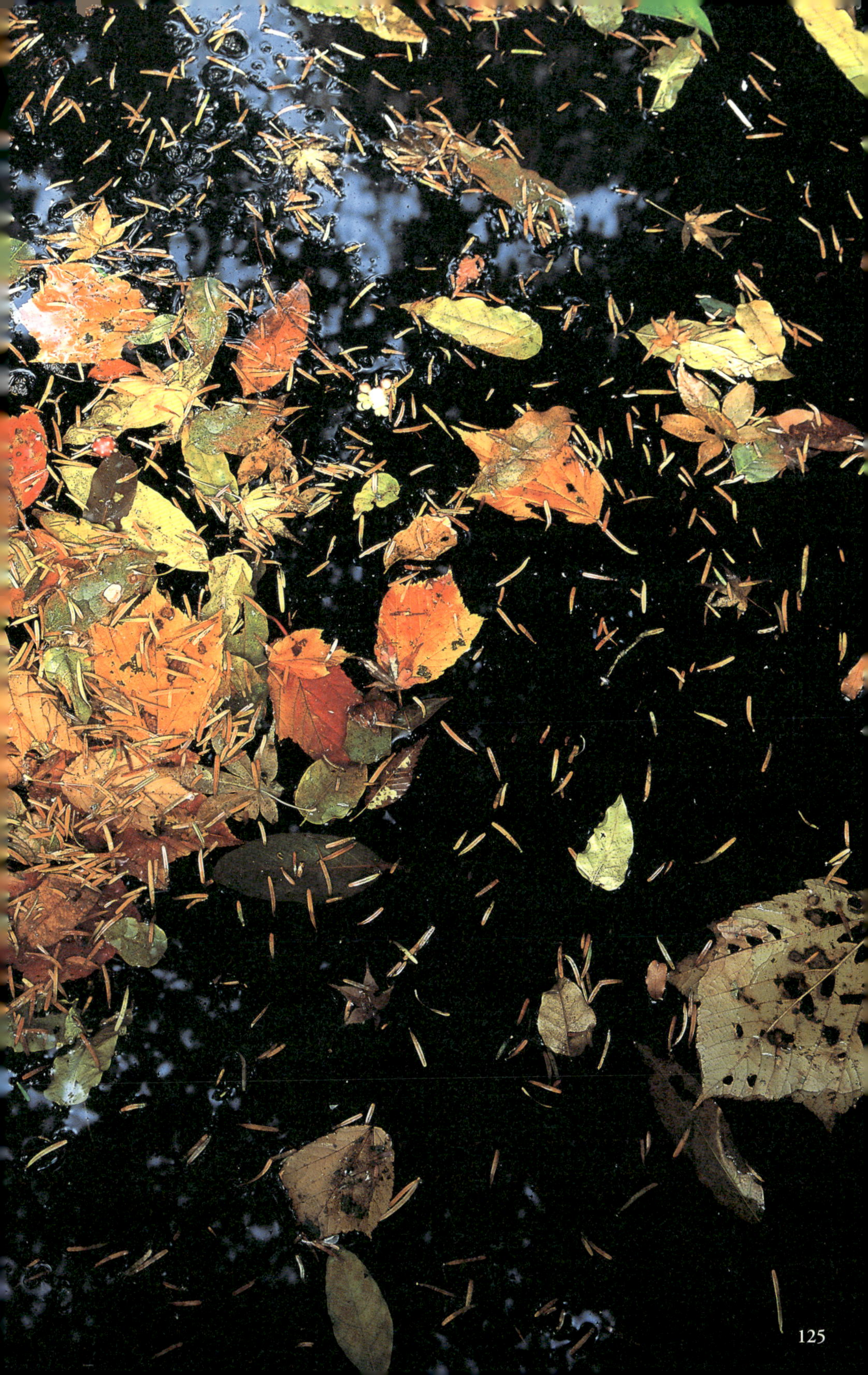

The autumn moon shines as it did
when I watched last year,
but my wife, who watched with me—
the drift of the year has taken her.

二二一

去年(こぞ)見てし秋の月夜(つくよ)は照らせども相見(あひ)し妹(いも)はいや年さかる

昨年は共に見た秋の月が、今年も同じように照っているけれども、妻ひとりは、ますます年とともに遠ざかることよ。

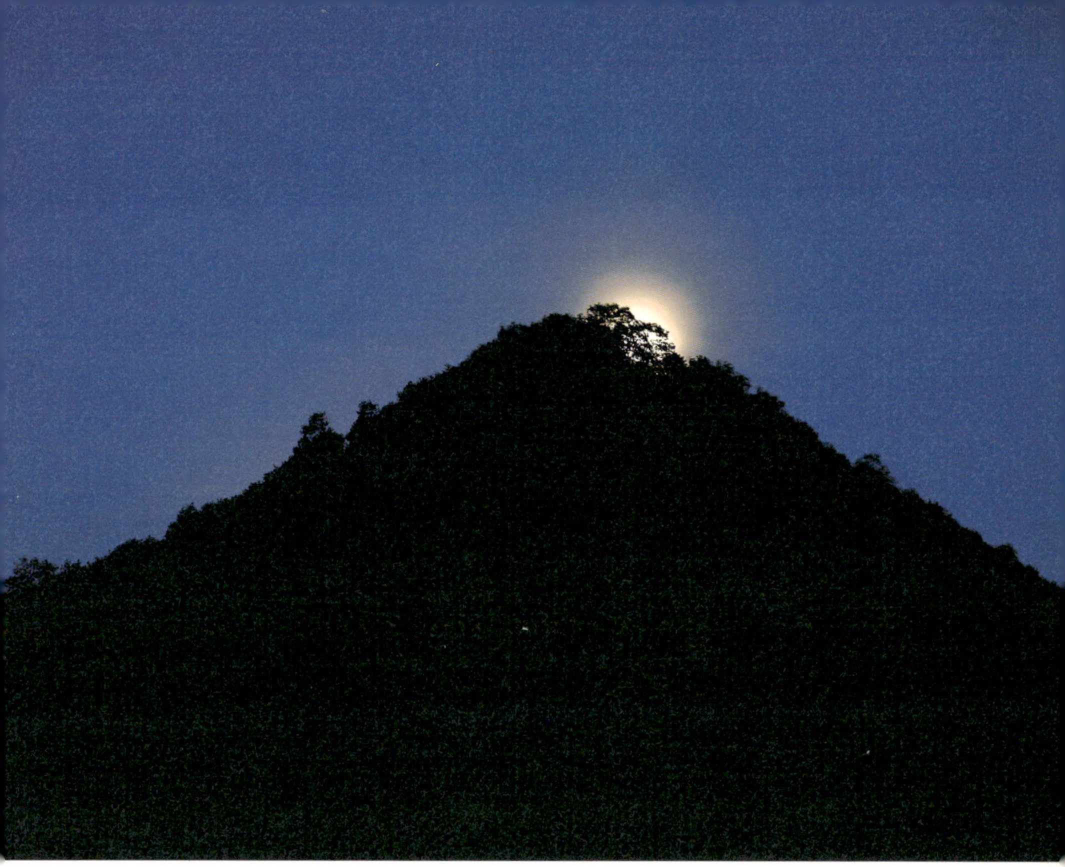

Envoy to poem by Kakinomoto Hitomaro upon seeing a dead man lying among the rocks on the island of Samine in Sanuki

Making a finely woven pillow
of the rocky shore
    where waves from the offing
        draw near,
you, who sleep there!

二二二

柿本朝臣人麻呂の作れる歌一首　に付随する反歌
讃岐の狭岑島に、石の中に死れる人を視て、

沖つ波来よる荒磯を敷栲の枕と枕きて寝せる君かも

沖の波がうち寄せる荒磯を、やわらかであるべき枕として寝ておられるあなたよ。

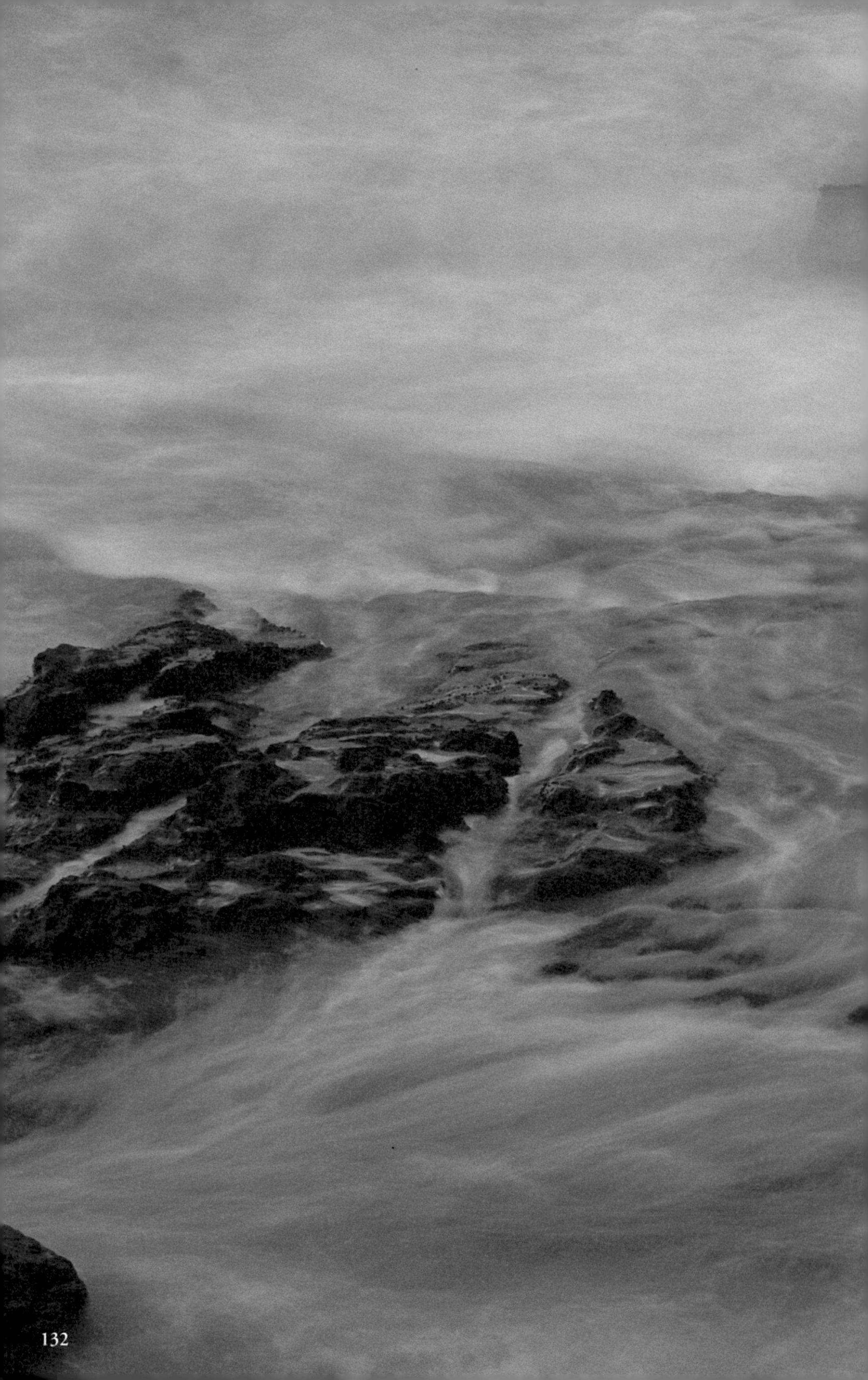

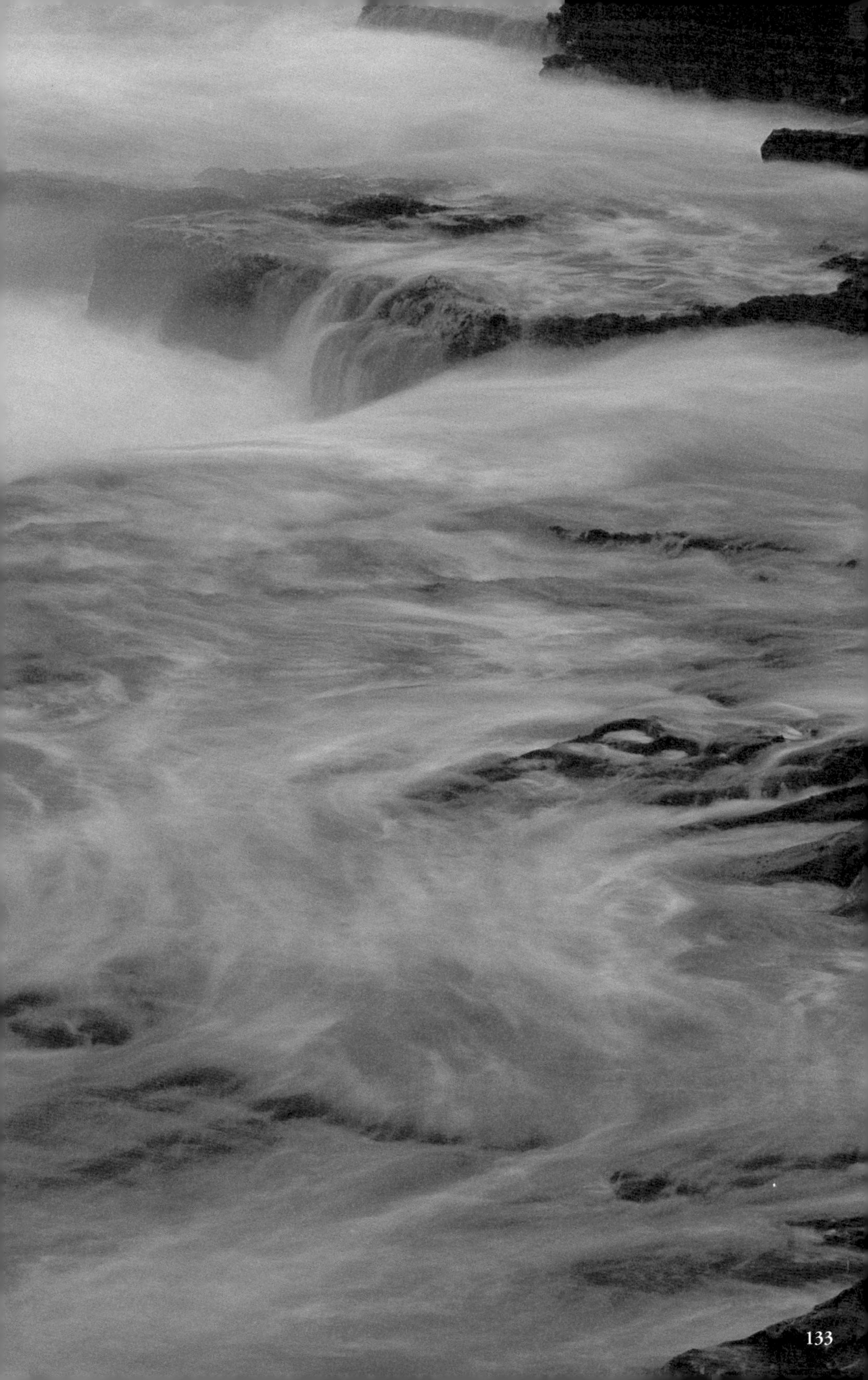

from
Poem upon the death of Prince Shiki in the ninth month, autumn, of the first year of Reiki (715)

"What flames are those?" I asked,
"what flames burning, bright
as field-fires on the spring plains,
by Takamato Mountain?"
One who came walking on that road
    straight as a jade spear
stopped, and with tears that fell
      like drizzling rain,
        drenching his white garments,
spoke to me:
"Why must you ask such a thing?
If you ask me,
  I shall cry out in my weeping.

If I speak it,
   it will pain my heart.
It is the torches they carry
in the funeral procession
of the Emperor's son
that make a profusion of light."

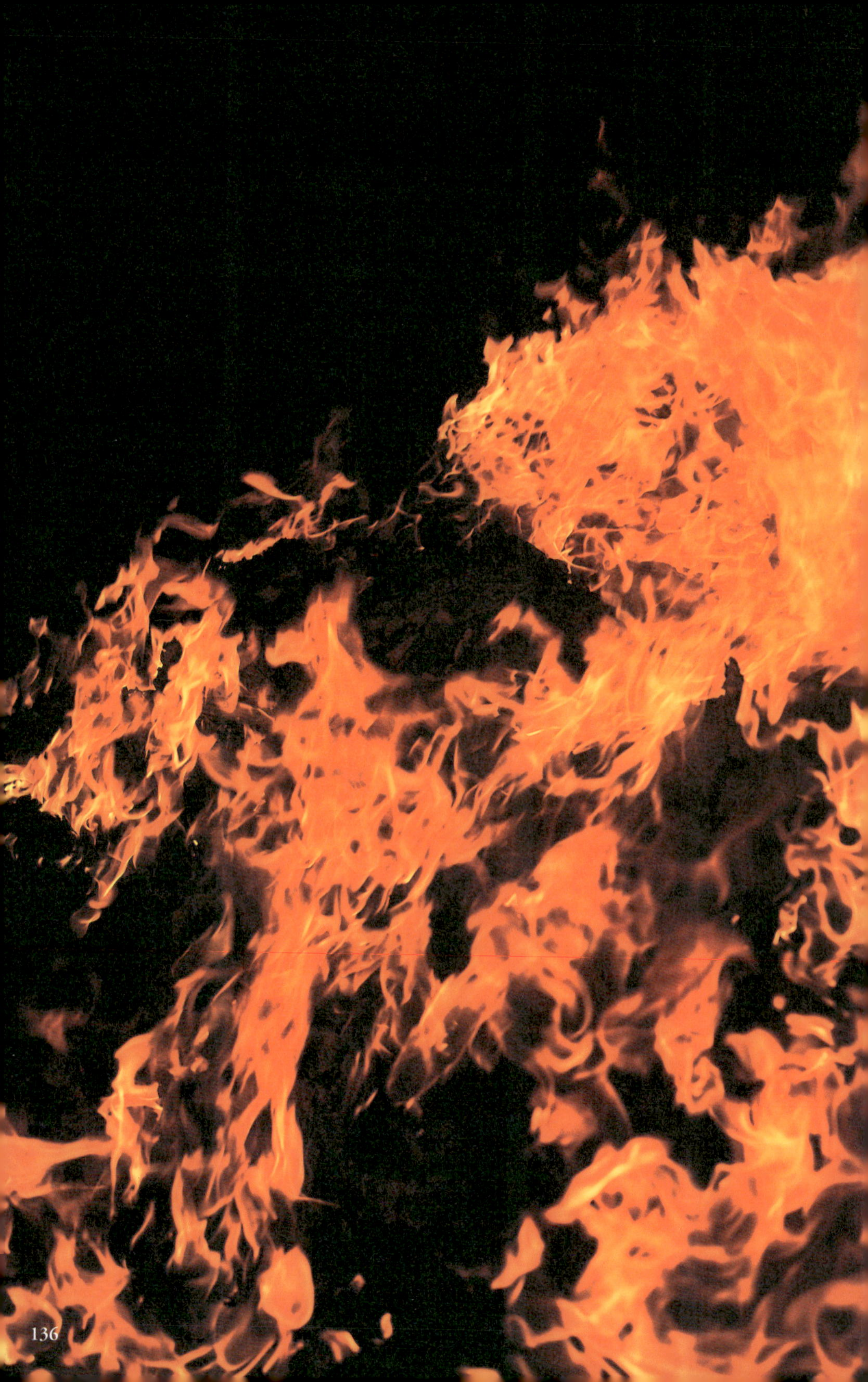

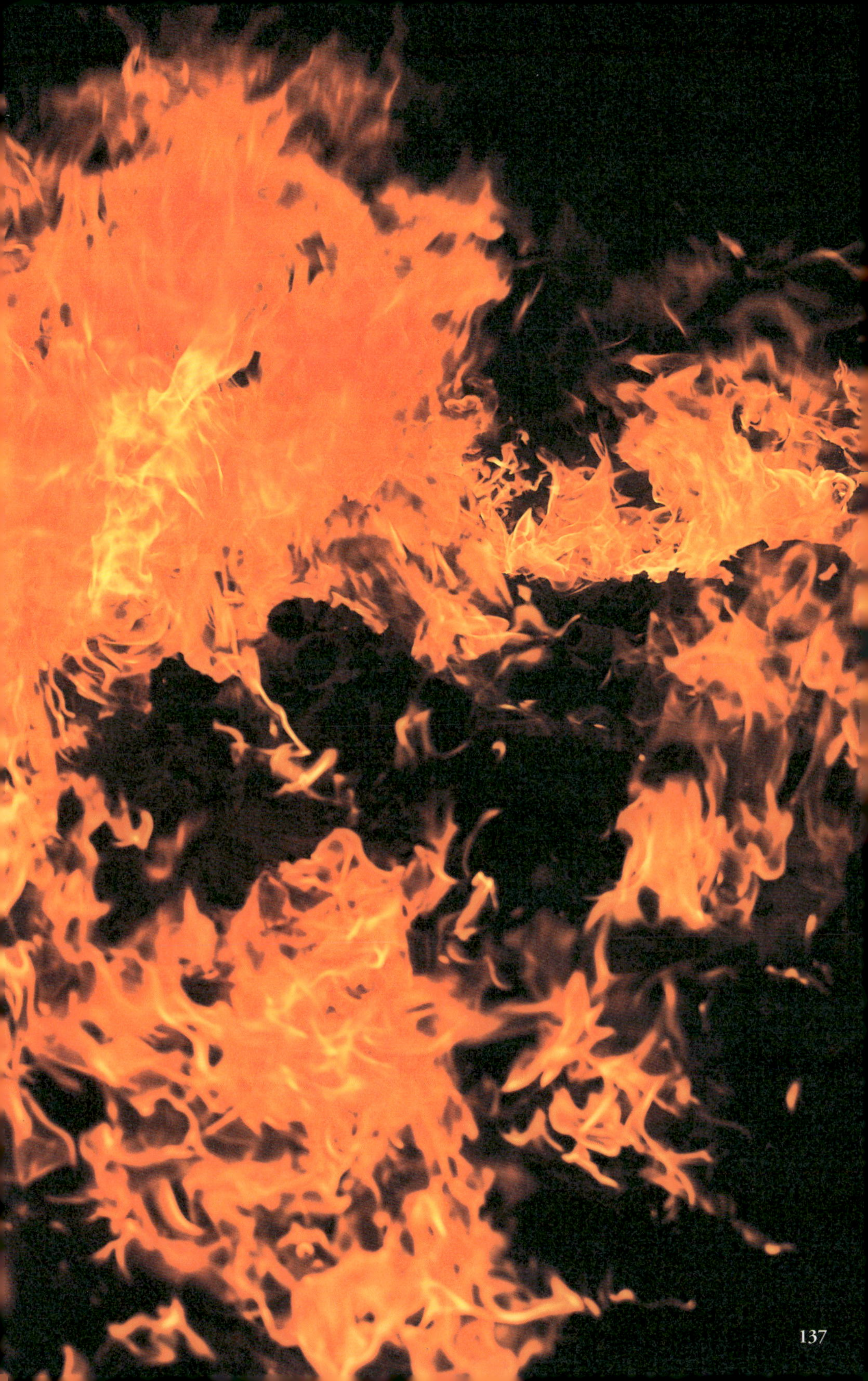

聞けば　哭（ね）のみし泣かゆ　語れば　心そ痛き　天皇（すめろき）の　神の御（み）
子の　いでましの　手火（たび）の光りそ　ここだ照りたる

高円山に、春の野を焼く火と思われるほど燃えている火を、「どうしたのか」と尋ねると、玉桙の道を来る人は、泣く涙を小雨のように降らし、白い衣濡らして立ちどまって私に語る。「どうしてか」と声をかけられるとまた涙もあらたになる。語ると心が痛む。あれは天皇の神の御子があの世におでましになる手火の光がおびただしく輝いて私に語る。「どうしているのだ」と。

二三〇

霊亀元年歳次乙卯の秋九月に、
志貴親王の薨りましし時の歌一首 より

高円山に 春野焼く 野火と見るまで もゆる火を いかにと
問へば 玉桙の 道来る人の 泣く涙 霑霂に降り 白栲の
衣ひづちて 立ち留り われに語らく 何しかも もとな唁ふ

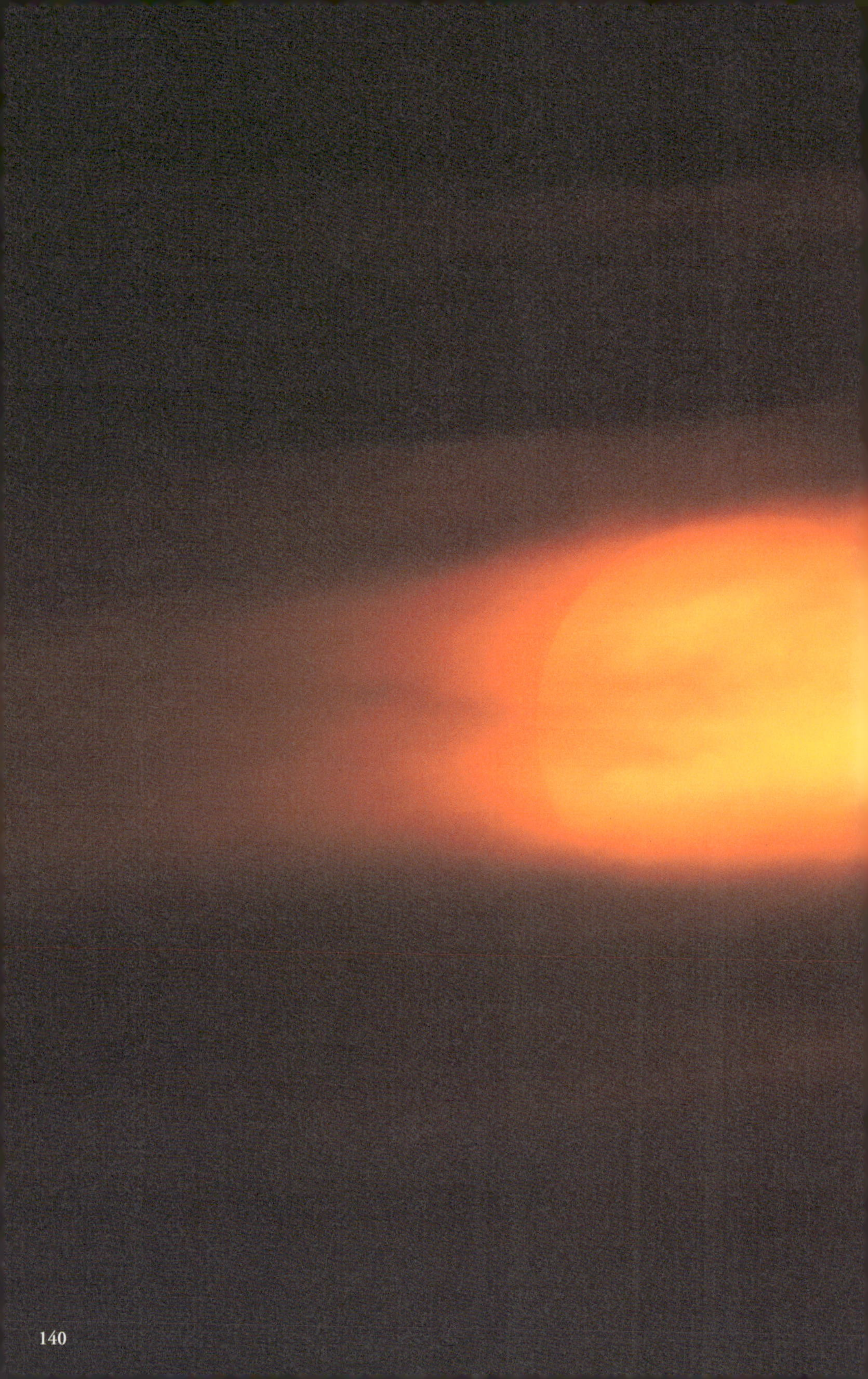

*One of eight poems of travel by
Kakinomoto Hitomaro*

Will I part rowing to the sun
that sinks into the Akashi Straits,
    bright with lampfires,
the land of home beyond my sight?

二五四

柿本朝臣人麿（かきのもとのあそみひとまろ）の羈旅（たび）の歌八首（その一首）

留火（ともしび）の明石（あかし）大門（おほと）に入（い）る日にか漕（こ）ぎ別れなむ家（いへ）のあたり見ず

ともしびの明るい明石海峡に入っていく日に、漕ぎ別れてゆくのだろうか、家のあたりを見ずに。

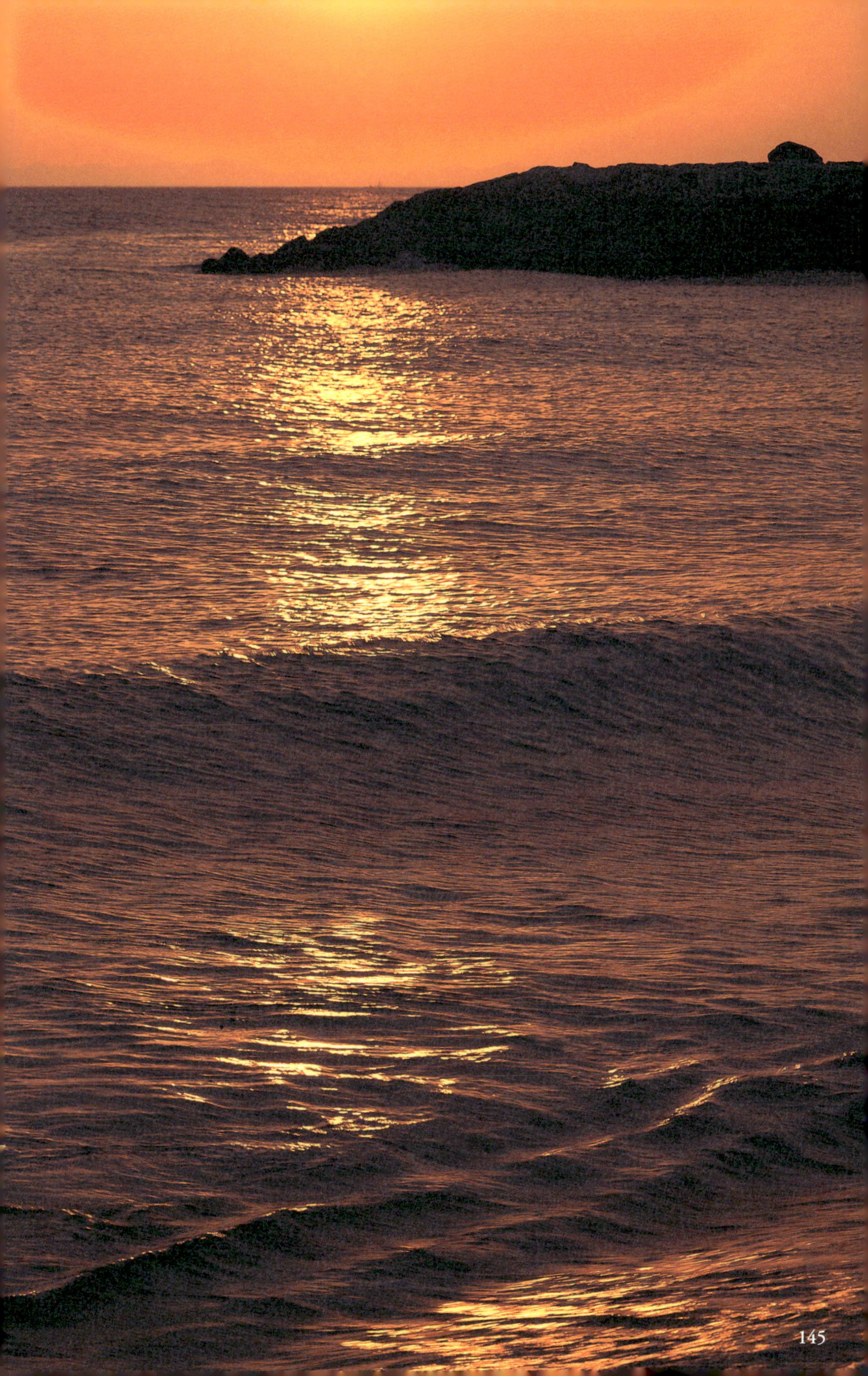

Poem by Kakinomoto Hitomaro

Plover skimming evening waves
on the Ōmi Sea,
when you cry
      so my heart trails
like dwarf bamboo
      down to the past.

二六六

柿本朝臣人麿の歌一首

淡海(あふみ)の海夕波(ゆふなみ)千鳥(ちどり)汝(な)が鳴けば情(こころ)もしのに古(いにしへ)思ほゆ

淡海の海の夕波を飛ぶ千鳥よ、お前が鳴くと心もしなえるように昔のことが思われる。

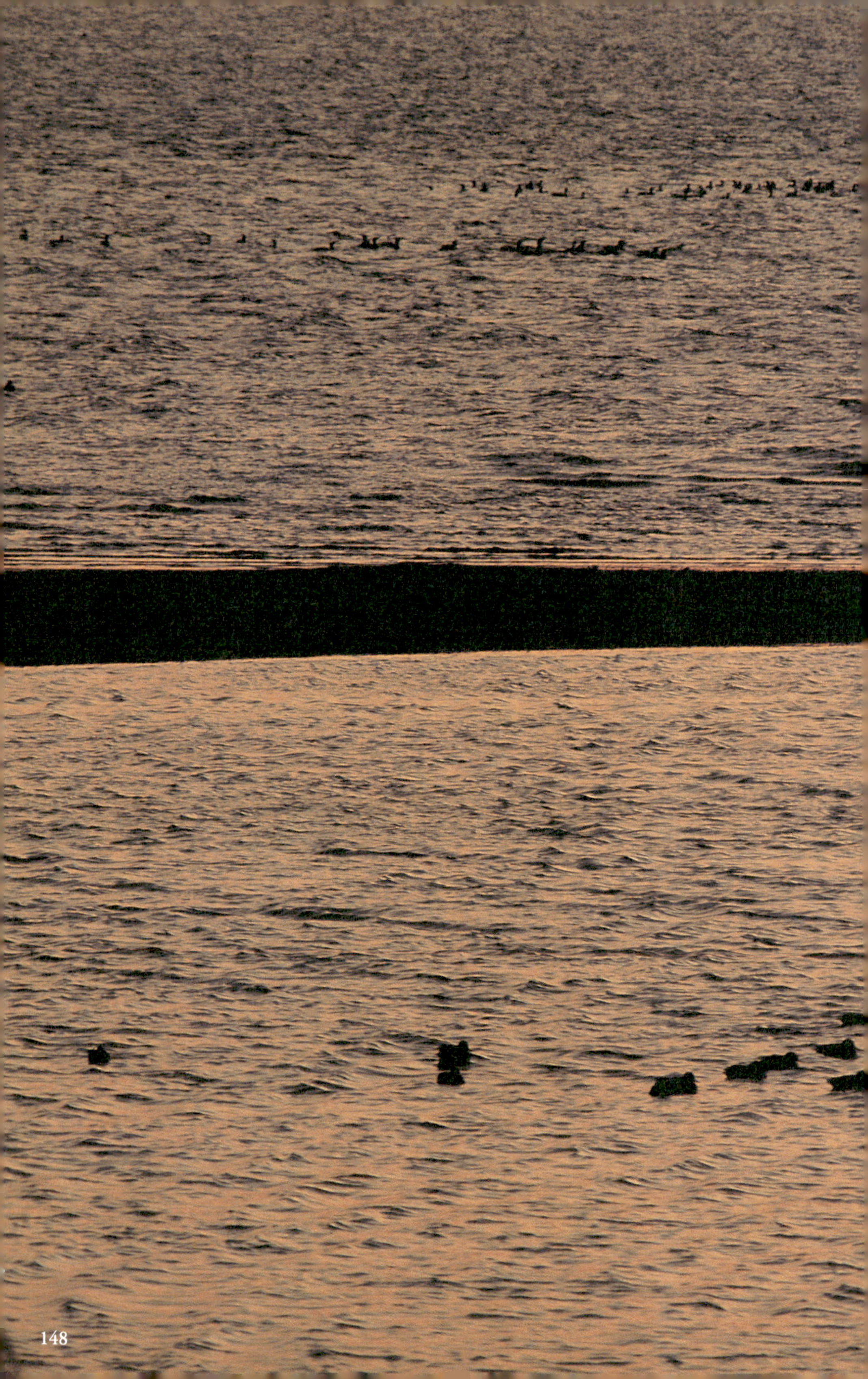

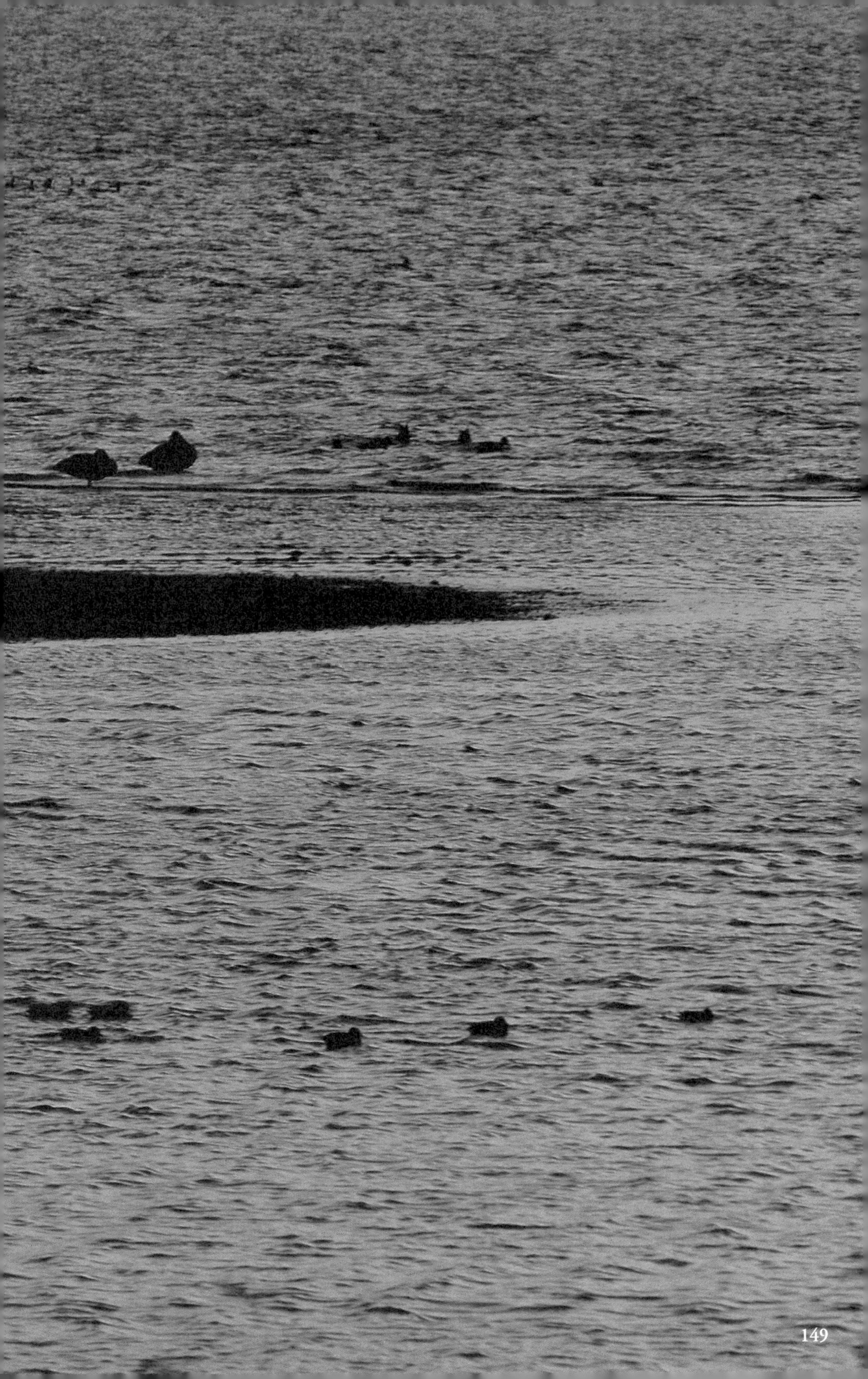

Envoy to poem by the councillor, Lord Ōtomo Tabito, written in response to an imperial command, during the procession to the detached palace at Yoshino in the late spring

Gazing now
on the stream at Kisa
that I gazed on in the past,
I see how, more and more,
it has become bright and clear.

316

三一六

暮春の月に芳野の離宮に幸しし時に、
中納言大伴卿の勅を奉りて作れる歌一首 に付随する反歌

昔見し象の小河を今見ればいよよ清けくなりにけるかも

昔見た象の小川は、今見るとますます清らかになっていることだ。

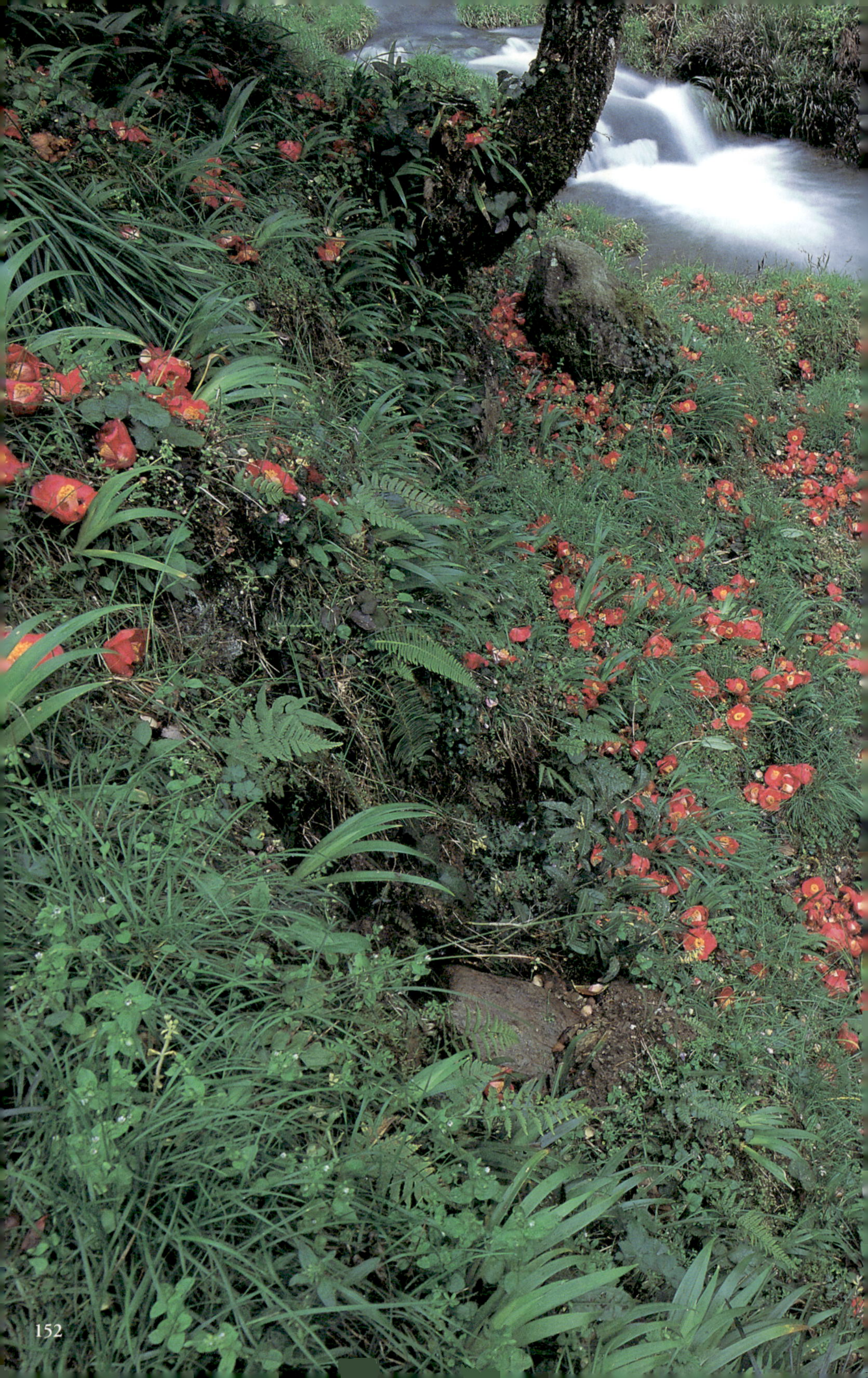

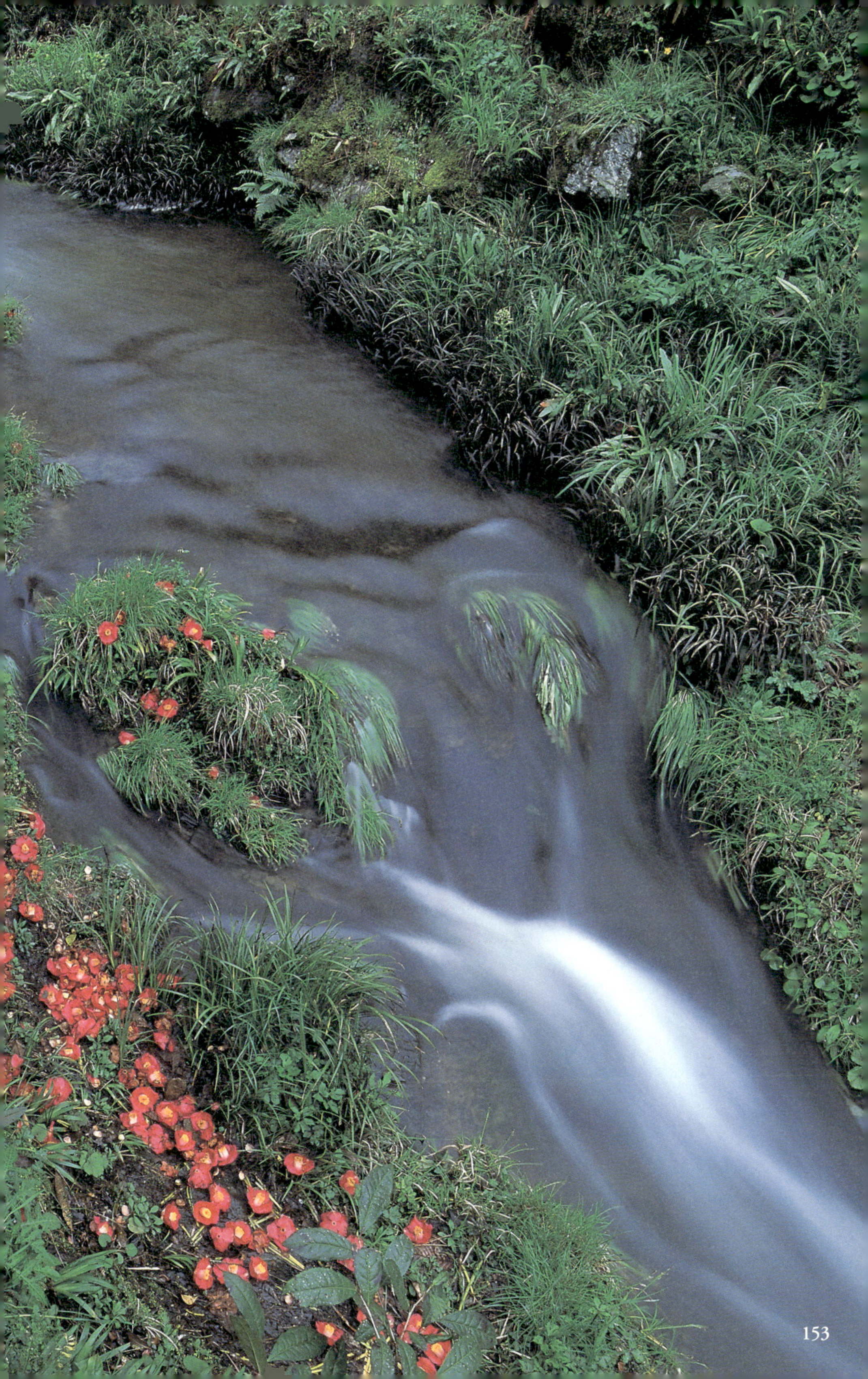

Poem on viewing Mount Fuji by Yamabe Akahito

Since the time
when heaven and earth split apart,
Fuji's lofty peak
has stood in the land of Suruga,
    high and noble,
      like a very god.

As I gaze up to it
through the fields of heaven,
I see it hides the light
of the sky-traversing sun,
and the very gleam of the moon
is invisible in its shadow.
It thwarts the white clouds

from their path,
and snow falls on its summit
outside the bounds of time.
Let us speak of it
and recount it to the ages—
Fuji's lofty peak!

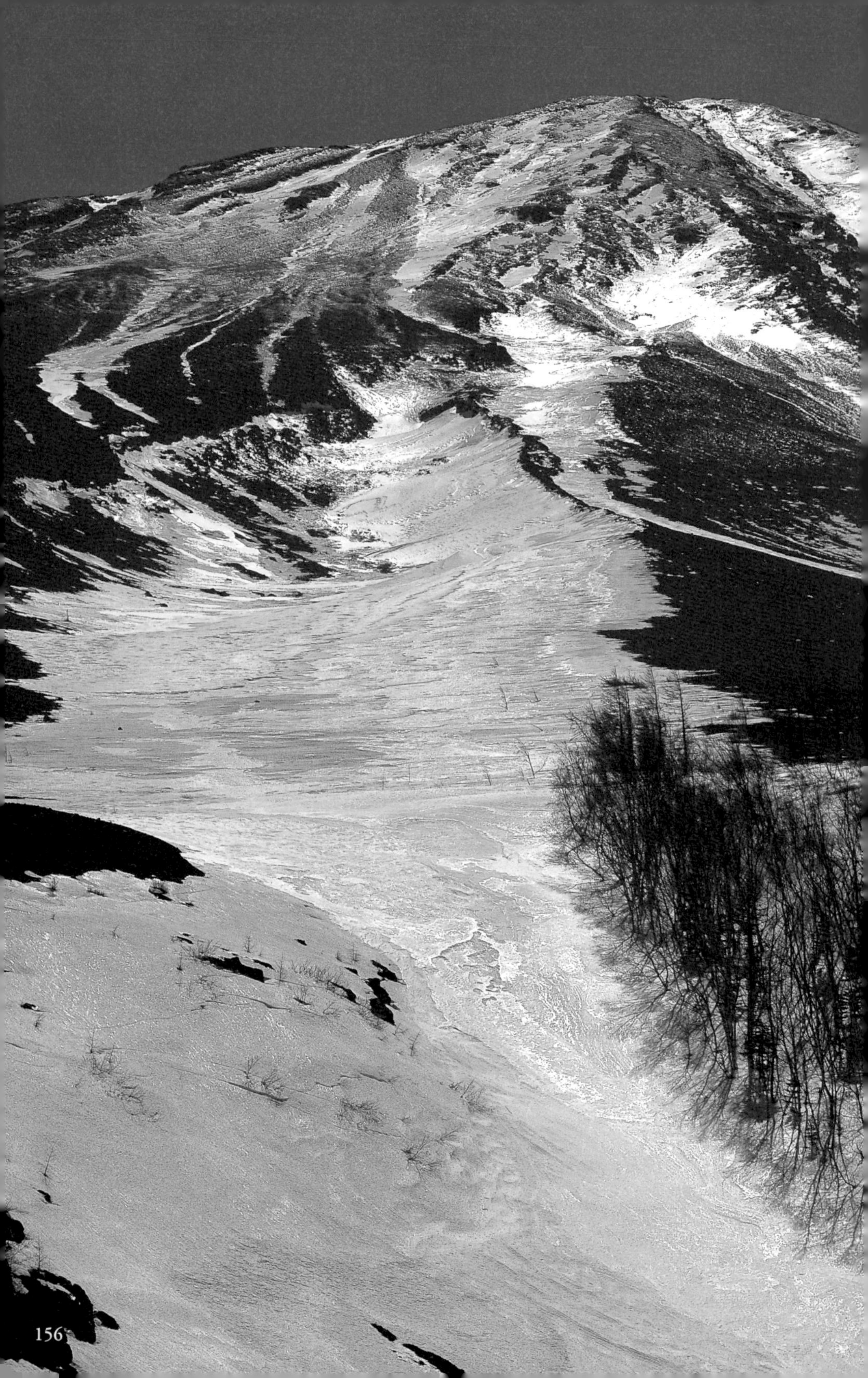

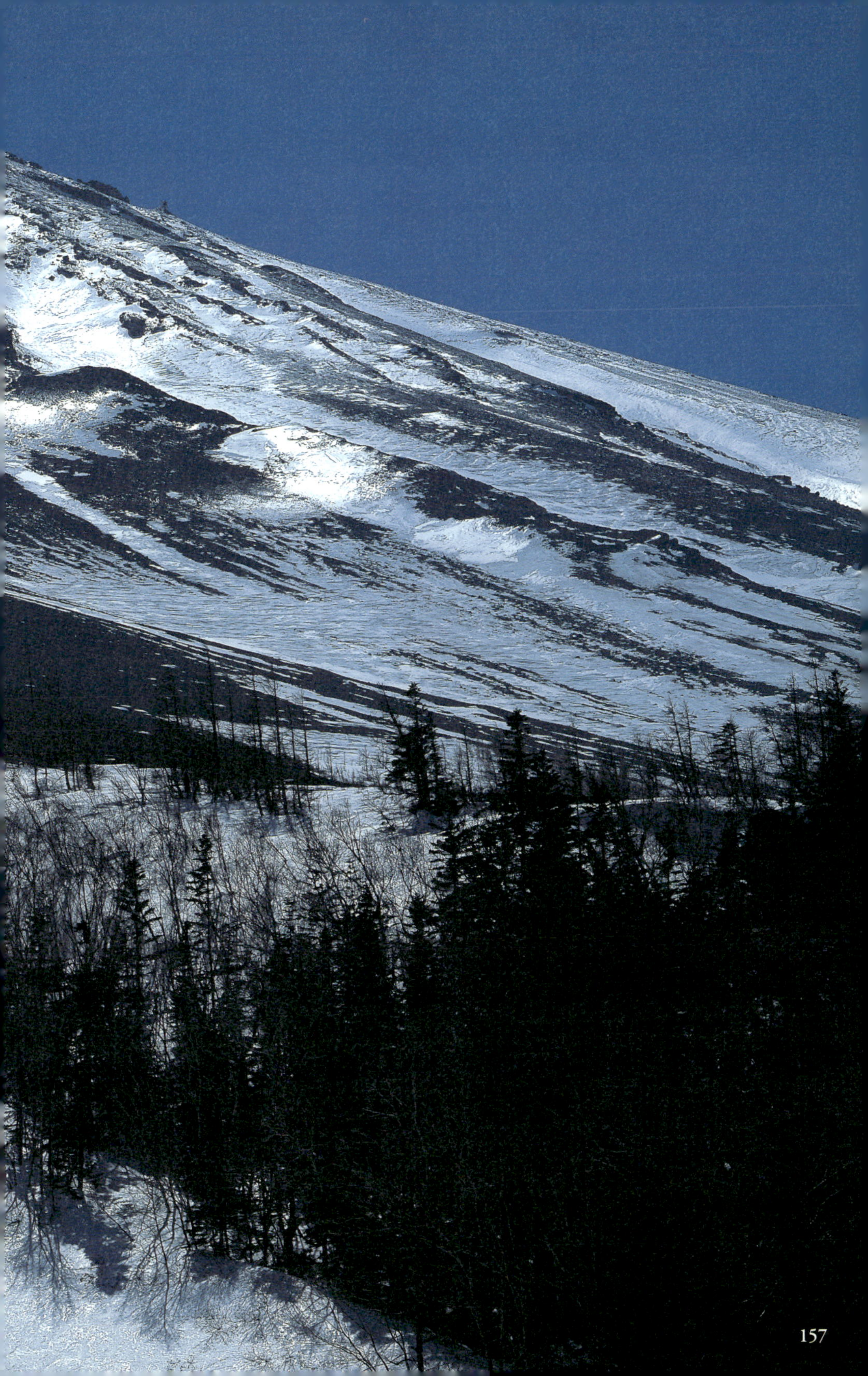

照る月の　光も見えず　白雲（しらくも）も　い行きはばかり　時じくそ
雪は降りける　語り継（つ）ぎ　言ひ継ぎ行かむ　不尽（ふじ）の高嶺（たかね）は

三一七

山部宿禰赤人の不尽山を望める歌一首 より

天地の　分かれし時ゆ　神さびて　高く貴き　駿河なる　布士
の高嶺を　天の原　振り放け見れば　渡る日の　影も隠らひ

天地の初めて分かれた時からずっと、神々しく高く貴い駿河の富士の高嶺を、天遠くふり仰いでみると、空渡る太陽の光もさえぎられ、白雲も流れなずんで、いつも雪が降っている。これからも語りつぎ、言いついでいこう、富士の高嶺は。頂に隠れ、照る月の光も

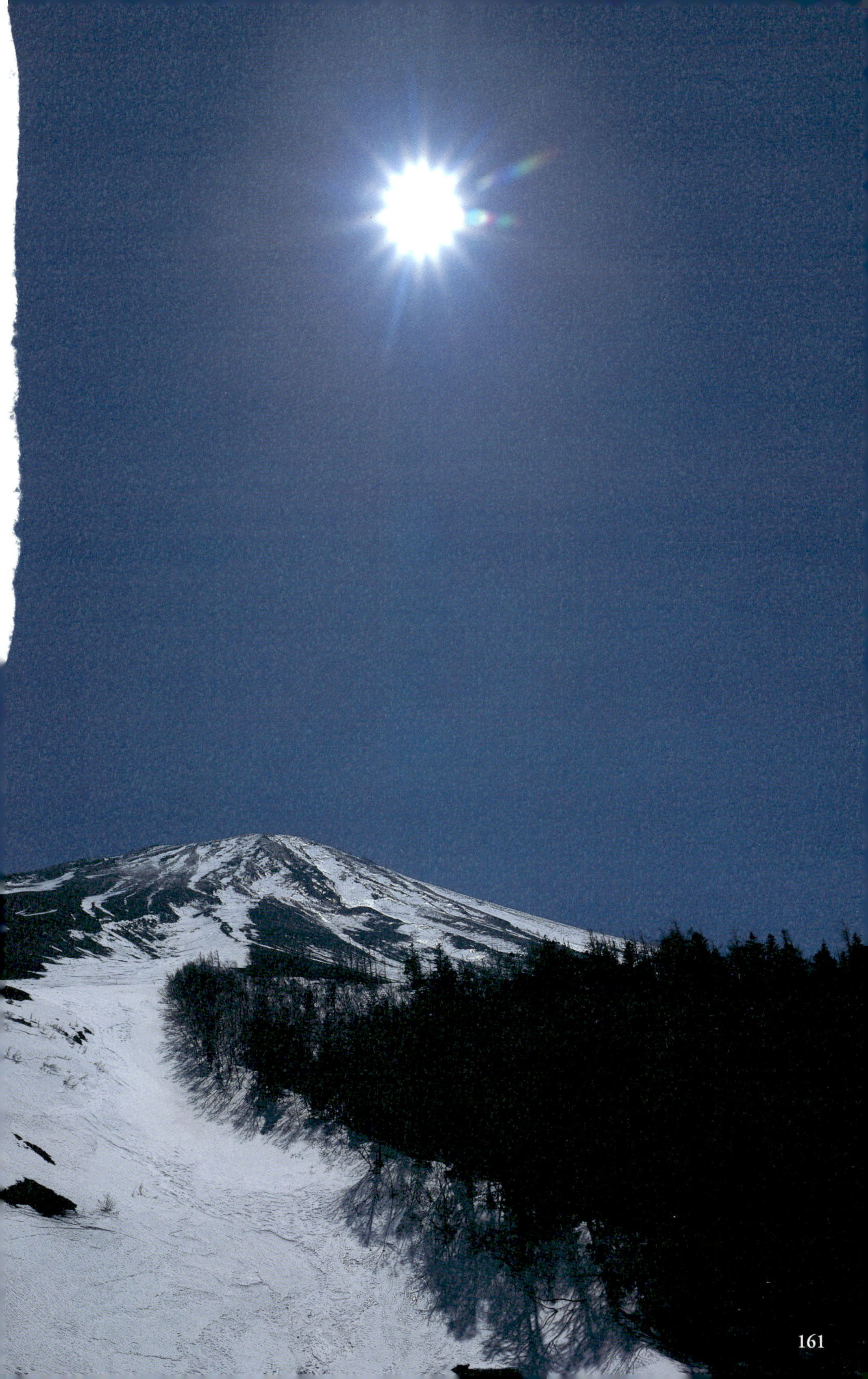

Envoy

Coming out
    from Tago's nestled cove,
I gaze:
    white, pure white
the snow has fallen
on Fuji's lofty peak.

三一八

反歌

田児(たご)の浦ゆうち出でて見れば真白(ましろ)にそ不尽(ふじ)の高嶺(たかね)に雪は降りける

田児の浦を通って出て見るとまっ白に富士の高嶺に雪が降っていたことだ。

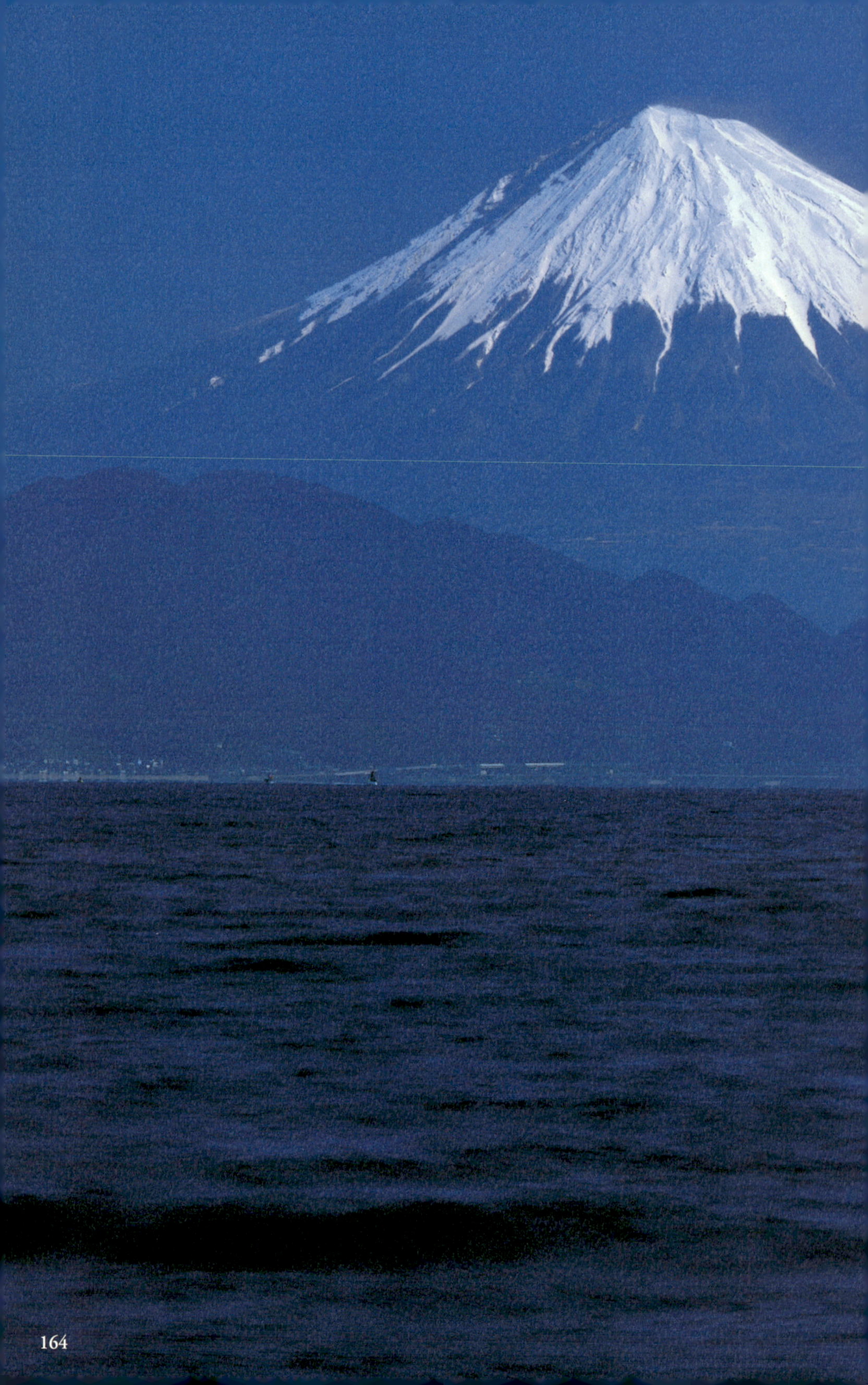

from
Poem about Mount Fuji

Rising between the lands of Kai,
   of the dark mountain pass,
and Suruga,
   where the waves draw near,
is Fuji's lofty peak.
It thwarts the very clouds
      from their path.
Even the birds
   cannot reach its summit
      on their wings.
There, the snow drowns the flame
and the flame melts the snow.
I cannot speak of it,
I cannot name it,
this occultly dwelling god!

三一九

不尽山を詠める歌一首 より

なまよみの 甲斐の国 うち寄する 駿河の国と こちごちの 国のみ中ゆ 出で立てる 不尽の高嶺は 天雲も い行きはばかり 飛ぶ鳥も 飛びも上らず 燃ゆる火を 雪もち消ち 降る雪を 火もち消ちつつ 言ひもえず 名づけも知らず 霊しくも います神かも

なまよみの甲斐の国と、高嶺は、天雲も流れたゆ波うち寄せる駿河の国と、たい、空とぶ鳥もそこまあちこちの国のまん中に ではのぼらず、頂に燃えそびえ立っている富士の うもなく、とおとくいる火は雪で消し、また降 っしゃる神であるよ。る雪を火によって消し、いいようもなく名づけよ

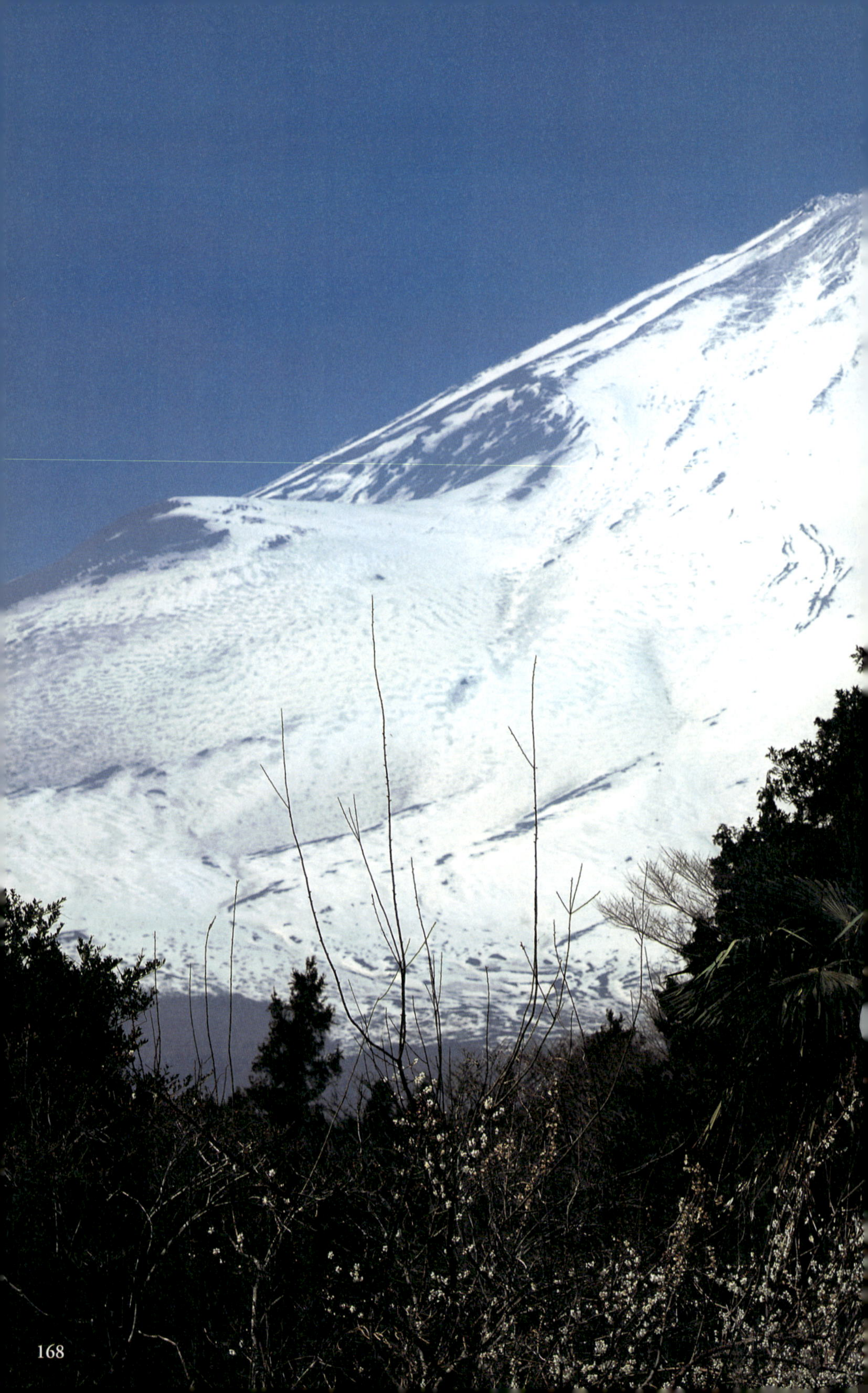

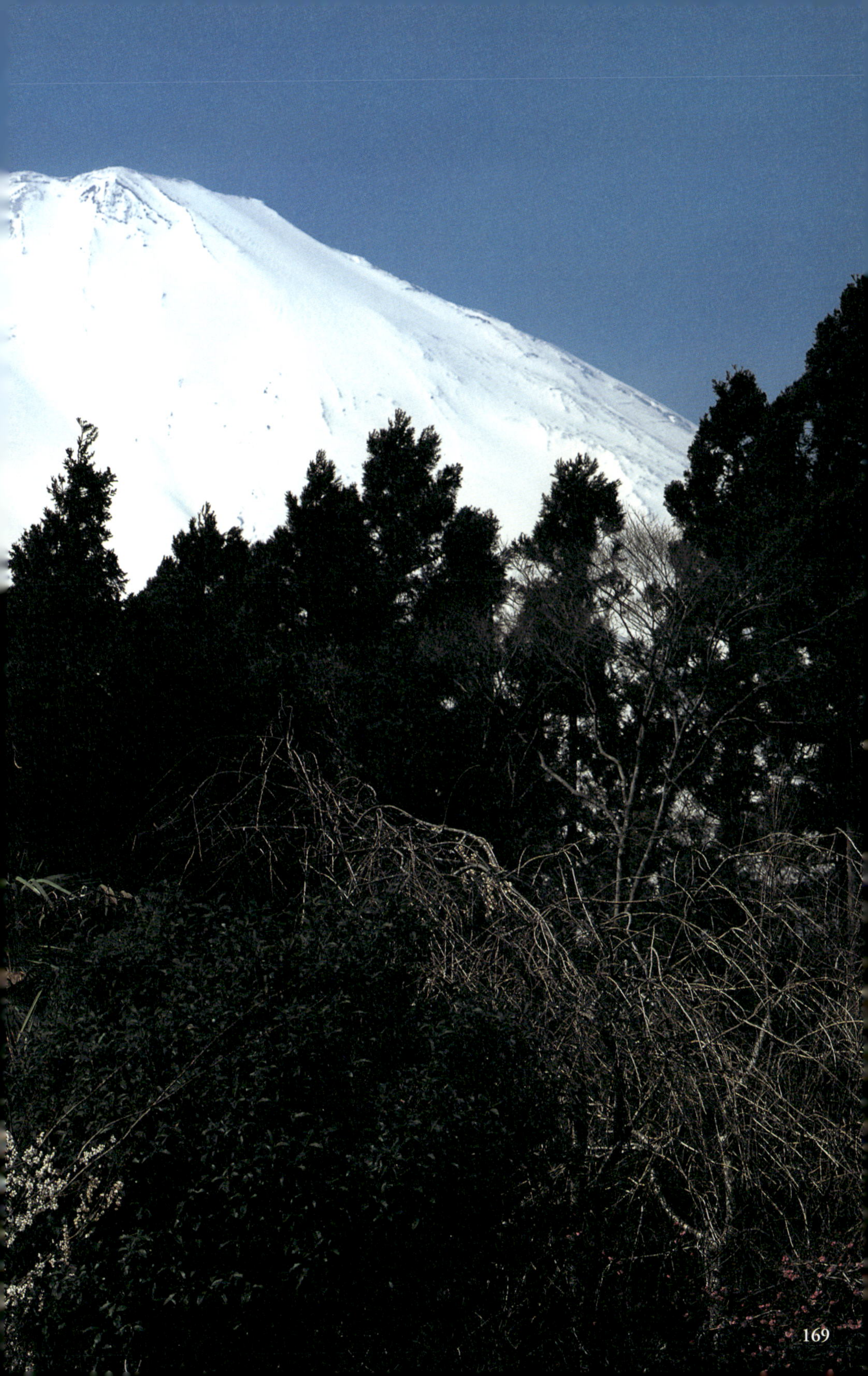

Envoy

Because of Fuji's lofty heights,
even the heavenly clouds,
    in their awe,
are thwarted from their path
and hang there trailing.

三二一

反歌

不尽の嶺を高み恐(かしこ)み天雲(あまぐも)もい行きはばかりたなびくものを

富士の山が高くおそれ多いので、天雲も流れたゆたって、頂にたなびくものを。

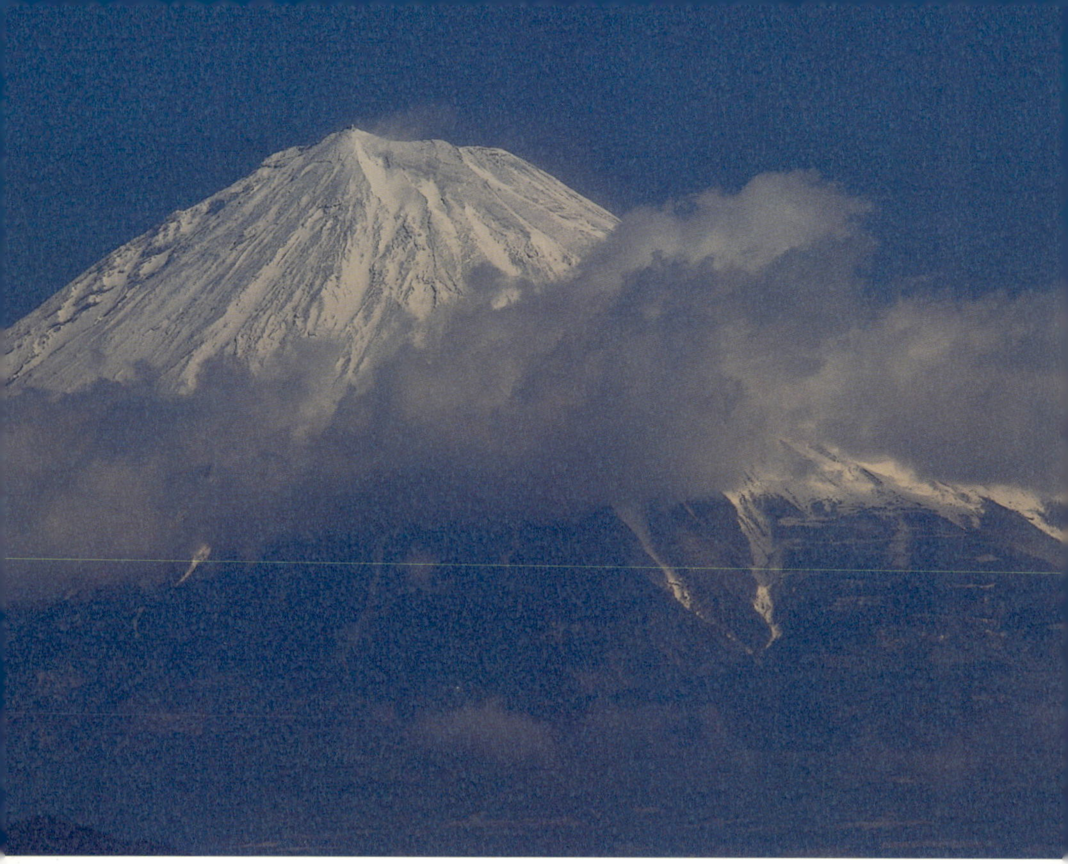

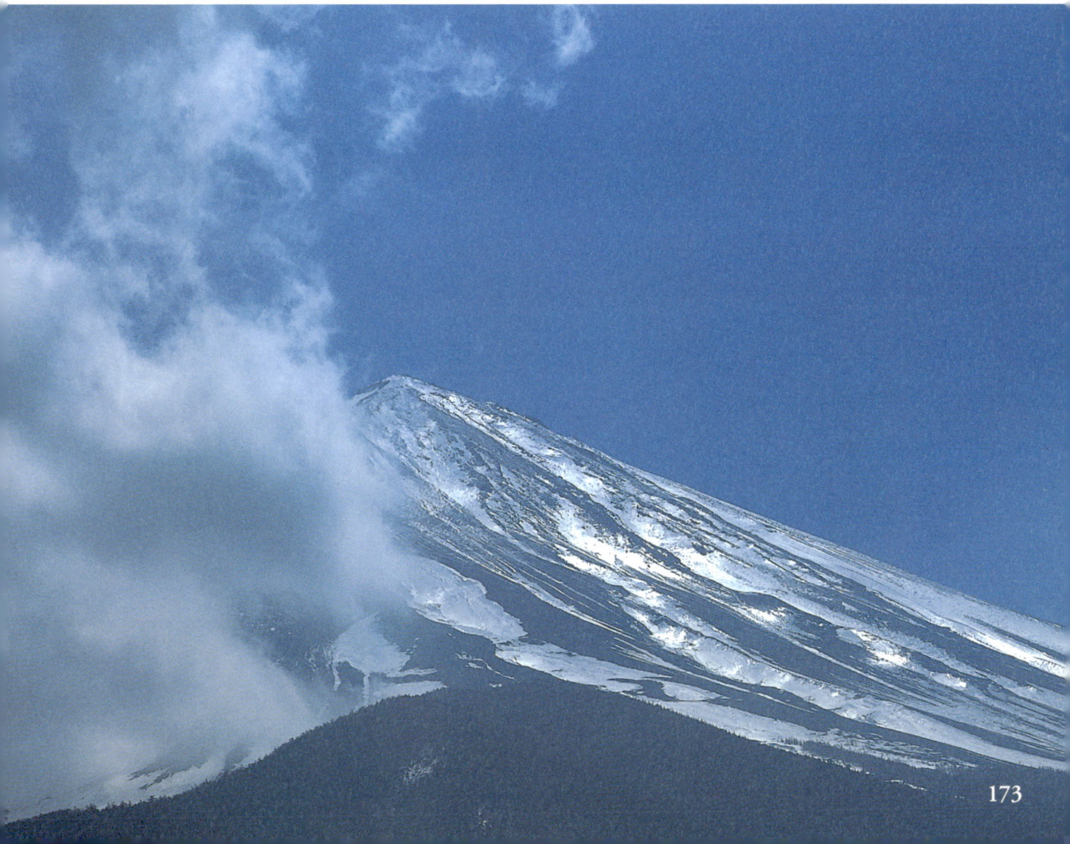

Poem by Ono Oyu, the Vice-Commander of the Dazaifu

The capital at Nara,
  beautiful in green earth,
flourishes now
like the luster
of the flowers in bloom.

三二八

大宰少弐小野老朝臣の歌一首
だざいのせうにをののおゆのあそみ

あをによし寧楽の京師は咲く花の薫ふがごとく今盛りなり

青丹も美しい奈良の都は、
咲きさかる花のかがやく
ように、今盛りである。

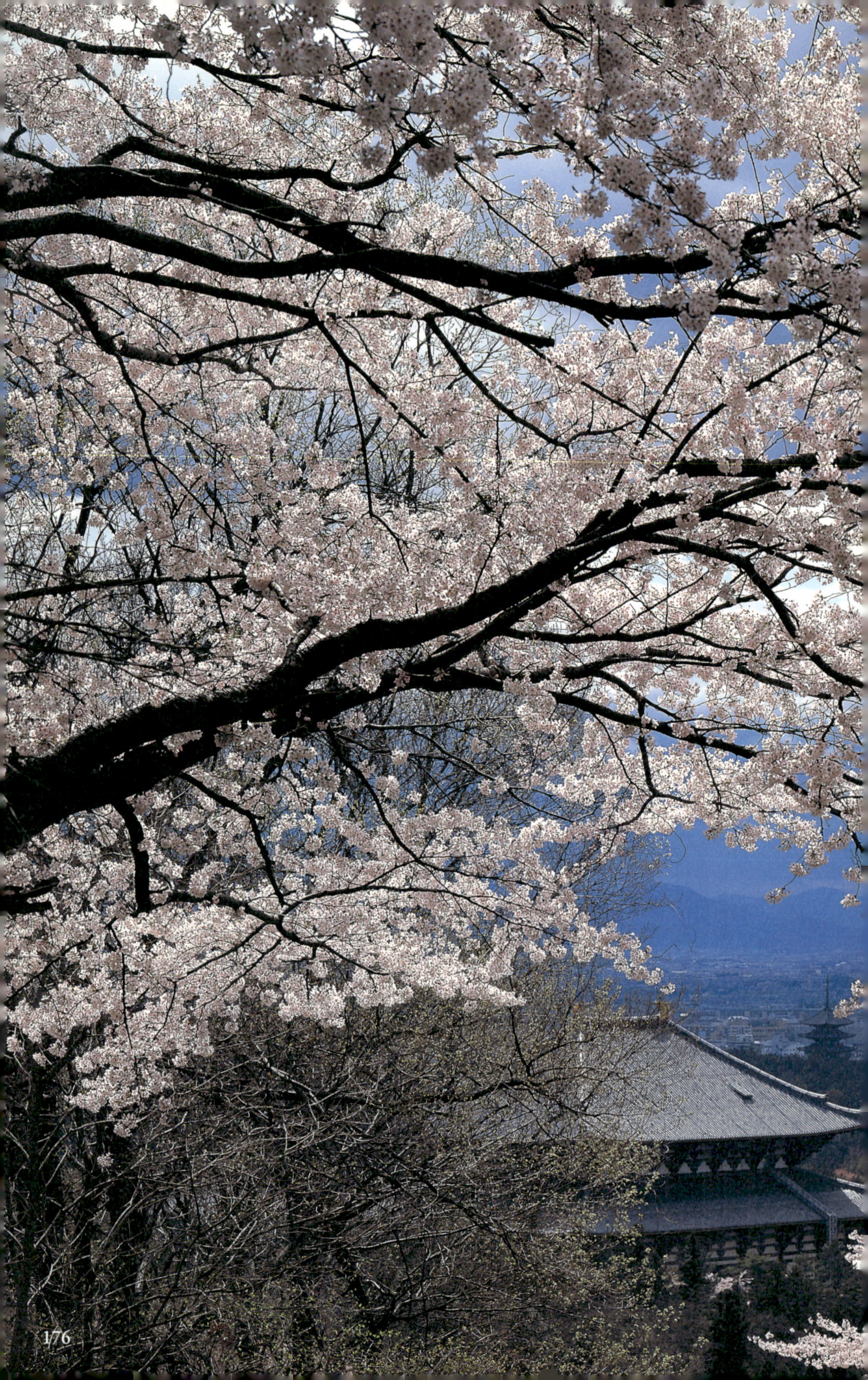

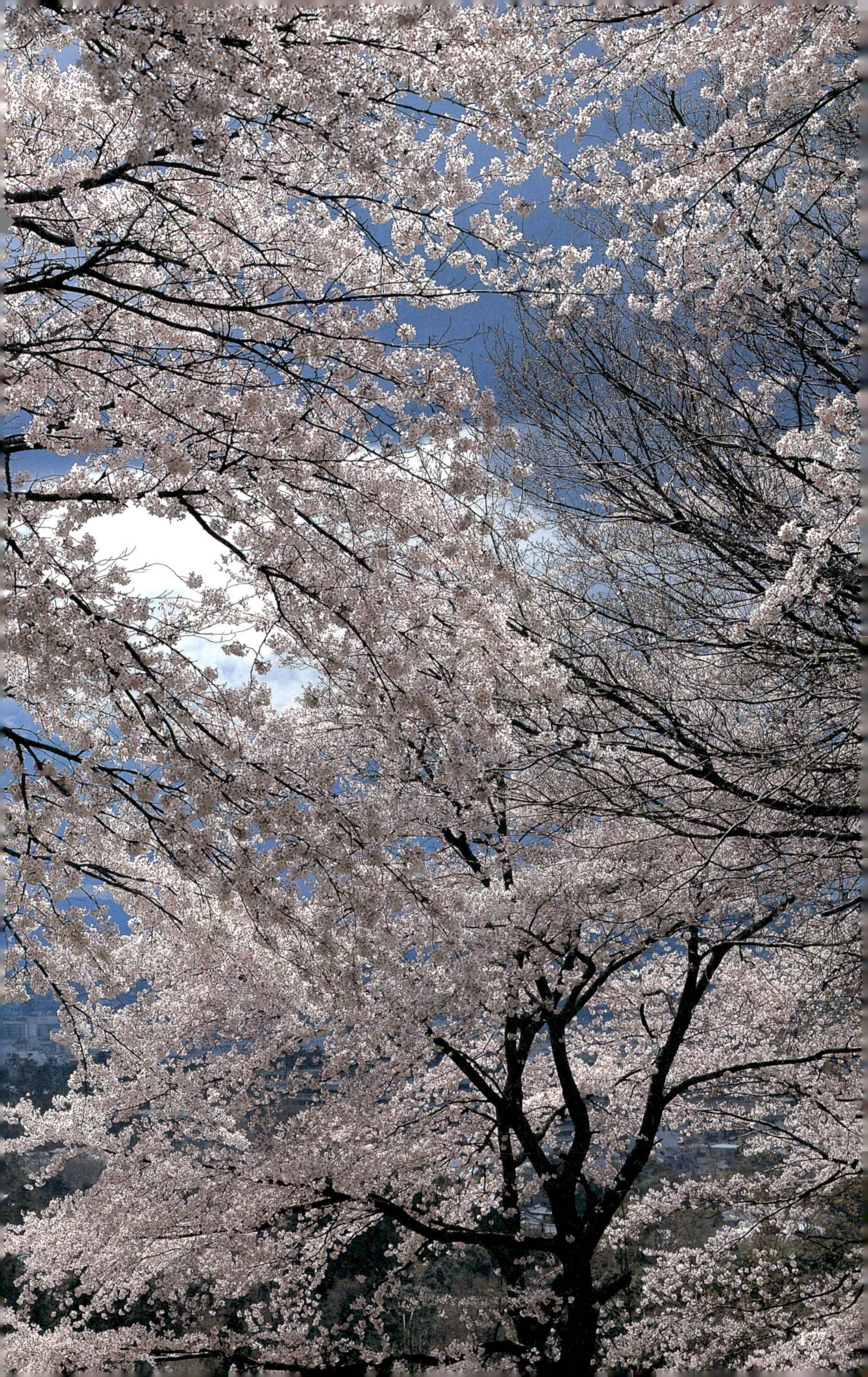

By Ōtomo Yotsuna, captain of the frontier guards at the Dazaifu

Now that the wisteria
are in full bloom,
sweeping down like waves,
do your thoughts, my Lord,
turn to the capital at Nara?

三三〇

防人司佑大伴四綱の歌二首（その一首）
さきもりのつかさのすけおほとものよつな

藤波の花は盛りになりにけり平城の京を思ほすや君
ふぢ　なみ　　　　　　　　　　　　　　　　なら　みやこ

藤の花が波うって盛りになったなあ。
奈良の都を恋しくお思いでしょうか。あなた。

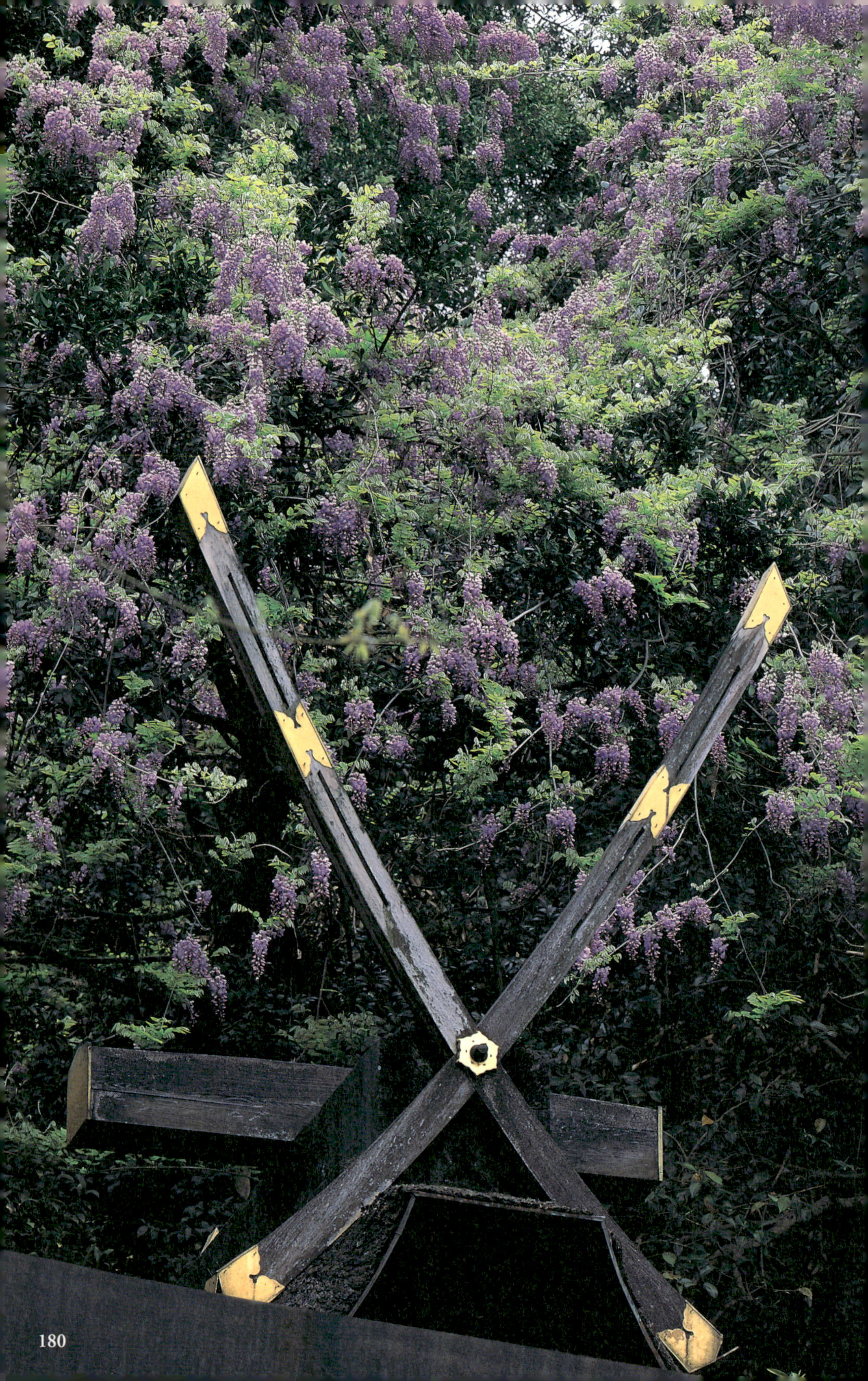

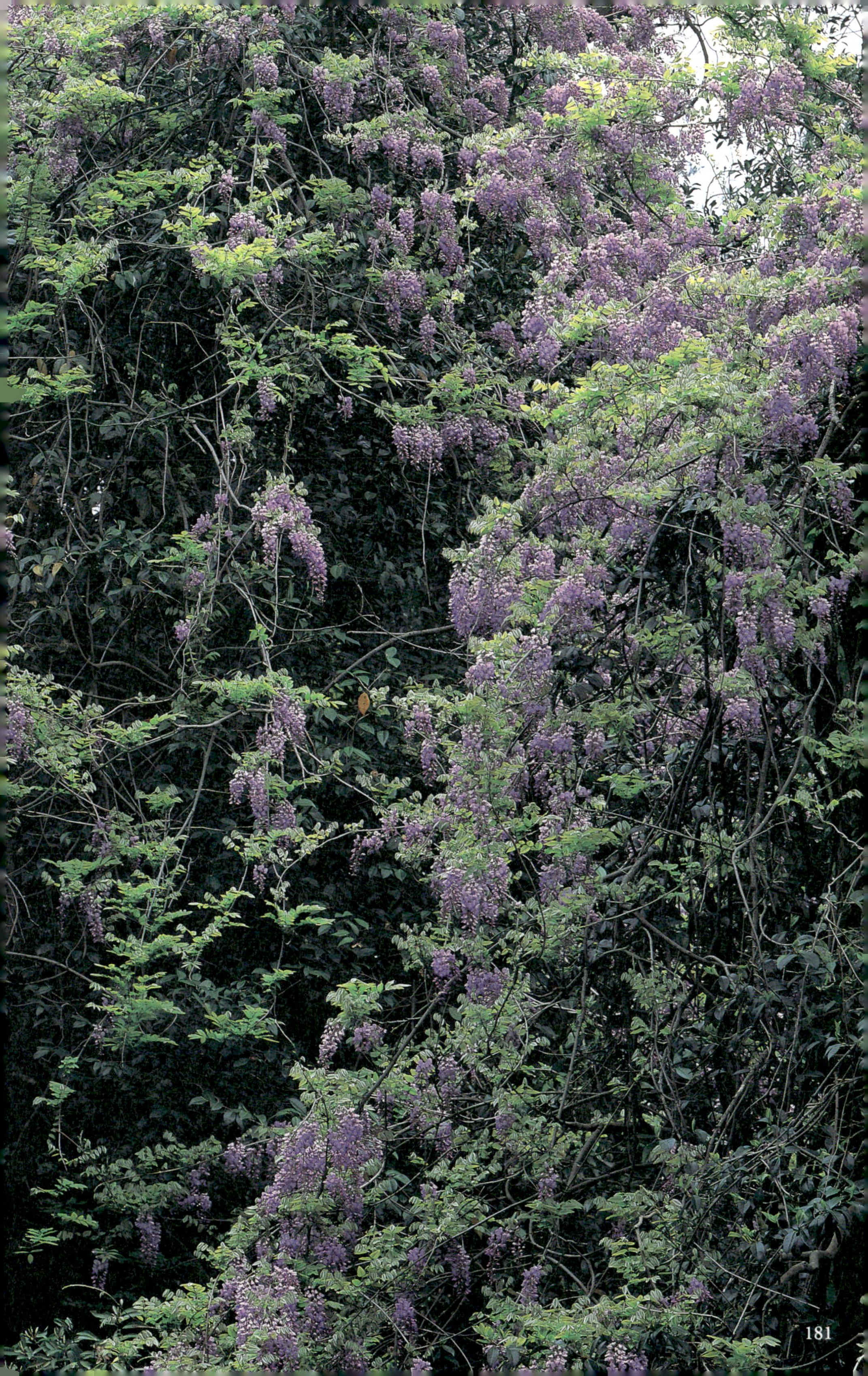

By Lord Ōtomo Tabito, Commander of the Dazaifu

Can I hope to regain
the full bloom of my youth,
or will I probably die
before I can ever see again
the capital at Nara?

三三一

帥大伴卿の歌五首（その一首）
そちおほとものまへつきみ

わが盛また変若めやもほとほとに寧楽の京を見ずかなりなむ
さかり　　　　をち　　　　　　　　　　なら　みやこ

私のいのちの盛りは、ふたたび若返って訪れることがあろうか。いやいや、ほとんど奈良の都を見ずじまいになってしまうだろう。

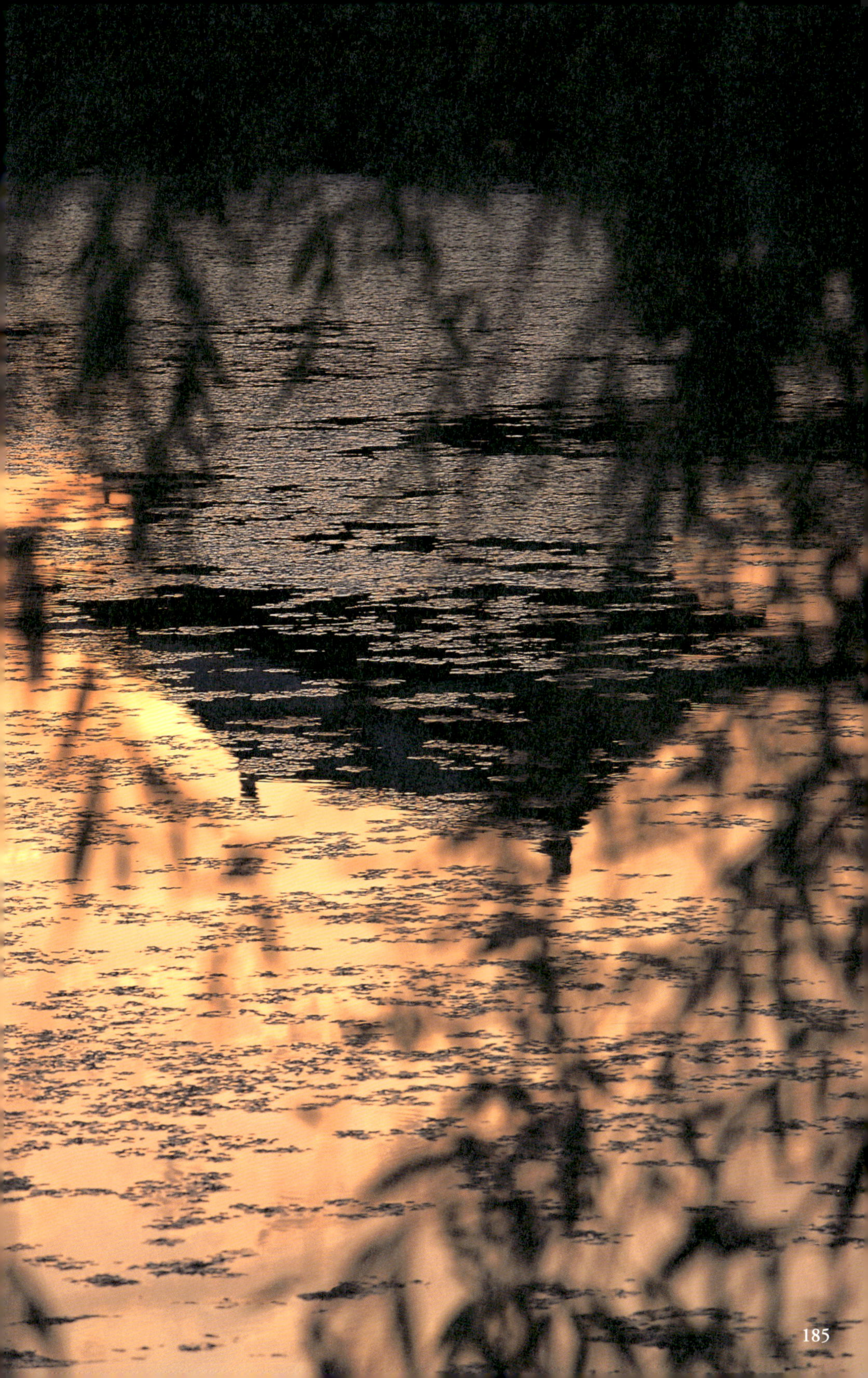

*Poem by Yamanoue Okura,
upon leaving a banquet*

Okura shall take his leave now.
My child must be crying
and its mother,
who bears it on her back,
must be waiting for me.

三三七
山上憶良臣の宴を罷るの歌一首

憶良らは今は罷らむ子泣くらむそのかの母も吾を待つらむそ

憶良はもう退出しましょう。子どもが泣いているでしょう。その子のあの母親も私を待っているでしょうよ。

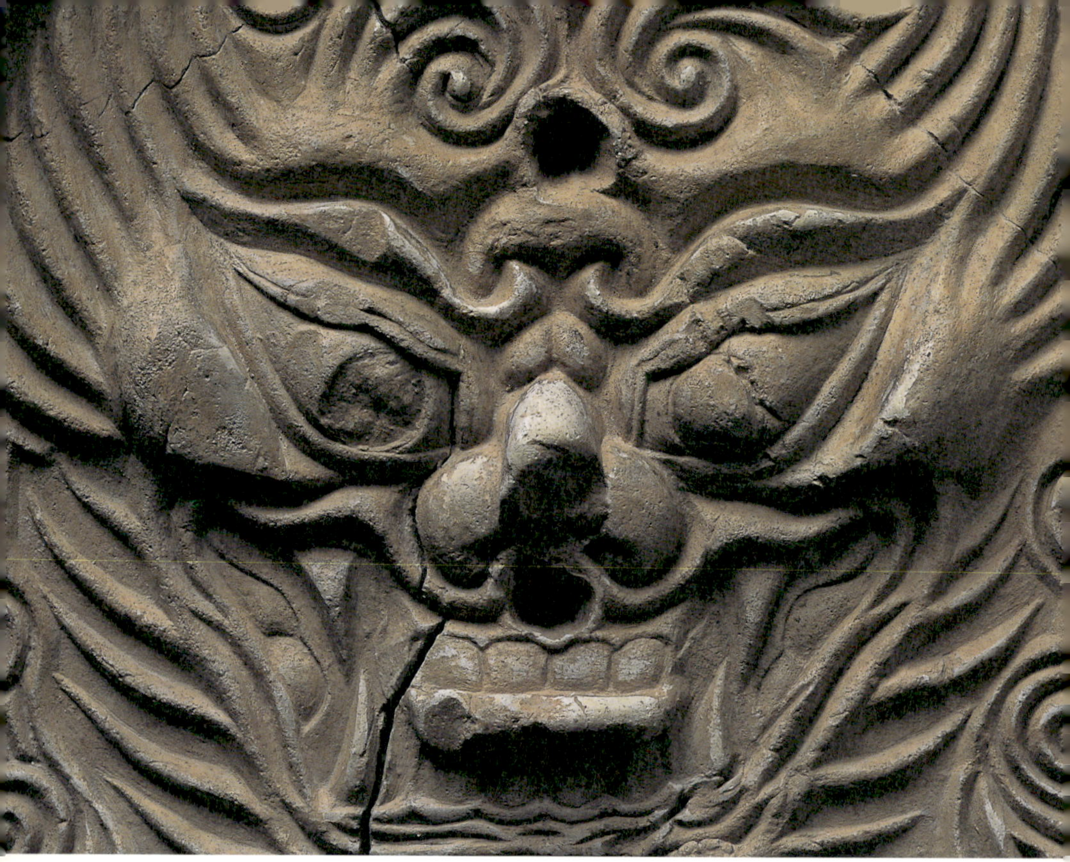

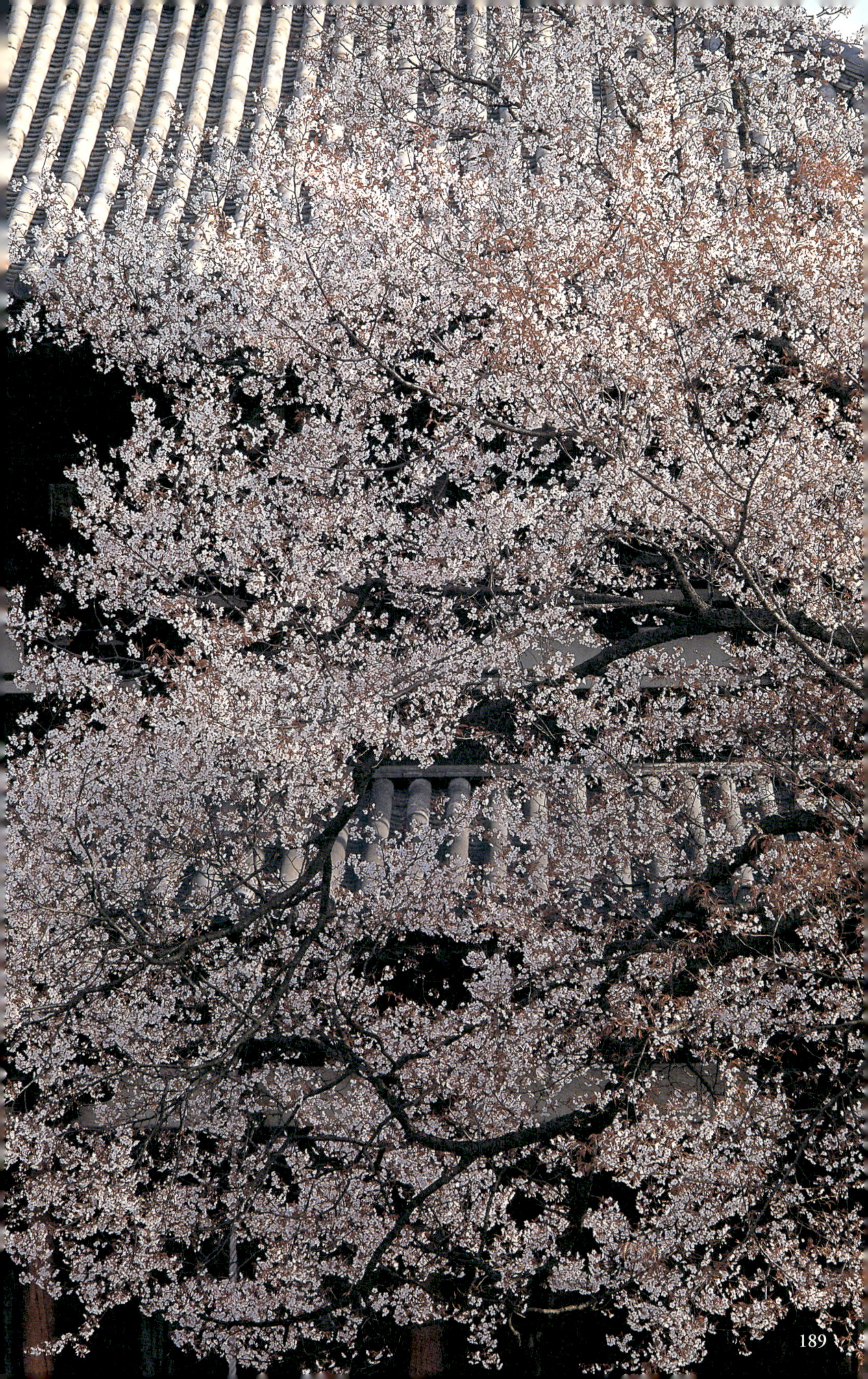

*Poem in praise of wine by Lord Ōtomo Tabito,
the Commander of the Dazaifu*

Great sages of the past
gave the name of "sage" to wine.
How well they spoke!

三三九

大宰師大伴卿の酒を讃(は)むるの歌十三首(その一首)

酒の名を聖(ひじり)と負(おほ)せし古(いにしへ)の大(おほ)き聖の言(こと)のよろしさ

酒の名を聖となづけた、昔の大聖人のことばのよさ。

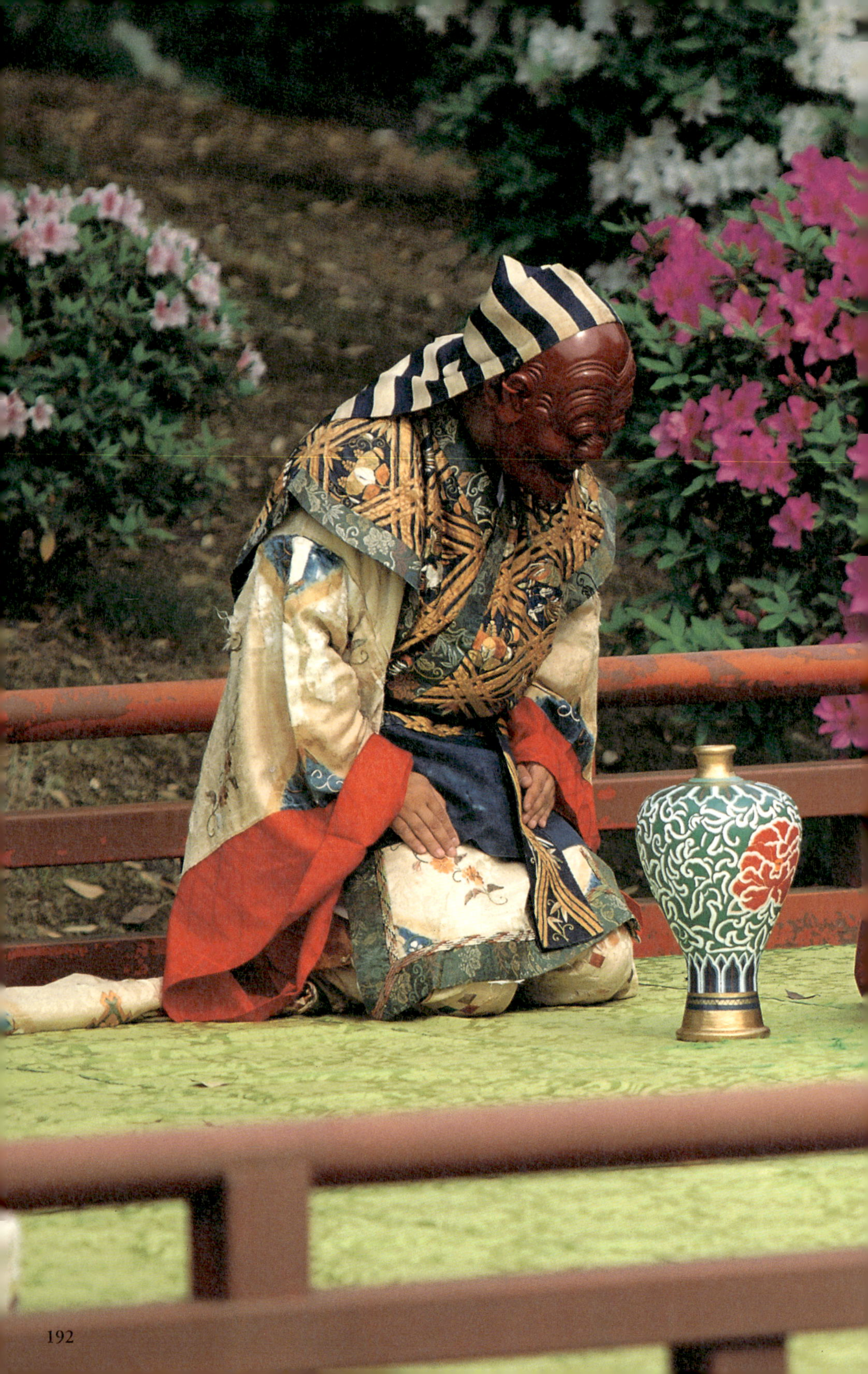

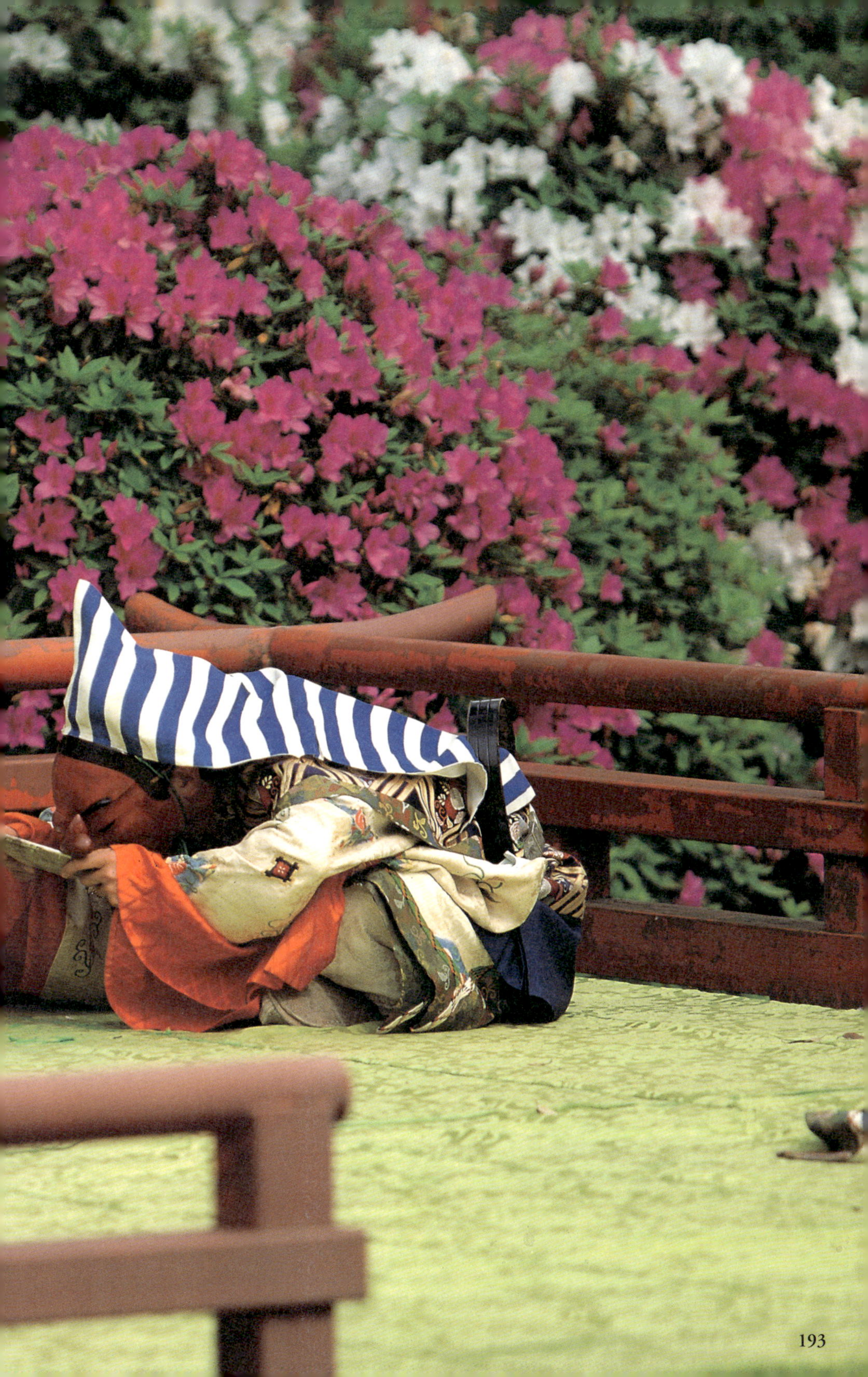

Poem by the Priest Mansei

To what shall I compare
    this life?
the way a boat
   rowed out from the morning harbor
      leaves no traces on the sea.

三五一

沙弥満誓の歌一首

世間を何に譬へむ朝びらき漕ぎ去にし船の跡なきがごと

この世を何にたとえよう。朝港を出ていった船の引く跡がわずかの間で跡形もなくなってしまうようなものだ、といおうか。

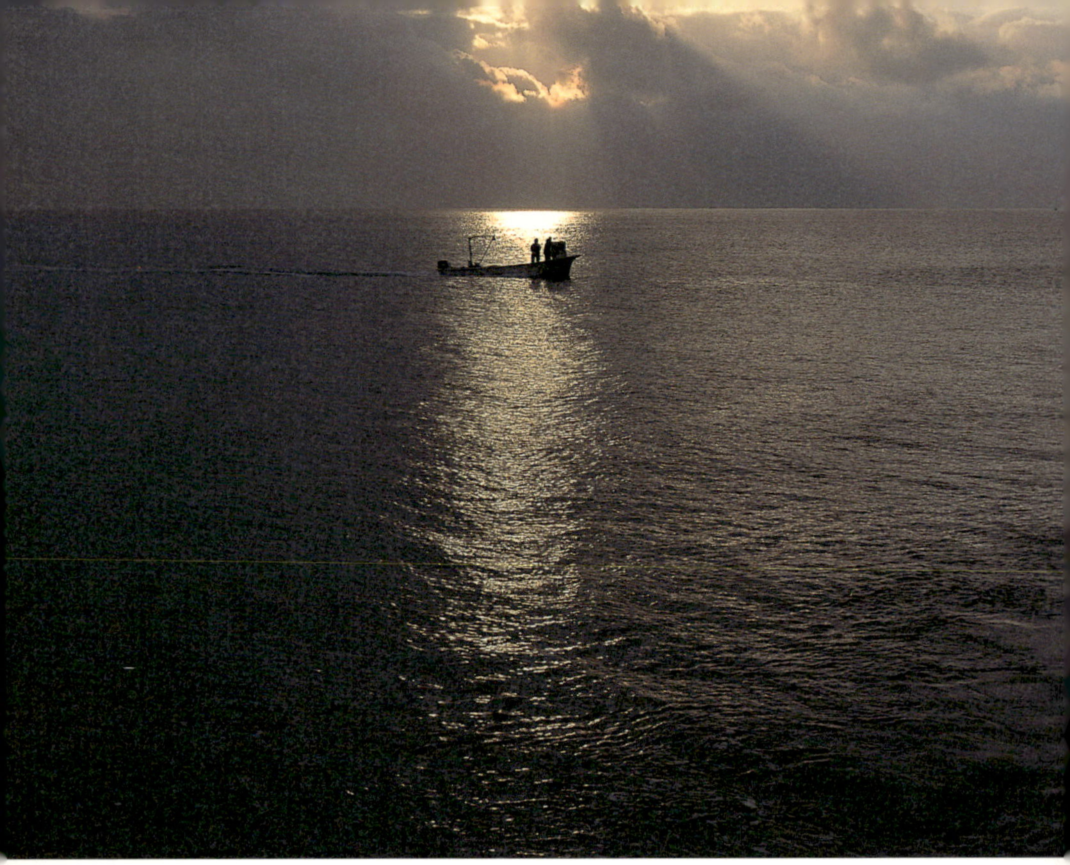

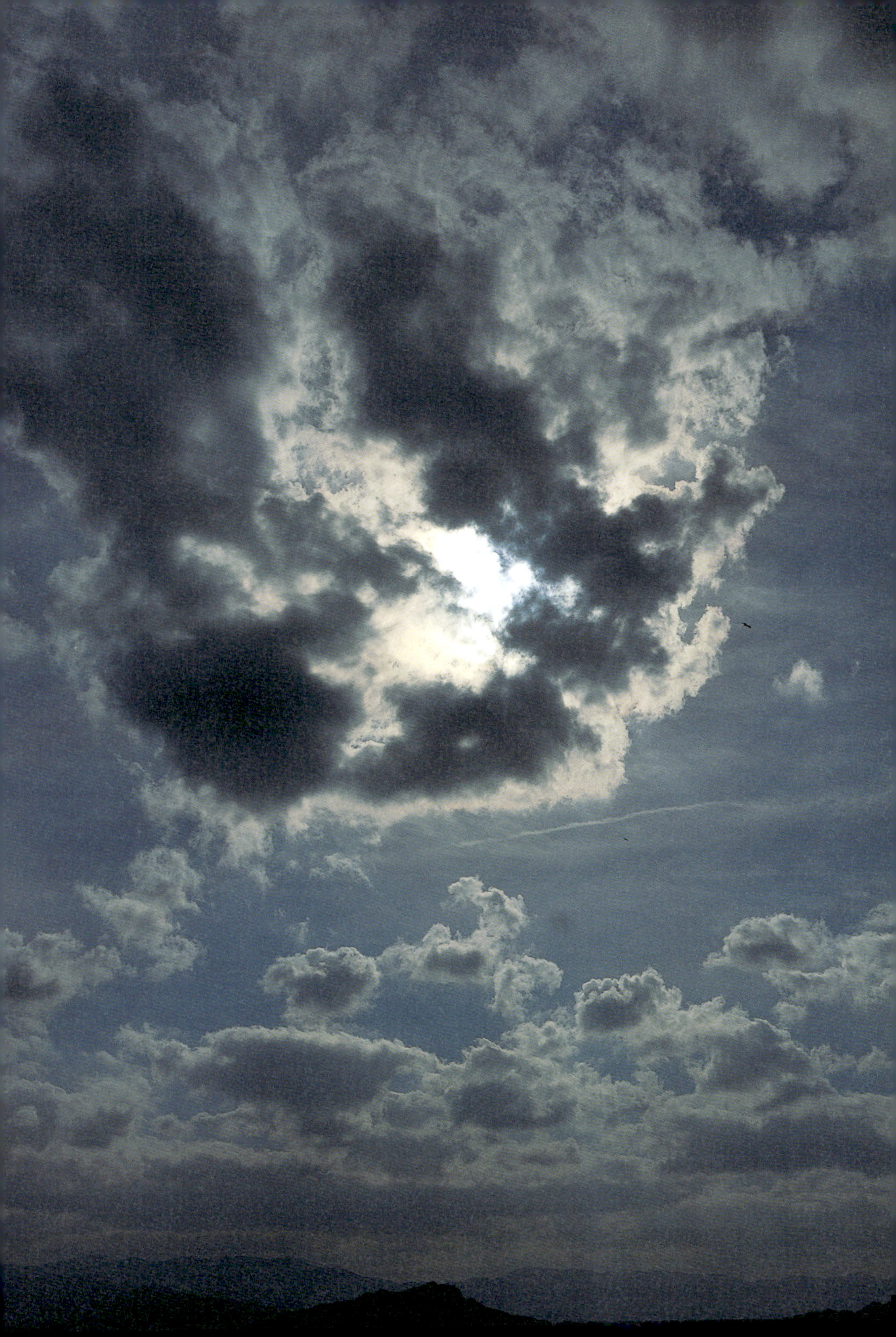

Poem by Prince Akayue

The cranes are crying
among the reeds.
Your harbor winds
must be blowing coldly,
      Cape Tsuo.

三五二

若湯座王の歌一首
わかゆゑのおほきみ

葦へには鶴が音鳴きて湖風寒く吹くらむ津乎の崎はも

葦べに鶴の鳴き声が寒々と聞こえて来る。港には風が冷たく吹いているであろう。津乎の崎よ。

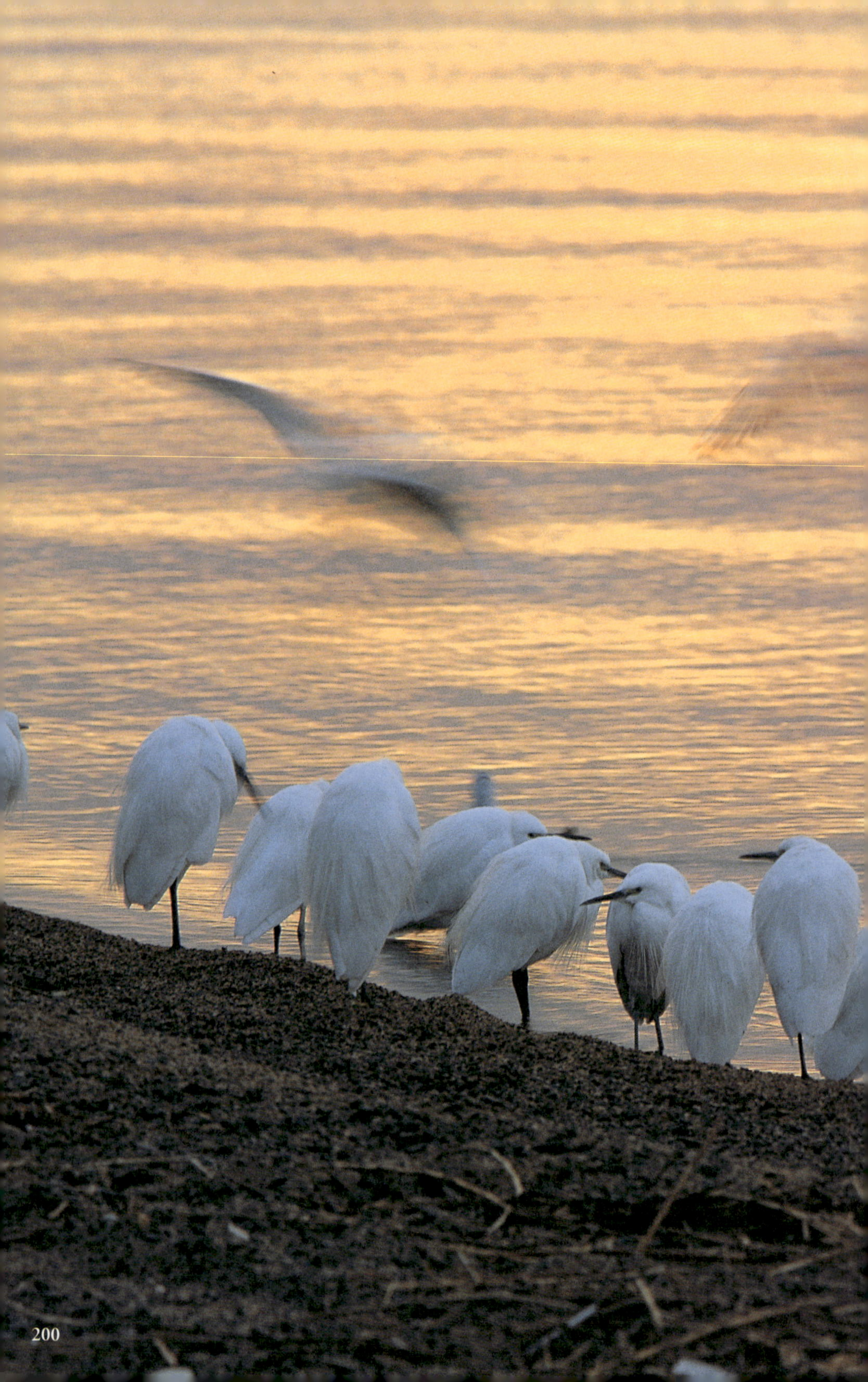

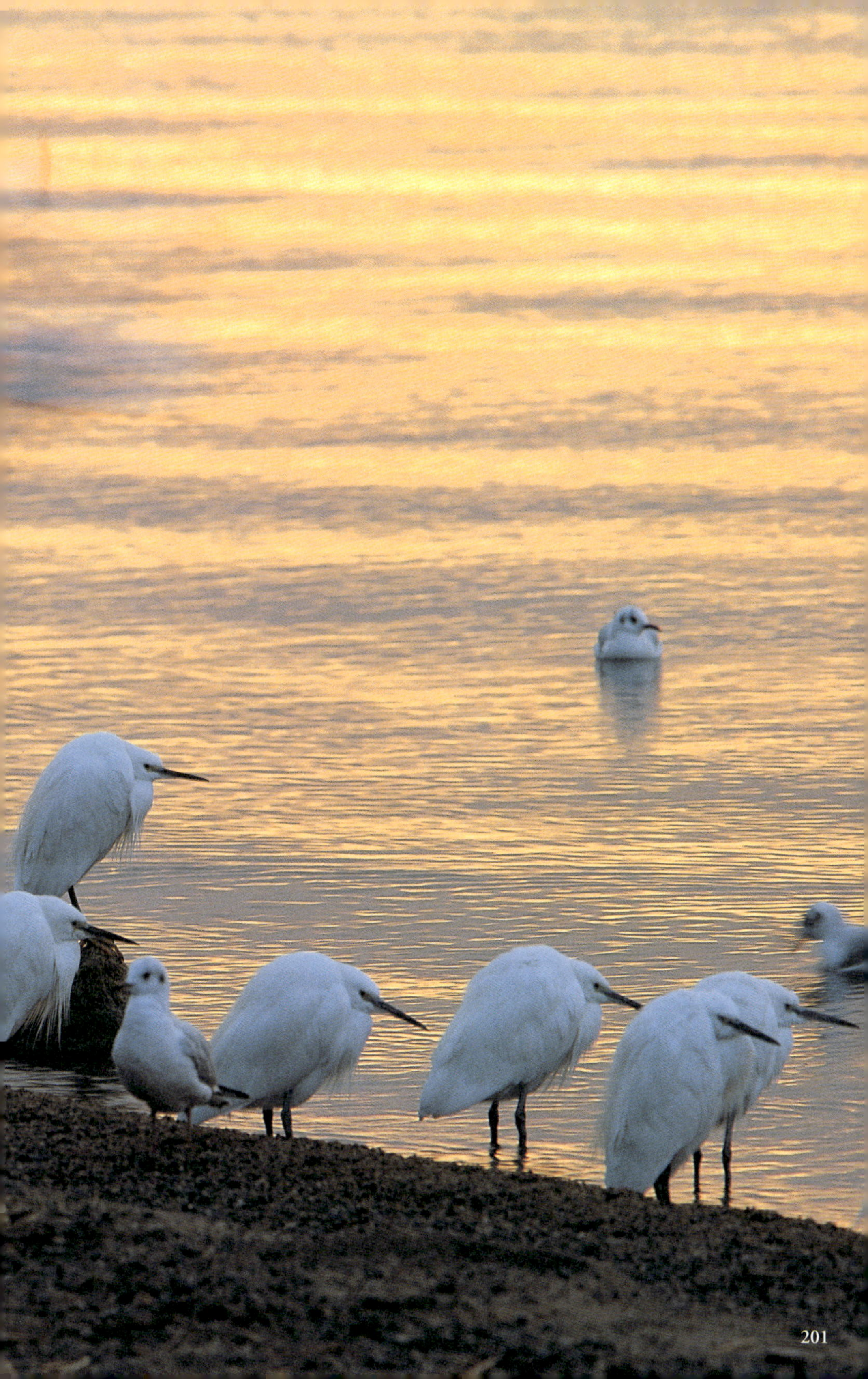

Poem by Prince Uenomiya Shōtoku, written in his grief when he found the body of a dead man on Tatsuta Mountain during his procession to Takaharanoi

If he were home
he would be pillowed
in his wife's arms,
but here on a journey
he lies with grass for pillow—
traveler, alas!

四一五

上宮聖徳皇子の竹原井に出遊しし時に、龍田山の死れる
人を見て悲傷びて作りませる御歌一首

家にあれば妹が手まかむ草枕旅に臥せるこの旅人あはれ

家にいたら妻の手を枕と
しているであろうに、草
を枕の旅路に倒れている
この旅人よ。ああ。

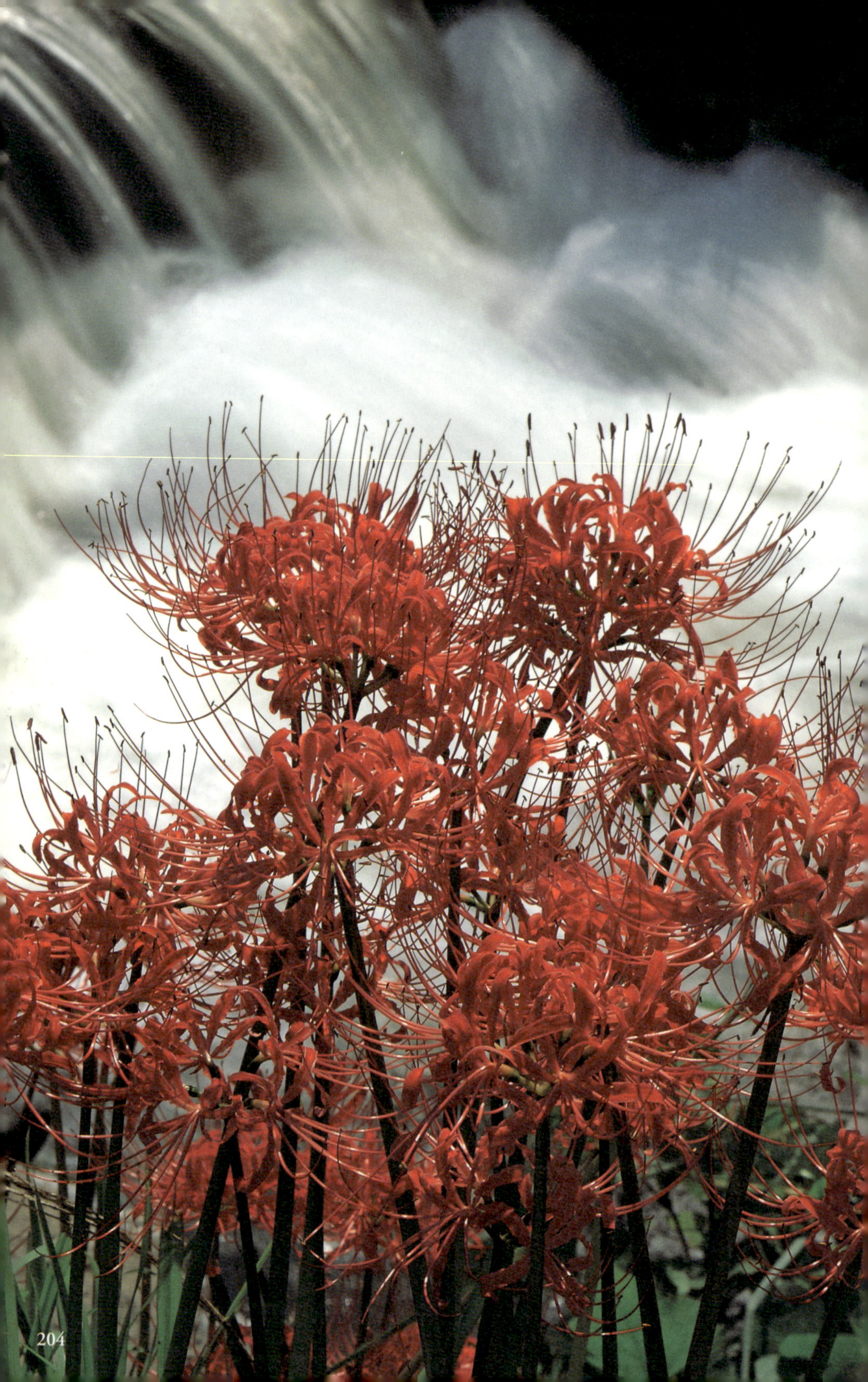

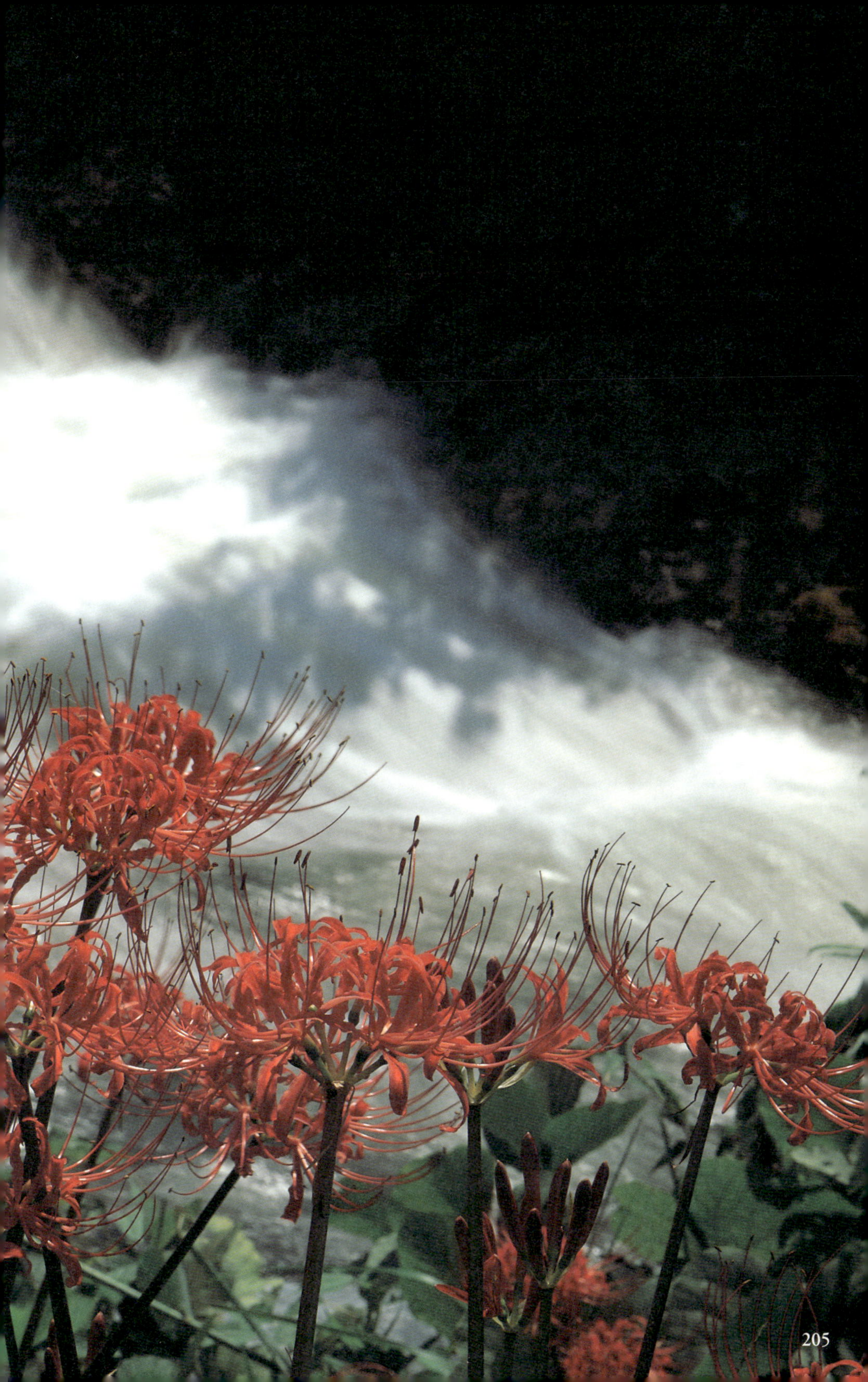

Poem by Prince Ōtsu, weeping on the banks of Iware Pond when he was about to be put to death

The duck that cries
in Iware Pond,
 where the vines
 crawl on the rocks:
will I see it just today,
and tomorrow be hidden in the clouds?

四一六

大津皇子の被死らしめらえし時に、磐余の池の般にして
涕を流して作りませる御歌一首

ももづたふ磐余の池に鳴く鴨を今日のみ見てや雲隠りなむ

百に伝う磐余の池に鳴く
鴨を見るのも今日を限り
として、私は雲の彼方に
去るのだろうか。

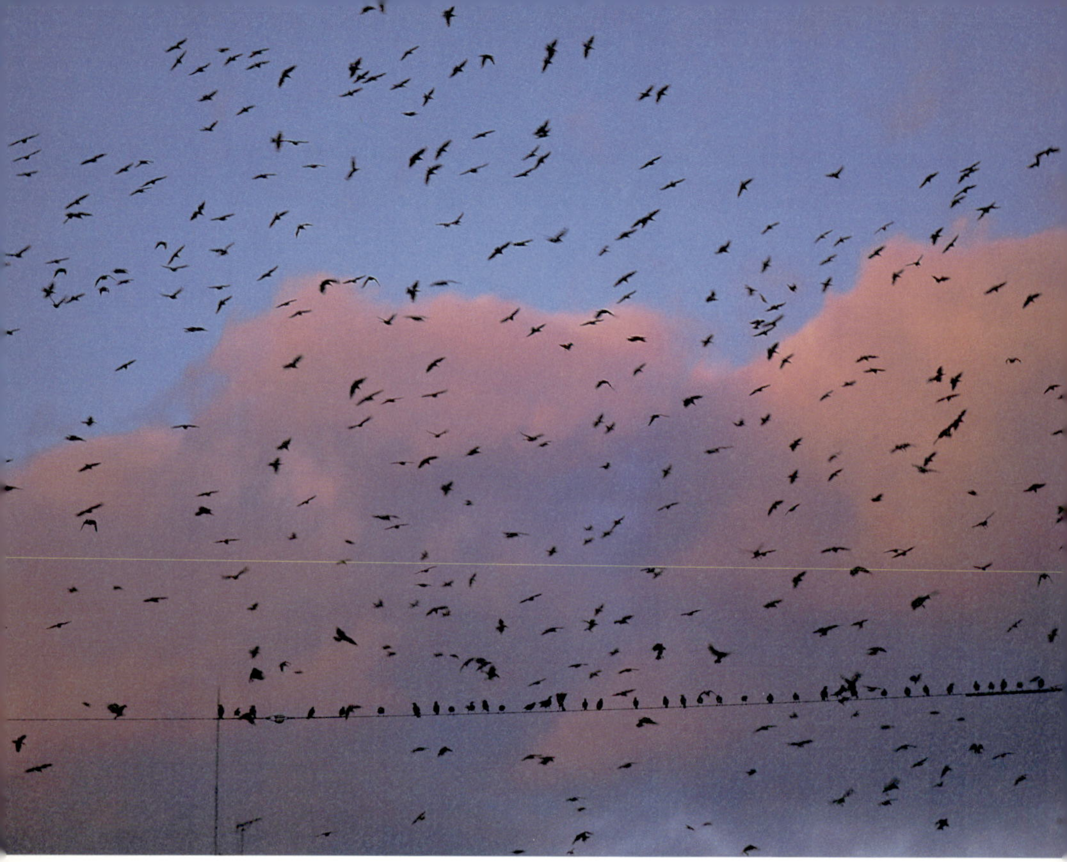

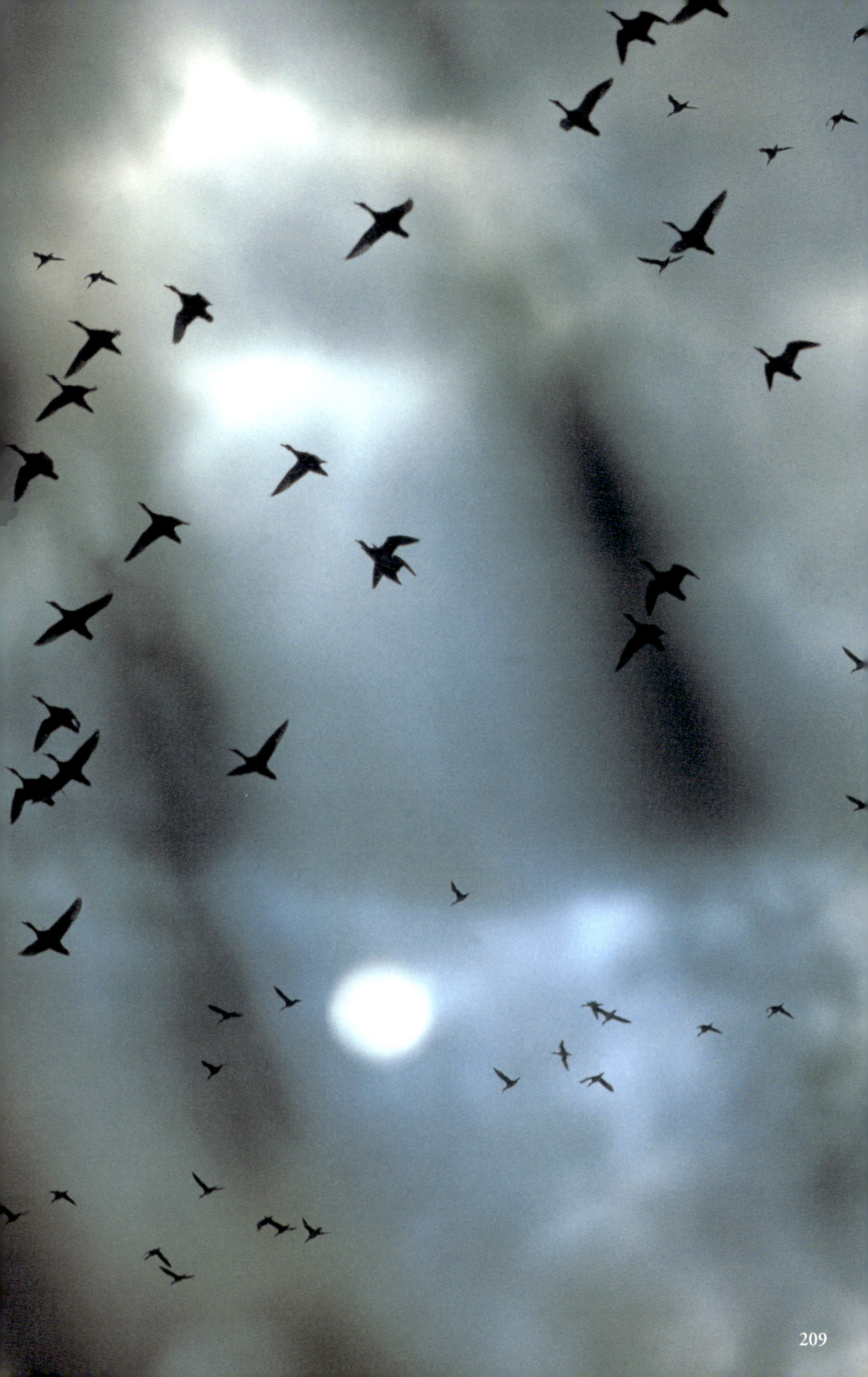

Upon returning to the home in one's native village

This empty house,
with no one here,
is more painful to be in
than to be on a lonely sojourn,
    with grass for pillow.

451

四五一

故郷(ふるさと)の家に還り入(い)りて、即ち作れる歌三首（その一首）

人もなき空しき家は草枕(くさまくら)旅にまさりて苦しかりけり

愛する妻もいない空しい家は、草を枕の旅以上に心みたされぬことよ。

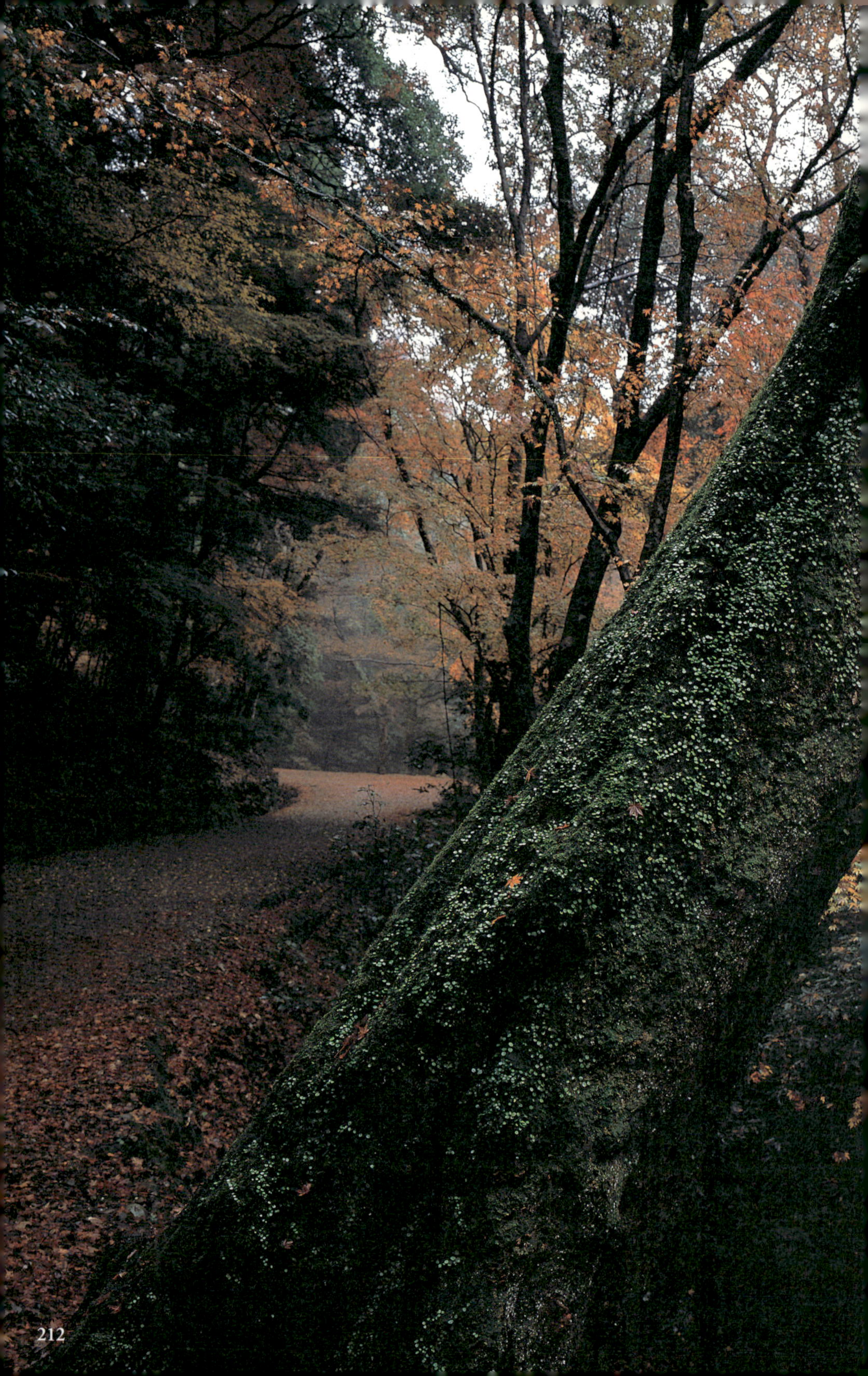

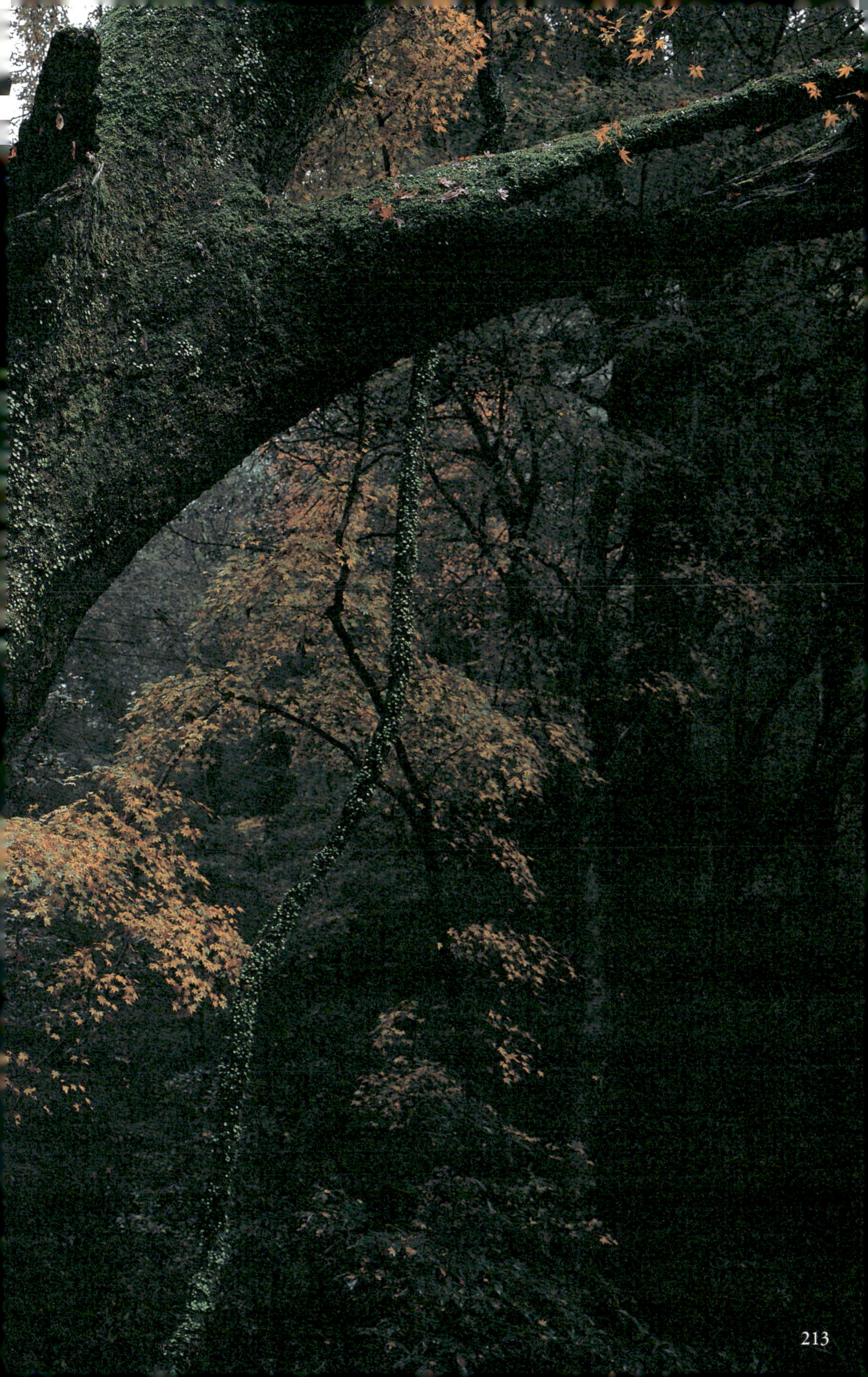

from
*Poem by Ōtomo Yakamochi, servingman to Prince
Asaka, when the Prince passed away in spring, the
second month, of the sixteenth year of Tempyō (744)*

Are these words of madness?
His servingmen
have donned white mourning robes
and have carried his palanquin
up Wazuka Mountain,
and he has ascended
to rule the far heavens.
I collapse,
I weep,
splattered with mud,
but there is nothing I can do.

四七五

十六年甲申。春二月に、安積皇子の薨りましし時に、内舎人大伴宿禰家持の作れる歌六首（その一首より）

逆言の　狂言とかも　白栲に　舎人装ひて　和豆香山　御輿立たして　ひさかたの　天知らしぬれ　こいまろび　ひづち泣けども　せむすべも無し

その時、さかしま言の戯れ言というのか、白布の喪服に舎人たちは装い、身を投げ出し、衣を濡らして泣くのだが、だがど和豆香山に皇子の輿をお立てになり、皇子は彼方の天を御支配なさってしまった。そこで舎人たちは大地にうしたらいいのかせん術もない。

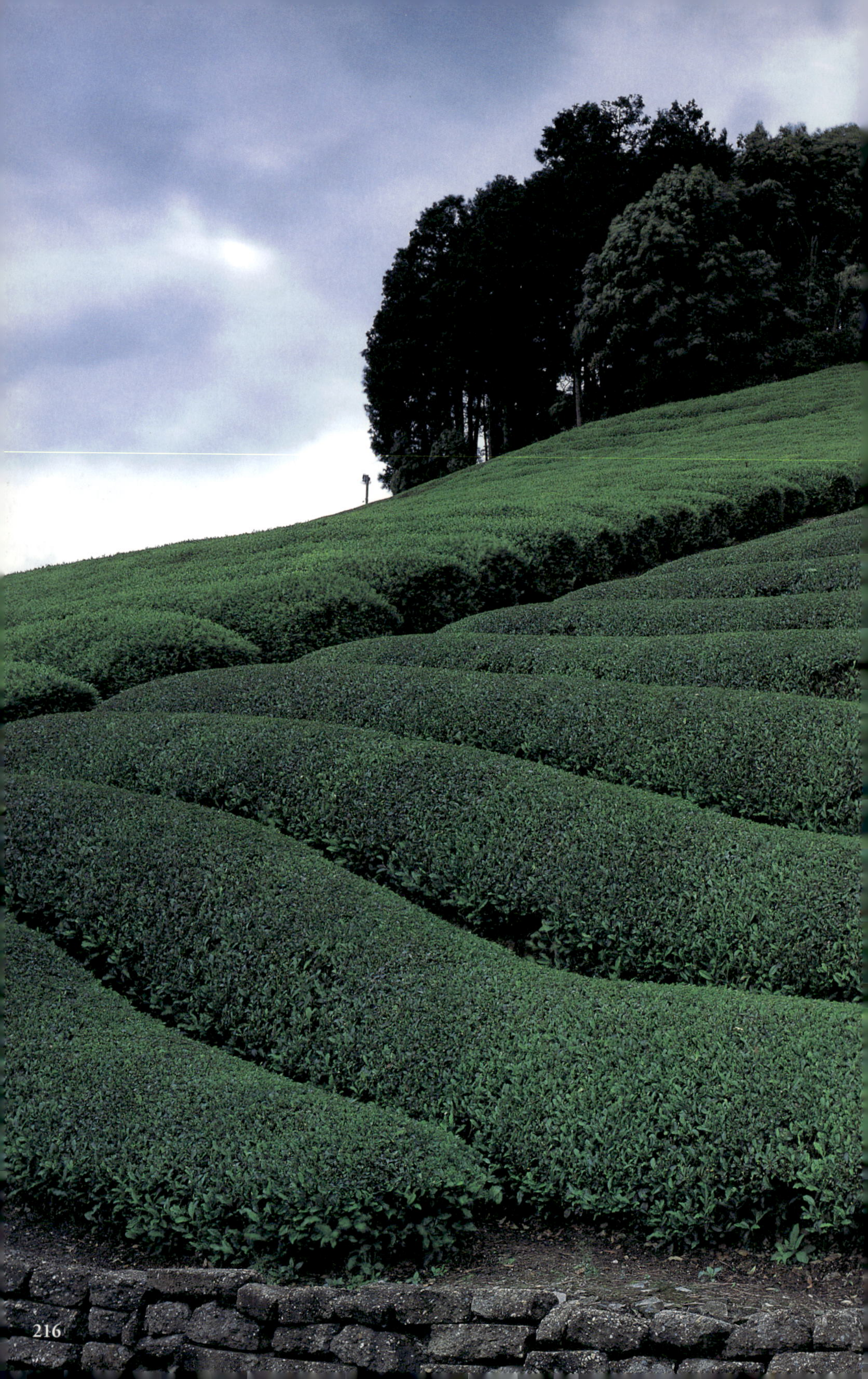

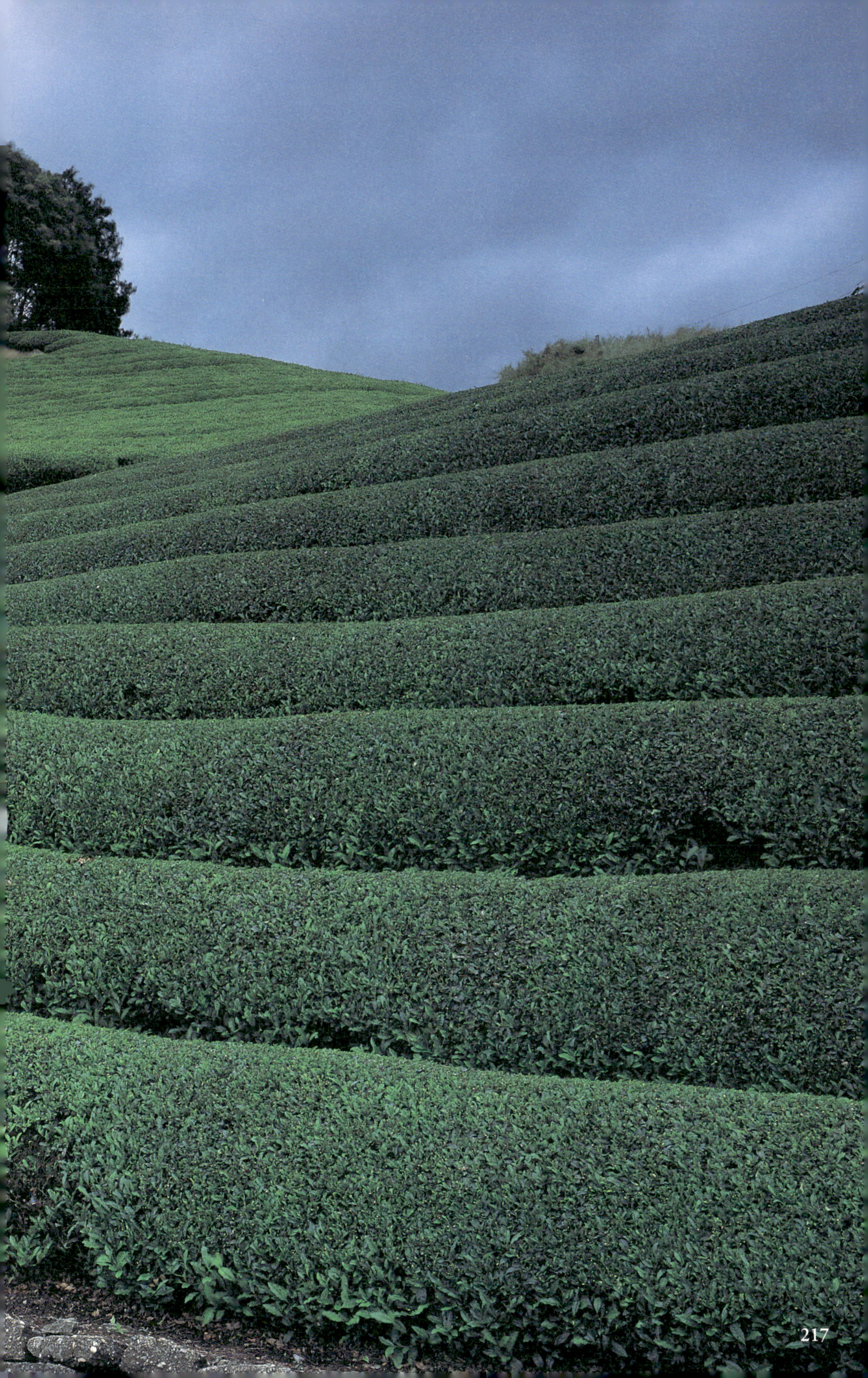

*By Lady Ōtomo in response to a poem
from Lord Fujiwara*

Would that,
even a single night a year,
your pitch-black steed would come,
    treading over the pebbles
    in the Saho River.

525

五二五

（京職、藤原大夫に）大伴郎女の和へたる歌四首（その一首）

佐保河の小石ふみ渡りぬばたまの黒馬の来る夜は年にもあらぬか

佐保河の小石を踏み渡って宵闇の中をあなたの黒馬の来る夜は、年に一度でもあってほしいものです。

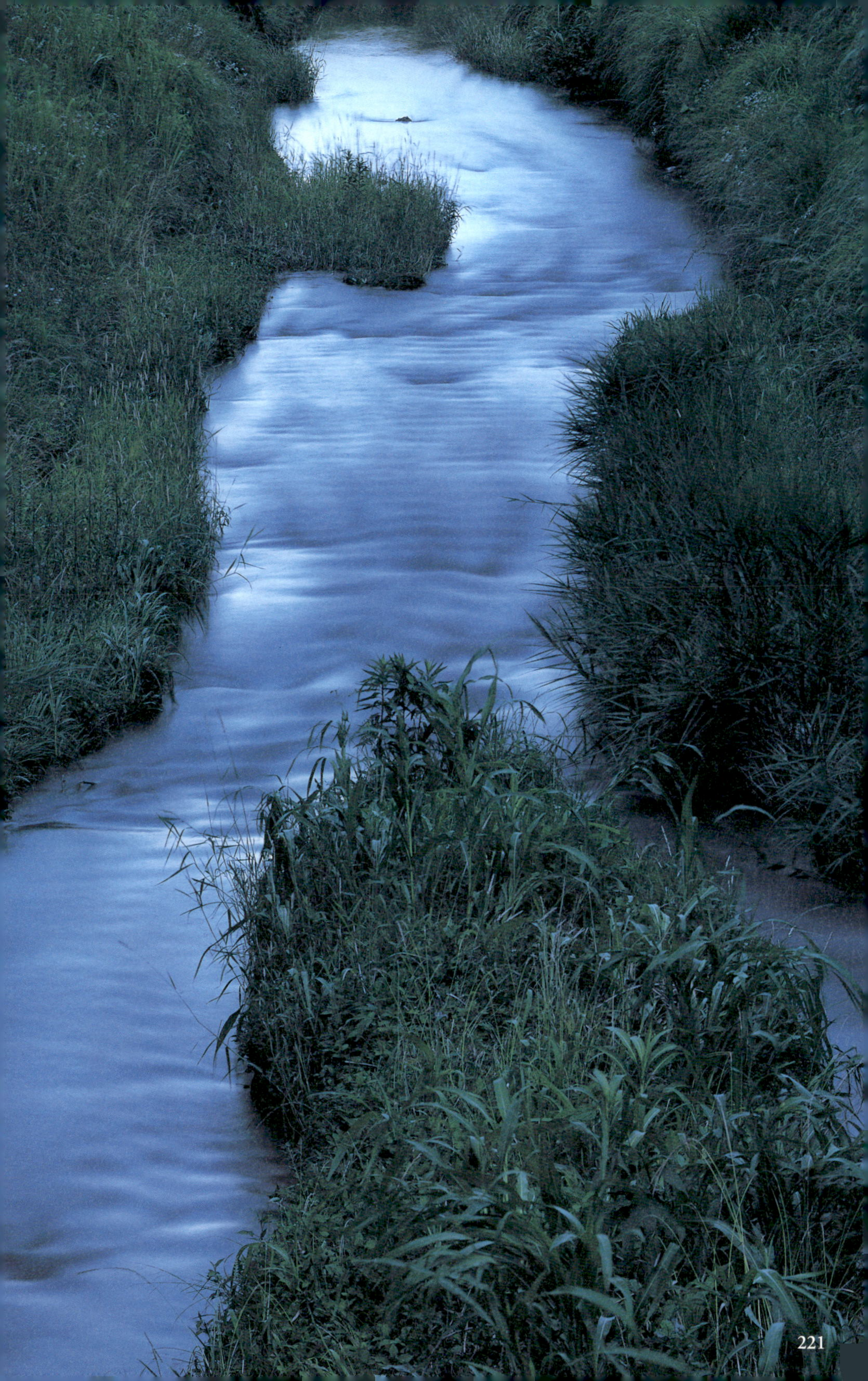

By Lady Ōtomo Sakanoue

Never until now
in this old life,
    when white hairs twine
      among the black,
have I fallen into longing like this.

563

五六三

大伴坂上郎女の歌二首（その一首）

黒髪に白髪交じり老ゆるまでかかる恋にはいまだ逢はなくに

黒髪に白髪がまじる老年の今日まで、こんな恋にまだ逢ったこともなかったのに。

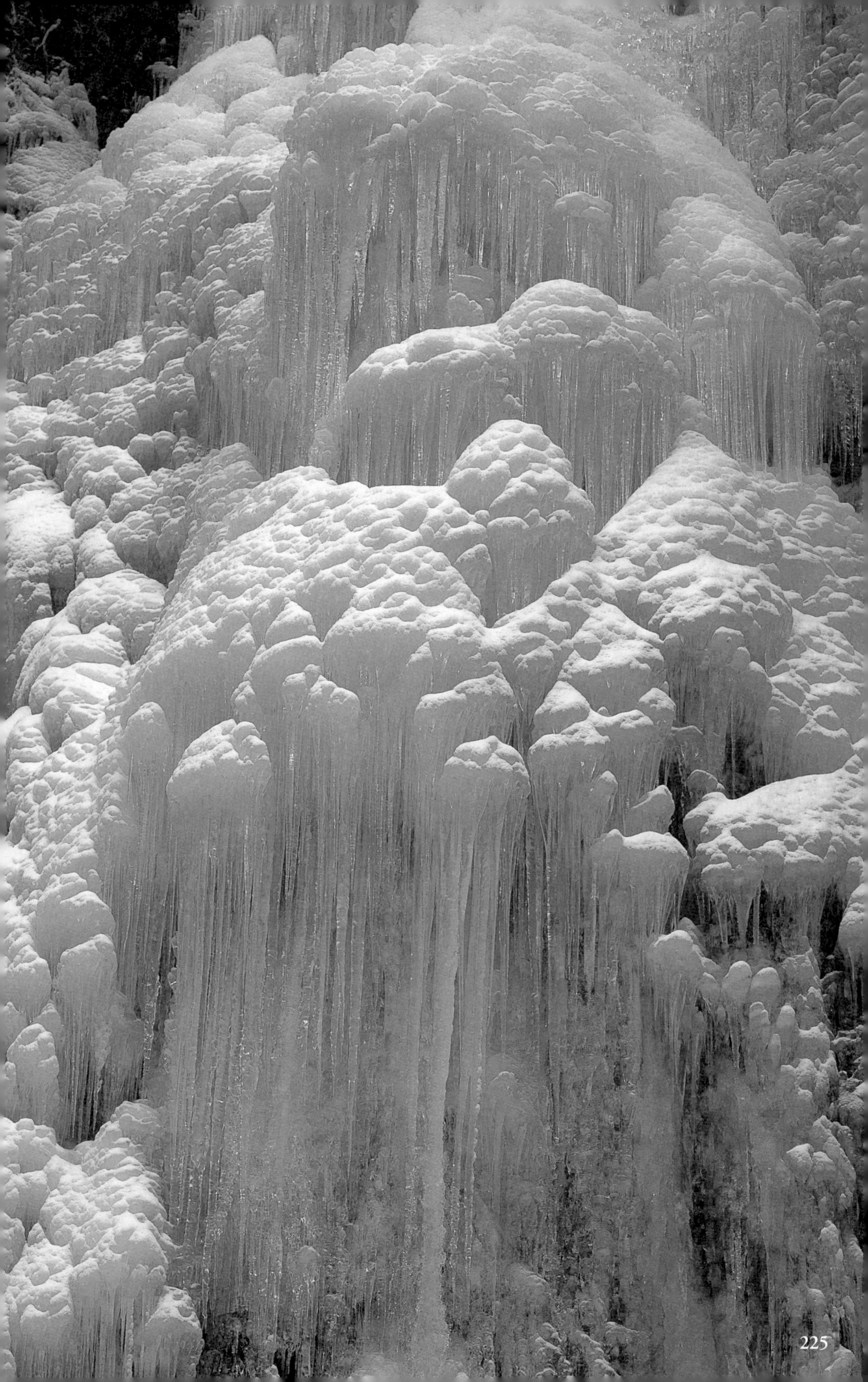

Sent to Ōtomo Yakamochi by Lady Kasa

To long for one
who does not long for you
is like kowtowing to hungry demons
    in the great temple
        from behind.

608

六〇八

笠女郎の大伴宿禰家持に贈れる歌二十四首（その一首）

相思はぬ人を思ふは大寺の餓鬼の後に額づくがごと

思ってもくれない人を思うなんて、大寺の役に立たぬ餓鬼像を、しかも後ろからひれ伏して拝むたいなものです。

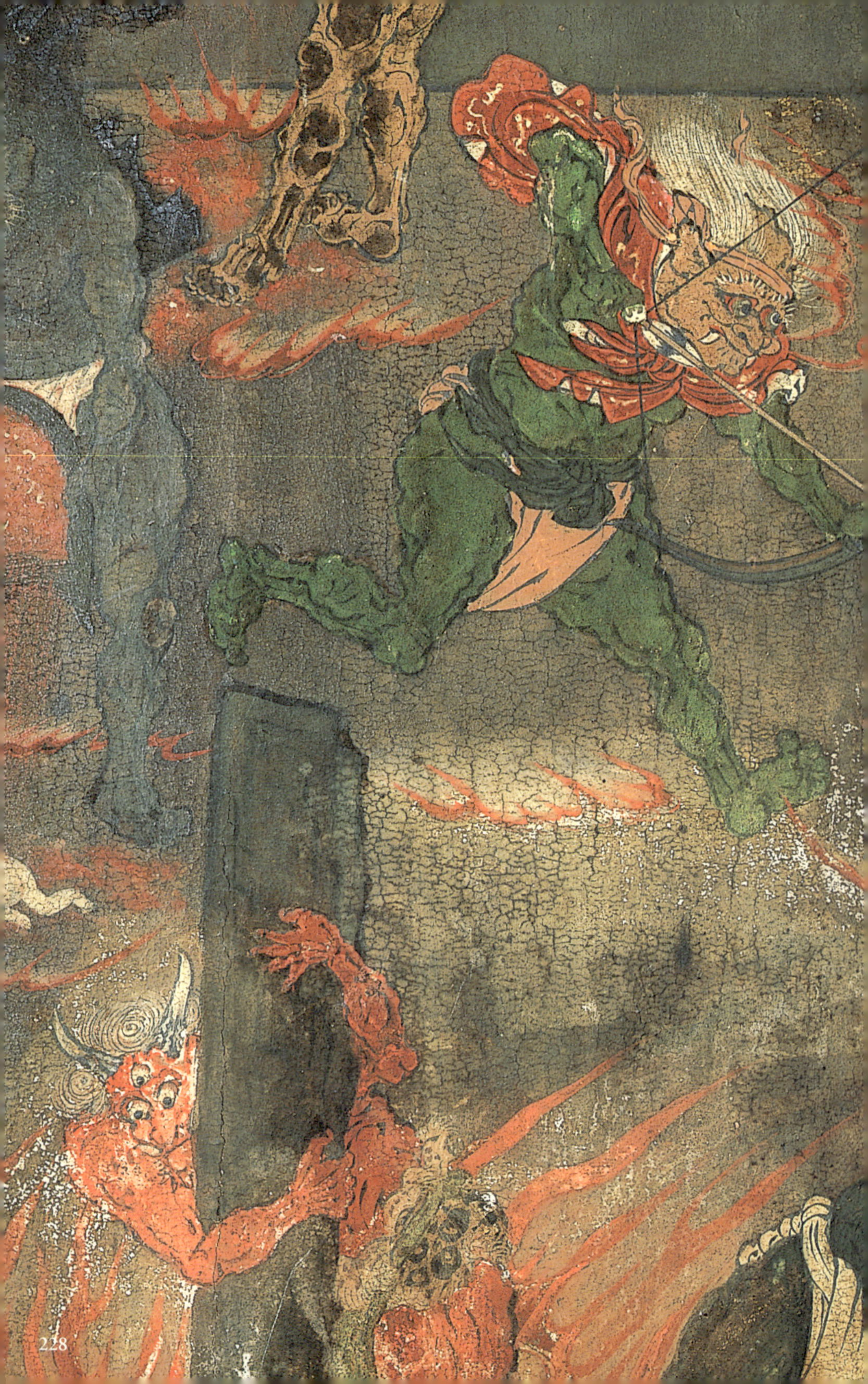

229

Poem presented to the Emperor by Princess Yashiro

Because of you, my Lord,
the talk flies thick about me.
I am going to the Asuka River,
 in my native village,
there to wash away the stains.

六二六

八代女王(やしろのおほきみ)の天皇に献(たてまつ)れる歌一首

君により言(こと)の繁(しげ)きを古郷(ふるさと)の明日香(あすか)の川に潔身(みそぎ)しに行く

あなたによって評判がうるさくたちました。故郷の明日香川に、それを清め流すために私は行きます。

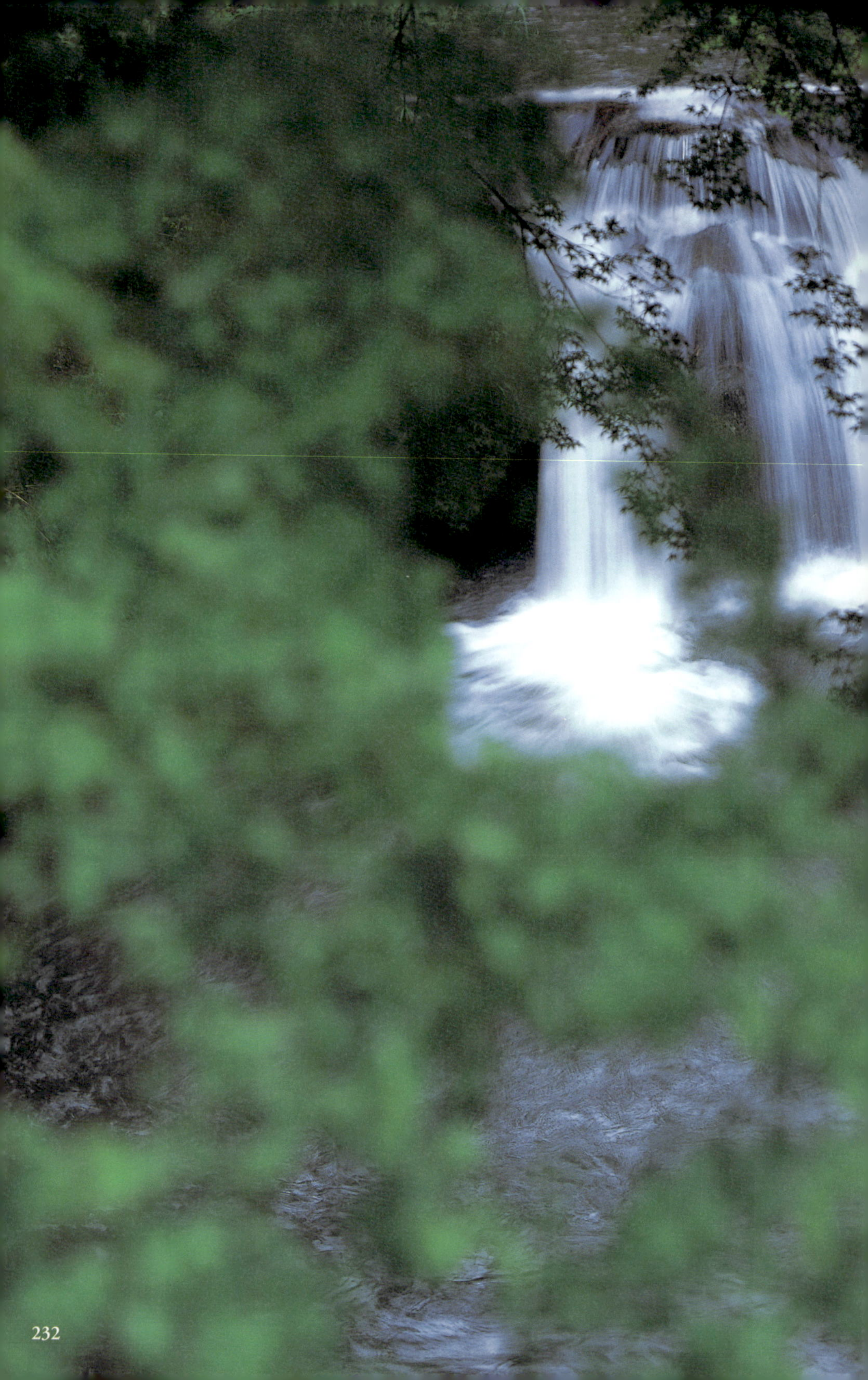

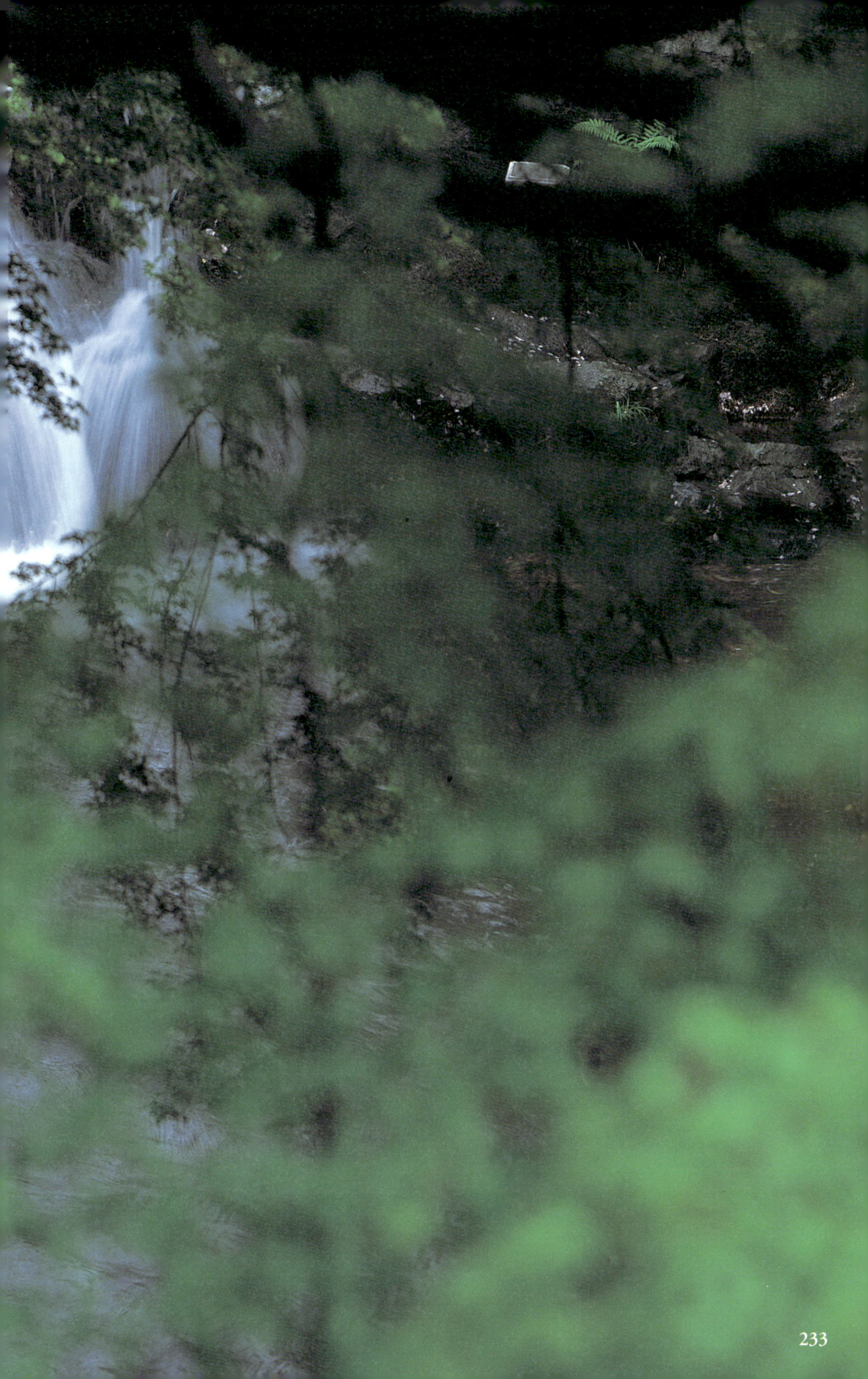

By the maiden Ōme of Taniwa

Is it a sin?
Have I touched the cedar
hallowed by the priests of Miwa,
　　　Miwa of sweet wine,
that meeting you should be so hard?

七一二

丹波大女娘子の歌三首(その一首)
<small>たにはのおほめのをとめ</small>

味酒を三輪の祝がいはふ杉手触れし罪か君に逢ひがたき
<small>うまさけ　みわ　はふり　てふ　つみ</small>

味酒よ神酒(みわ)──三輪の神官がまつる杉に手を触れるようなことをしたのか、その罪によって君に逢いがたいことよ。

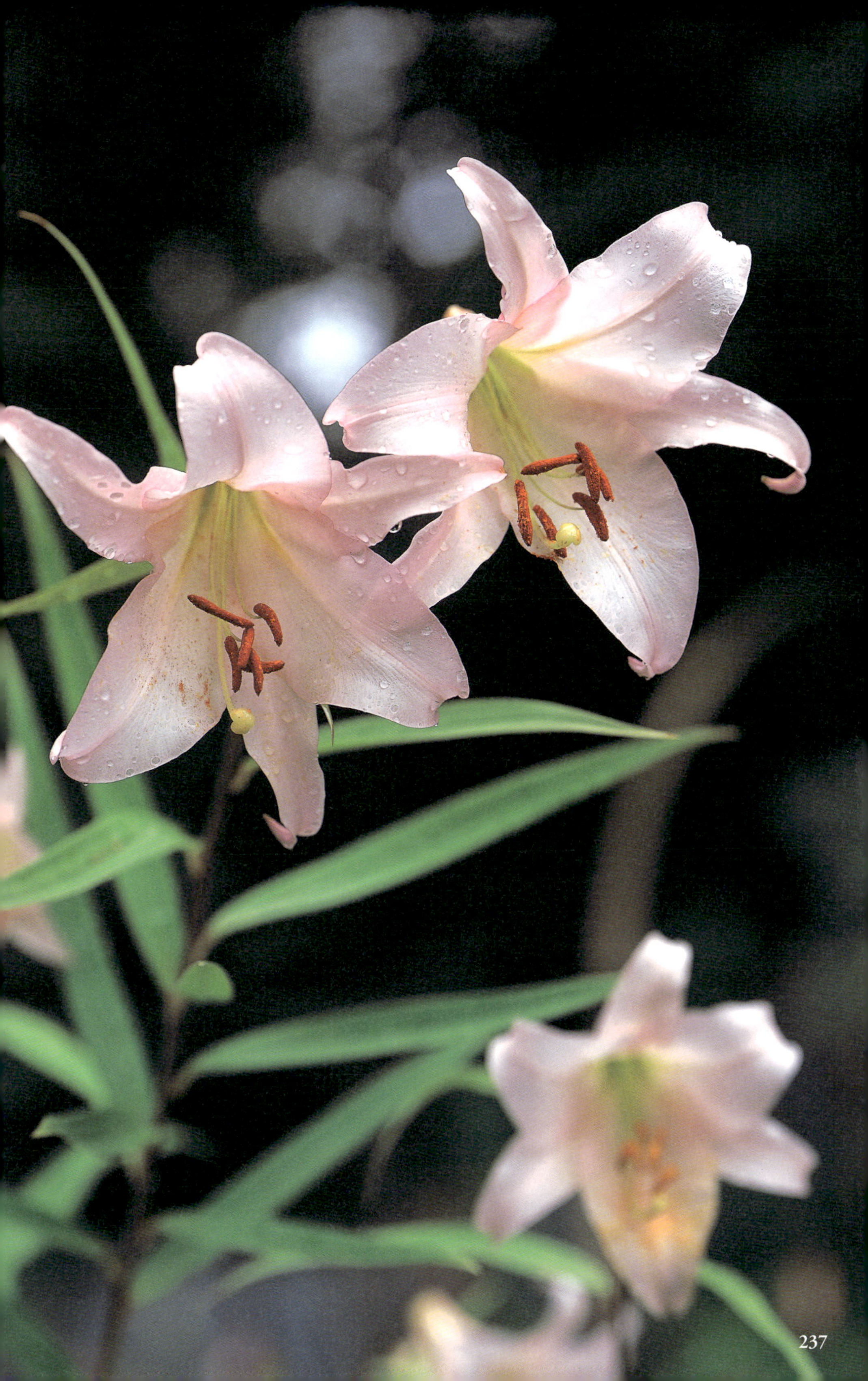

Sent to a maiden by Ōtomo Yakamochi

When can I make my way to you,
urging my horse
    across the crystal shallows
        of the Saho ford,
          where the plover cries?

715

七一五

大伴宿禰家持の娘子に贈れる歌七首（その一首）

千鳥鳴く佐保の河門の清き瀬を馬うち渡し何時か通はむ

千鳥の鳴く佐保川の渡しの清らかな瀬を、馬を渡して、私はいつ通うことだろう。

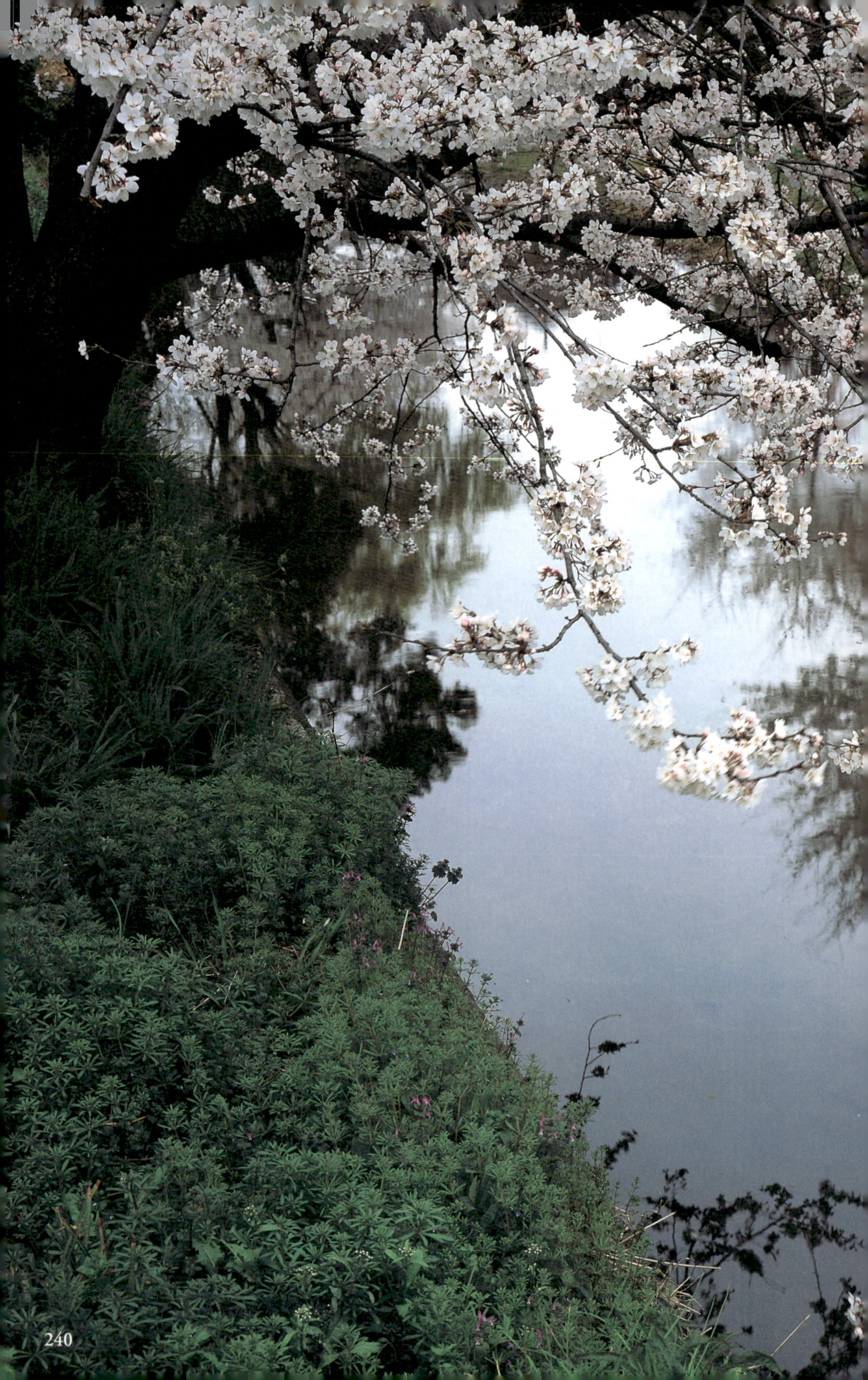

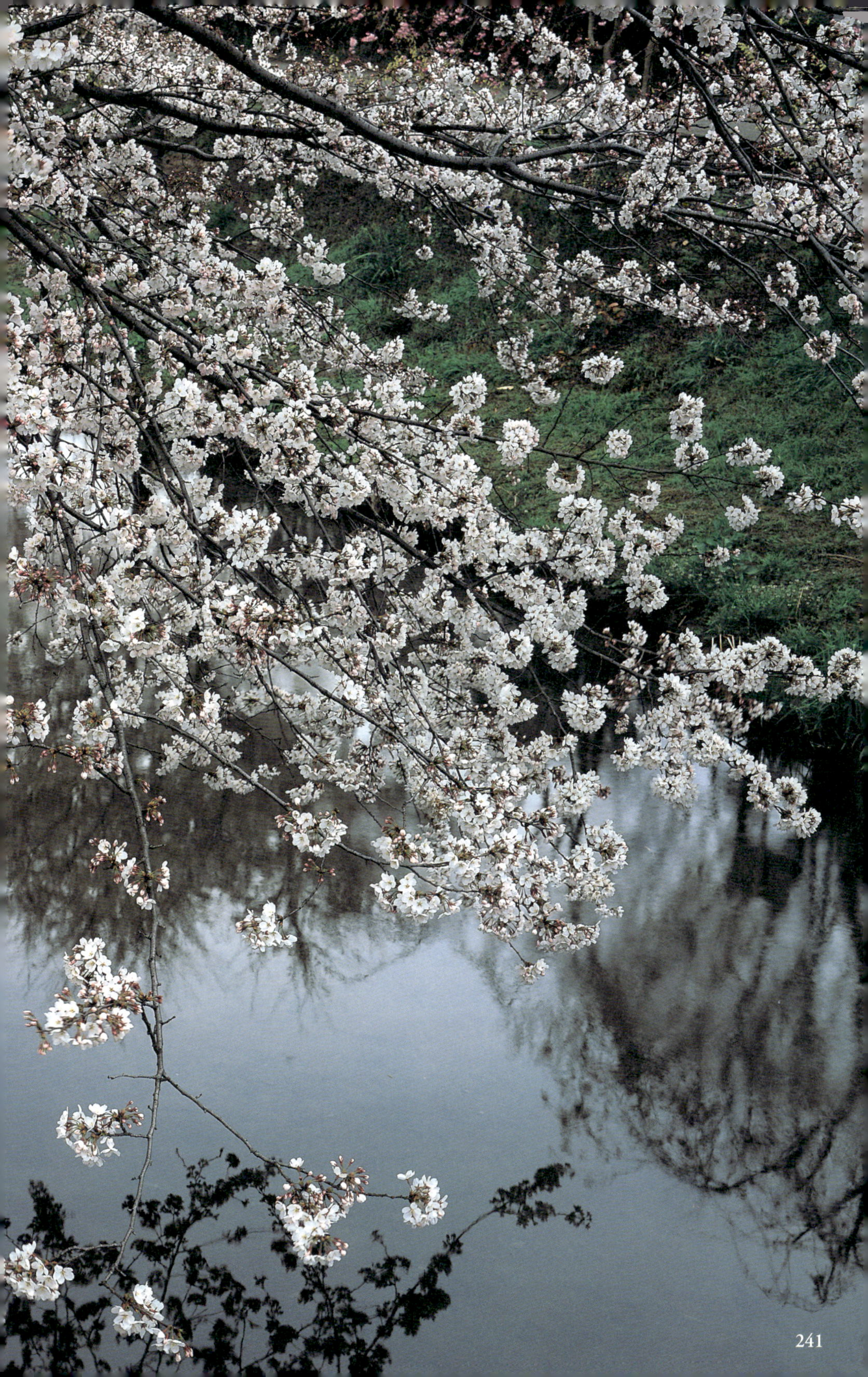

*Sent to the elder daughter of the Sakanoue house
by Ōtomo Yakamochi*

Let my longing be as great
as seven boulders
each a thousand men must haul
all hung upon my neck—
I leave it to the gods.

743

七四三

さらに、大伴宿禰家持の坂上大嬢に贈れる歌十五首（その一首）

わが恋は千引の石を七ばかり首に繋けむも神のまにまに

わが恋こそ千人引きの岩を七つだって首にかけましょうよ。
神様の思召しのままに。

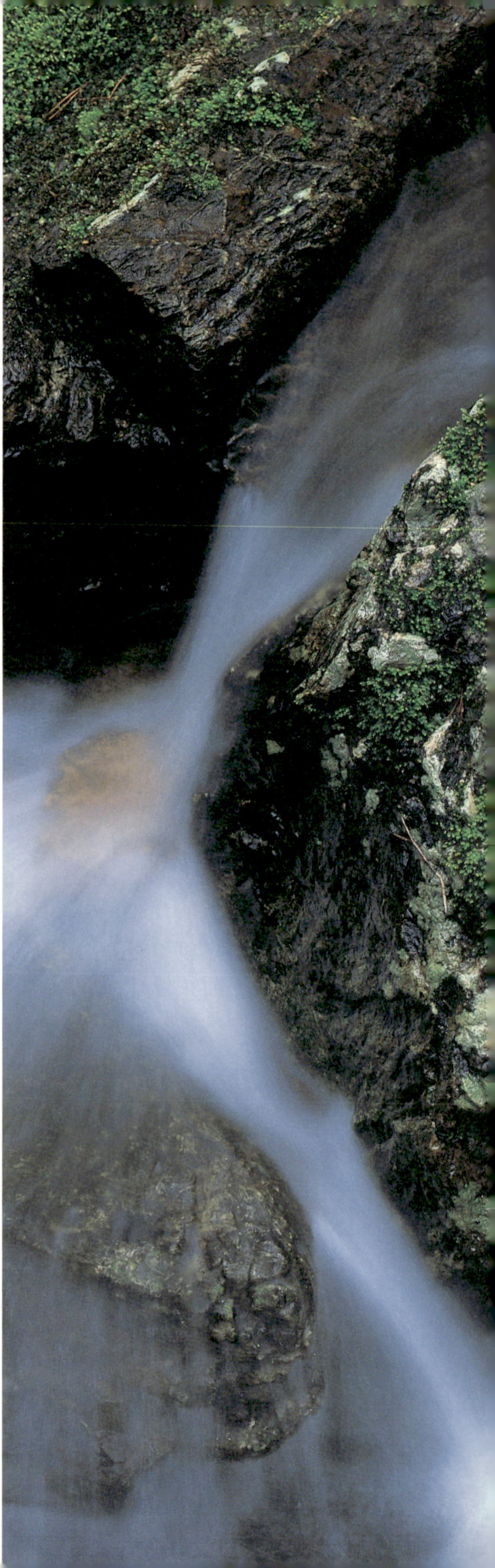

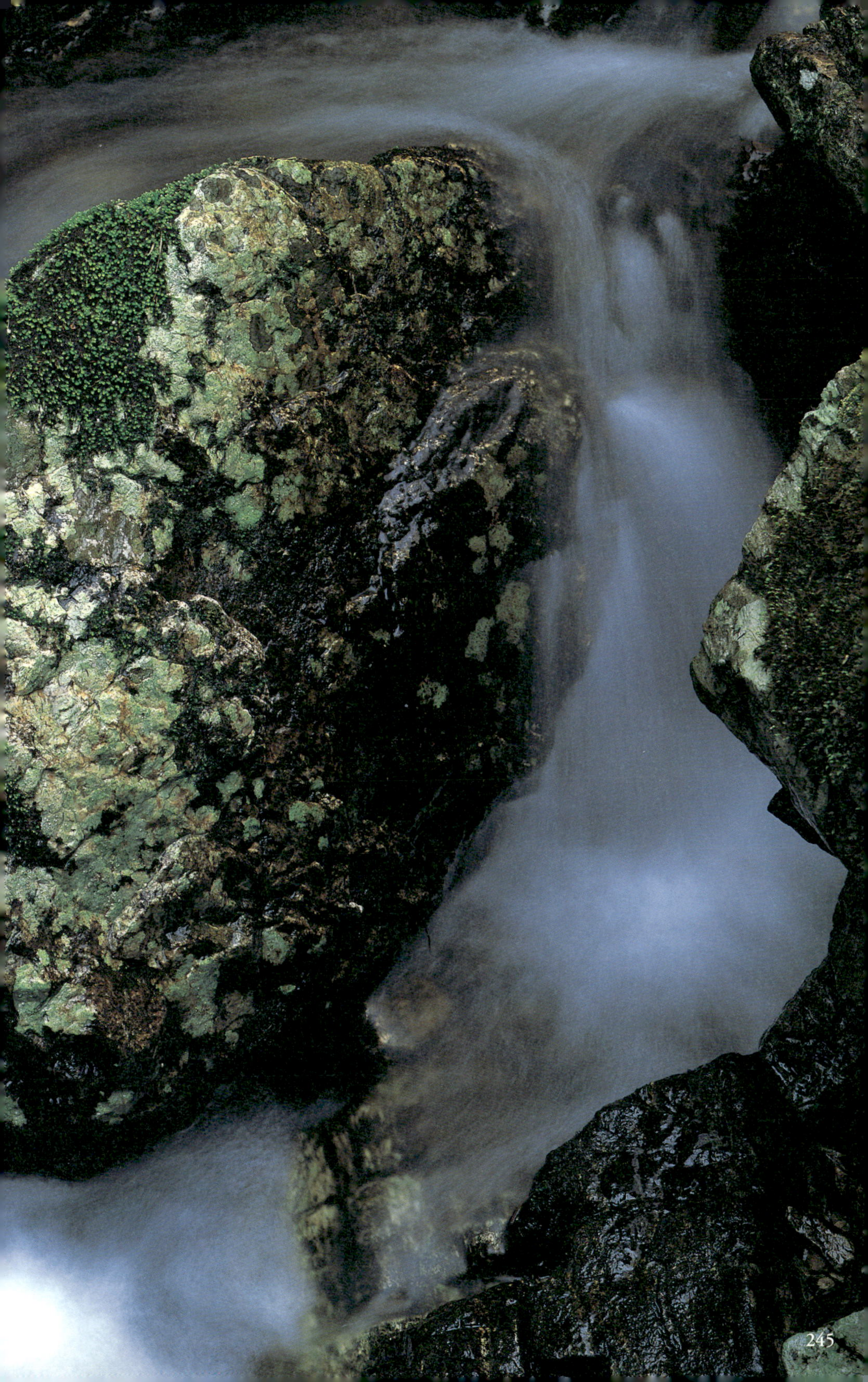

Poem by Lord Ōtomo Tabito, Commander of the Dazaifu, in response to the dreadful news that his wife had died

Afflictions pile one upon another, and dreadful news gathers in a heap. I am constantly filled with sadness enough to rend the heart, and alone I weep gut-wrenching tears. Only because of the great assistance the two of you have given me have I somehow been able to keep my aged body alive. My brush is unable to express all I wish to say — the grief of ancient and modern alike.

When I realize
this world is an empty thing,
then all the more I feel
a deeper and deeper sorrow.

七九三

大宰帥大伴卿の、凶問に報へたる歌一首

禍故重畳し、凶問累集す。永に崩心の悲しびを懐き、独り断腸の泣を流す。
ただ両君の大きなる助に依りて、傾命を繊に継ぐのみ。(筆の言を尽さぬは、古今の嘆く所なり)

世の中は空しきものと知る時しいよいよますますかなしかりけり

わざわいが重なり、不吉な知らせがしきりに集まりました。
長く心も崩れるような悲しみを懐き、ひとり腸を断つような涙を流します。

ただあなた方二人の大きな助けによって、傾きかけた命を、わずかにつなぐばかりです。
(筆がいいたいことを十そ、いよいよ、ますます分表わさないのは、古来悲しかったことだ。

人々の嘆いたところです)

この世が空(くう)だとはじめて思い知った時こ

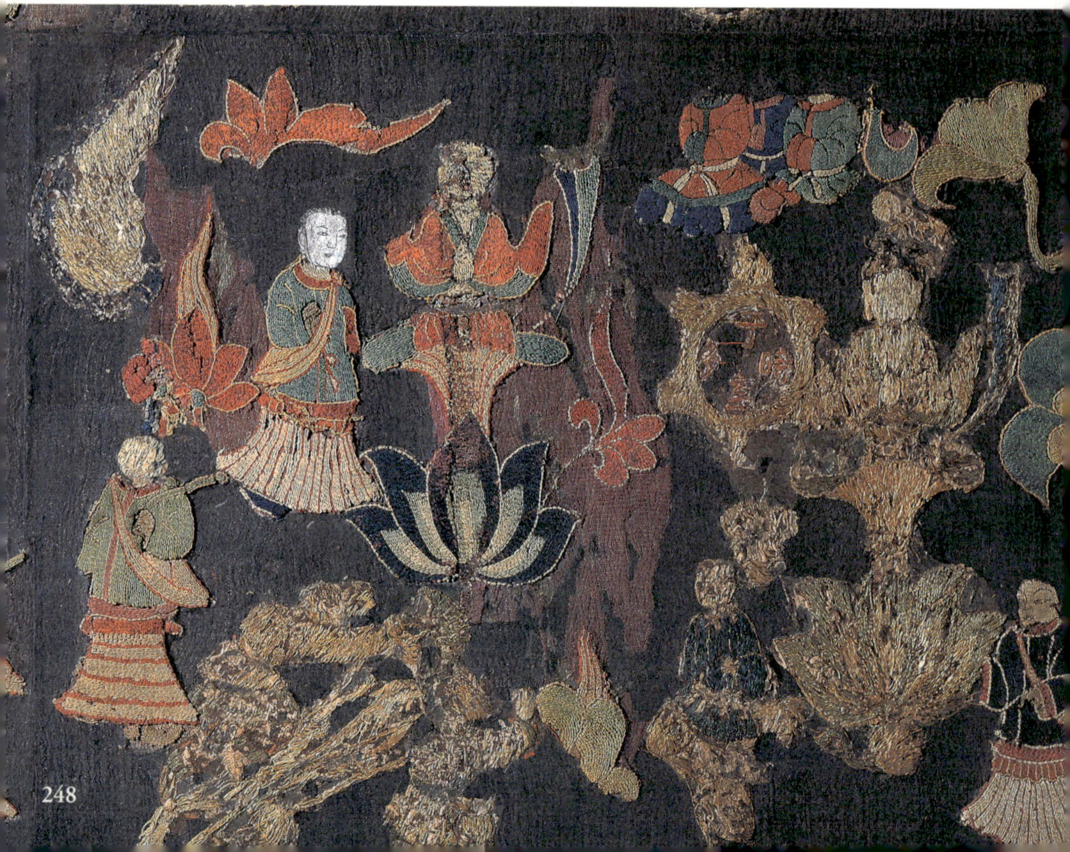

249

Poem on thinking of his children
by Yamanoue Okura

Preface

Sakyamuni expounds truthfully from his golden mouth, "I love all things equally, the way I love my child Rāhula." He also teaches us, "No love is greater than the love for one's child." Even the greatest of saints cherishes his child. Who, then, among the living creatures of this world could fail to love his children?

When I eat a melon,
I think of my children.
When I eat chestnuts,
I long for them even more.
Where do they possibly come from?
Their mischief flickers
       before my eyes
and keeps me from my sleep.

八〇二

山上臣憶良の子らを思へる歌一首并せて序

釈迦如来の、金口に正に説きたまはく「等しく衆生を思ふことは、羅睺羅の如し」と。又説きたまはく「愛びは子に過ぎたるは無し」と。至極の大聖すら、尚ほ子を愛ぶる心ます。況むや世間の蒼生の、誰かは子を愛びざらめや。

瓜食めば　子ども思ほゆ　栗食めば　まして思はゆ　何処より
来りしものそ　眼交に　もとな懸りて　安眠し寝さぬ

釈迦如来が口ずから説かれることには「なべて衆生を思うことは、わが子ラゴラのごとくである」と。また説かれて「子を愛する以上の愛はない」と。悟達の大聖人ですら、

やはり子を愛する煩悩をもっておられる。まして世間の凡人の誰が、子をかわいいと思わないでいうものはどういう因縁によって来たものだろう。目の先にちらついては、

とが思われる。栗を食べるとましてしのばれてならない。一体、子どもというものはどういう因縁によって来たものだろう。目の先にちらついては、

瓜を食べると子どものこ
私を安眠させない。

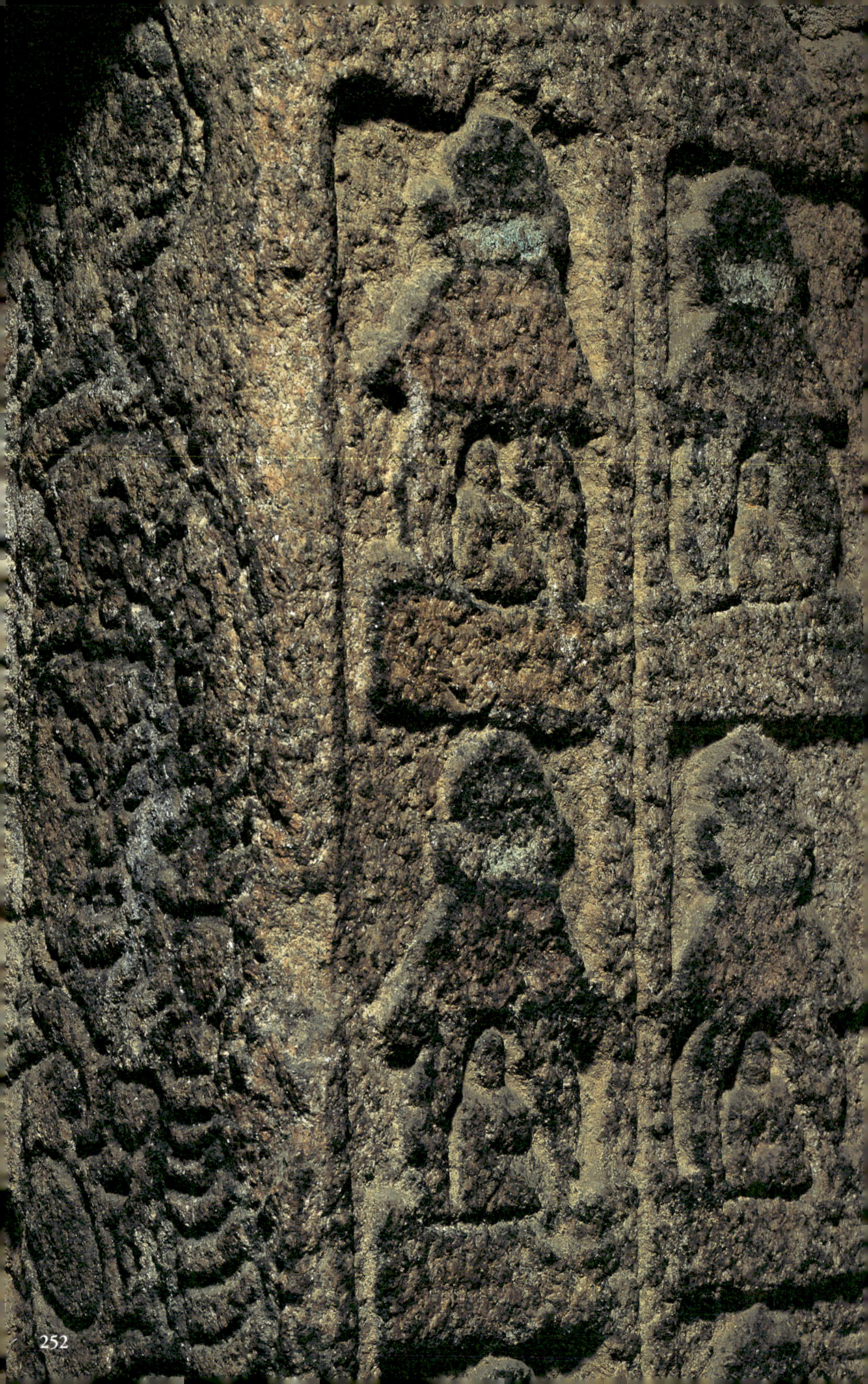

253

Envoy

What do I need
      with silver,
      with gold and gems?
Could the most precious jewel
      be equal to my child?

八〇三

反歌

銀も金も玉も何せむに勝れる宝子に及かめやも

銀も金も、玉とても、何の役に立とう。すぐれた宝も子に及ぶことなどあろうか。

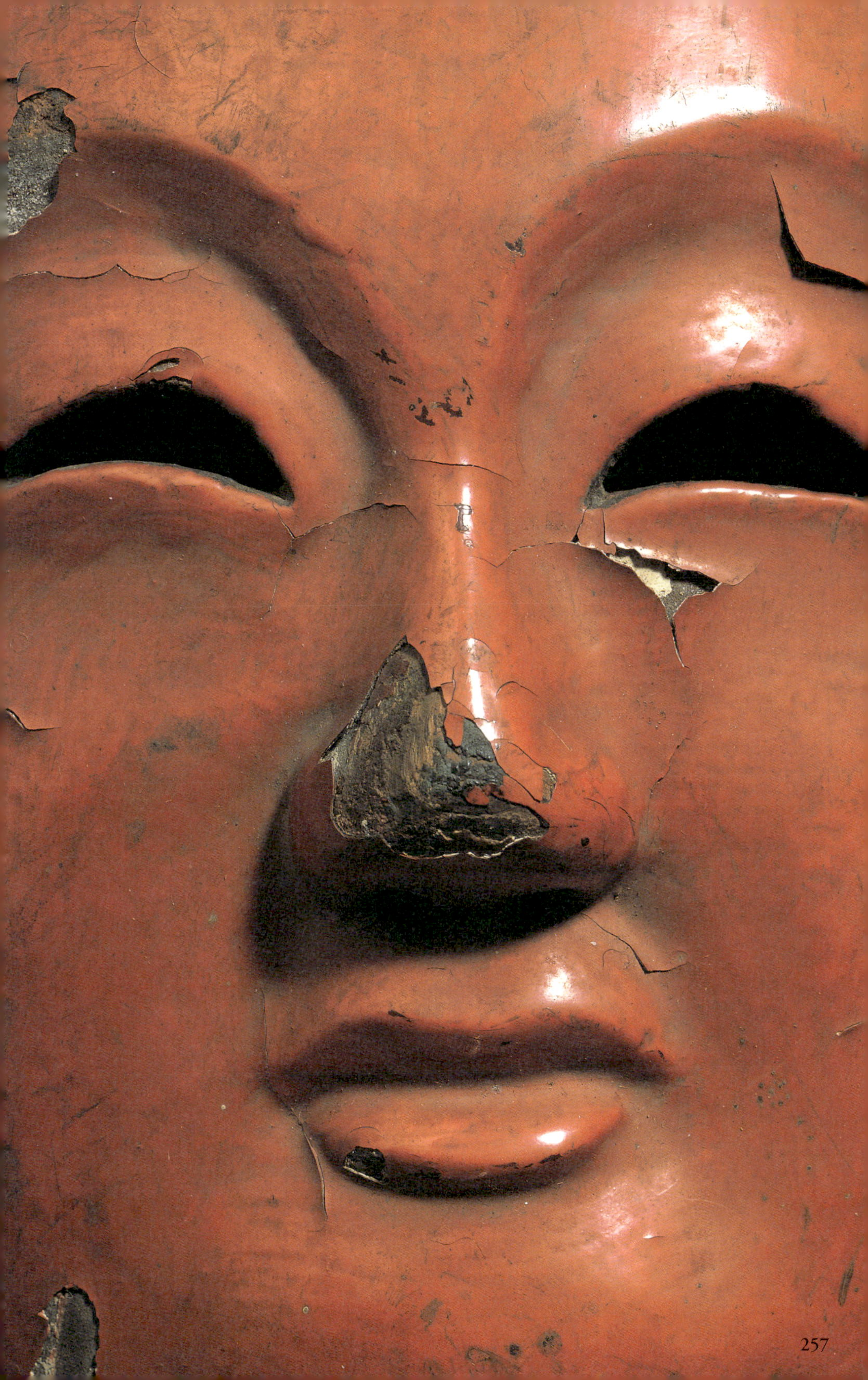

from
*Poem sorrowing on the impermanence of life
in this world by Yamanoue Okura*

We cannot hold time
   in its blossoming:
      when young girls,
to be maidenly,
wrapped Chinese jewels
around their wrists
and, hand in hand
with companions of their age,
must once have played.
When has frost fallen
on hair as black
as the guts of river snails?

804

八〇四

山上臣憶良の世間の住り難きを哀しびたる歌一首

并せて序 より

少女らが　少女さびすと　唐玉を　手本に纏かし　同輩児らと

手携りて　遊びけむ　時の盛りを　留みかね　過し遣りつれ

蜷の腸　か黒き髪に　何時の間か　霜の降りけむ

少女たちが初々しい少女らしく唐玉を手首に纏い、同じ年ごろの子と手を携えて遊んだであろう盛りの時期を、留めることができず過ごしやってしまったので、蜷の腸のように黒々とした髪には、何時の間に霜がおりたのだろう。

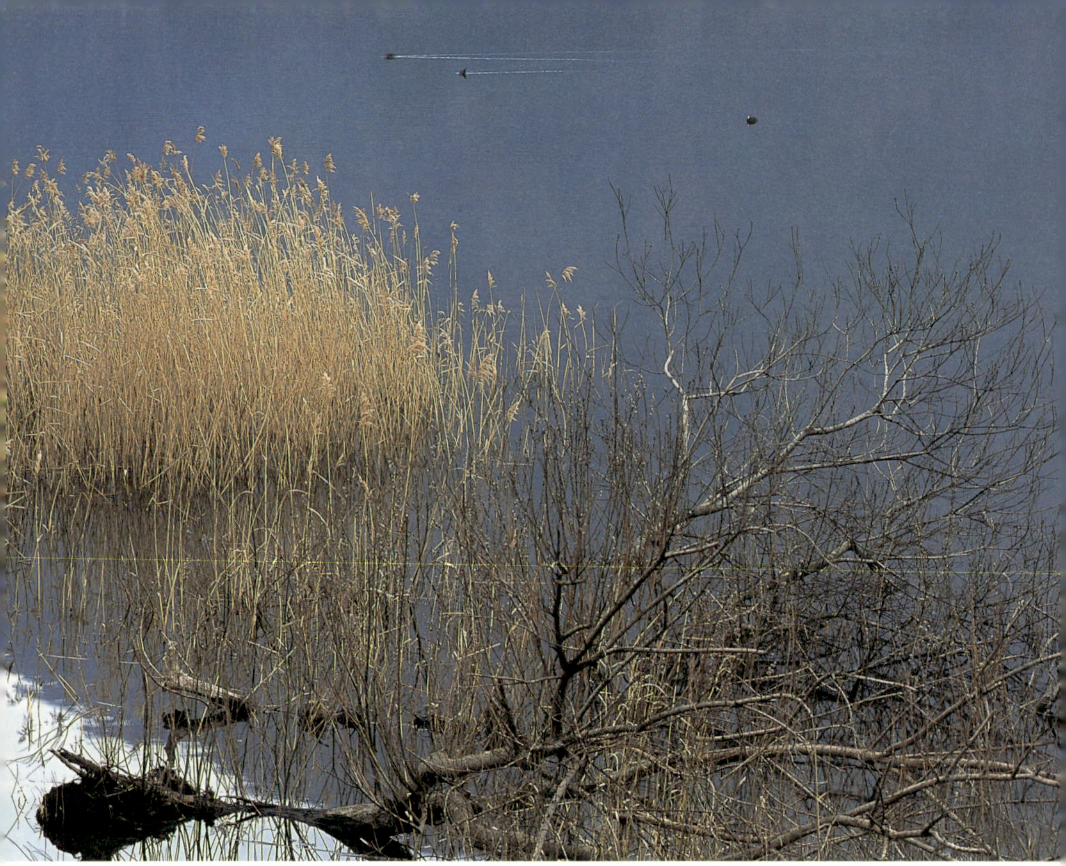

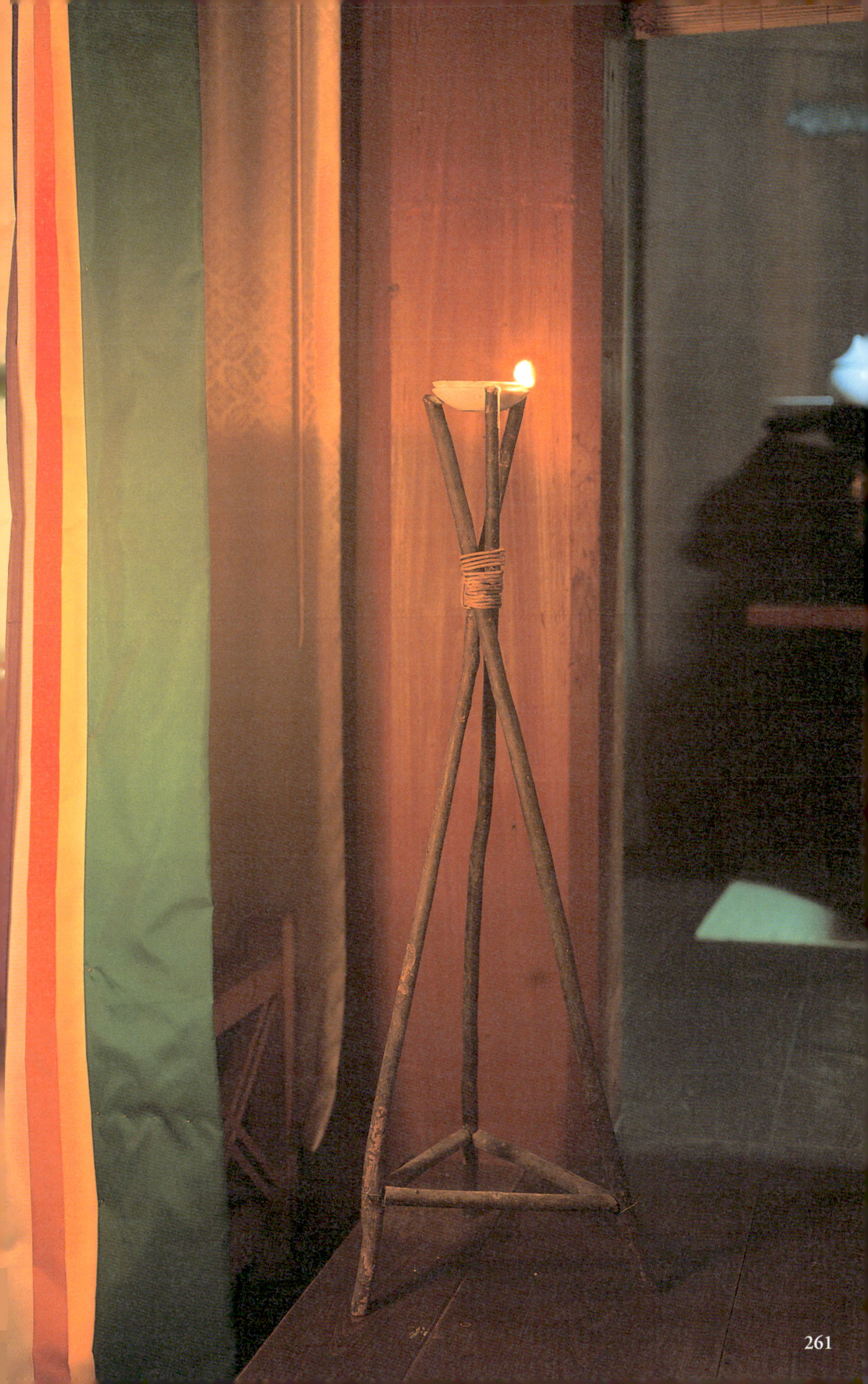

from
Thirty-two poems on the plum blossoms

Plum blossoms by my house,
first to bloom
              when spring arrives:
will I be watching them alone
as this spring day yields to dusk?

By Yamanoue Okura, Governor of Chikuzen

八一八

大宰帥大伴卿の宅の宴の梅花の歌三十二首（その三首）

春さればまづ咲く宿の梅の花独り見つつや春日暮さむ

筑前守山上大夫

春になると最初に咲くわが家の梅花、私一人で見つつ一日をすごすことなど、どうしてしようか。

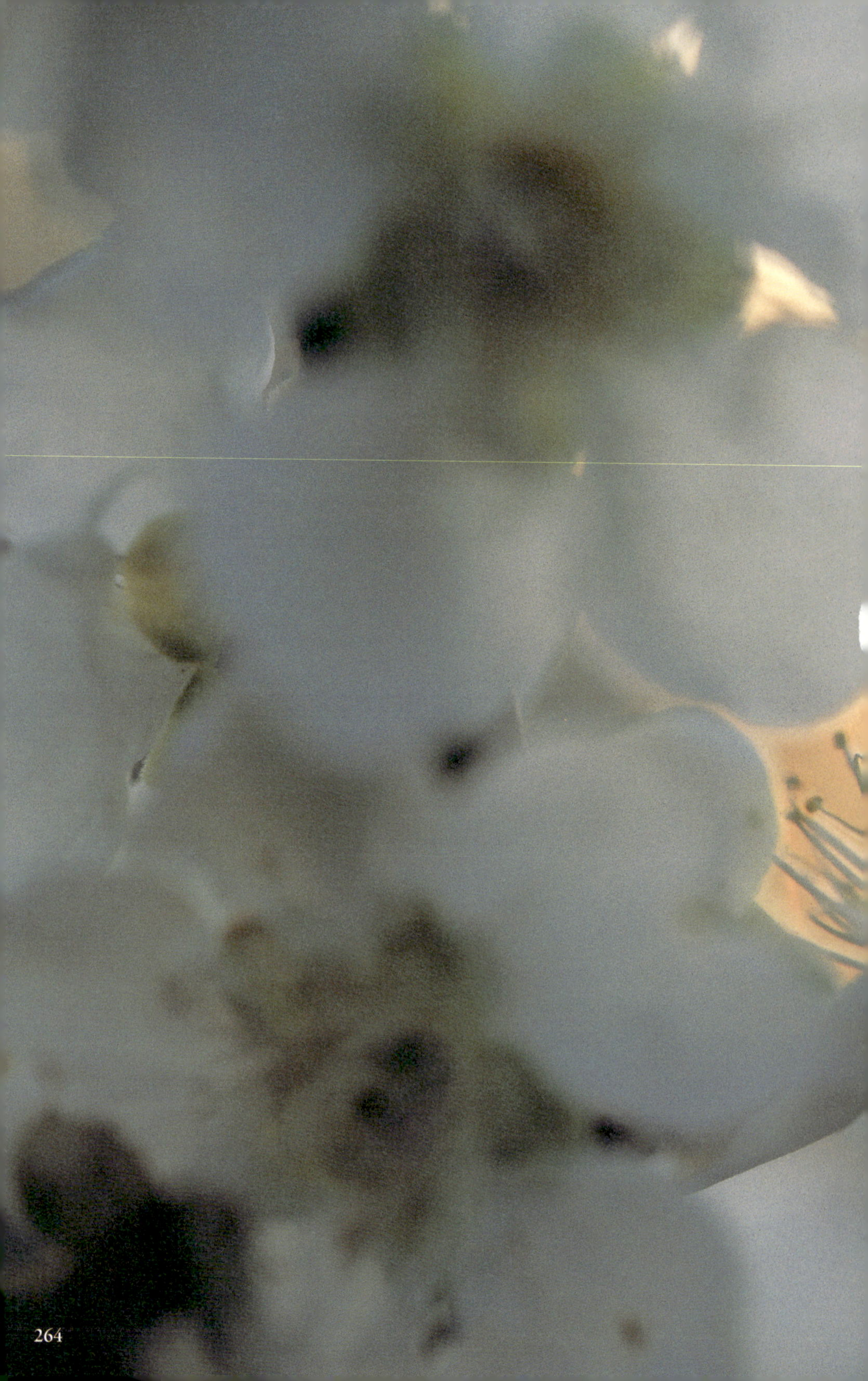

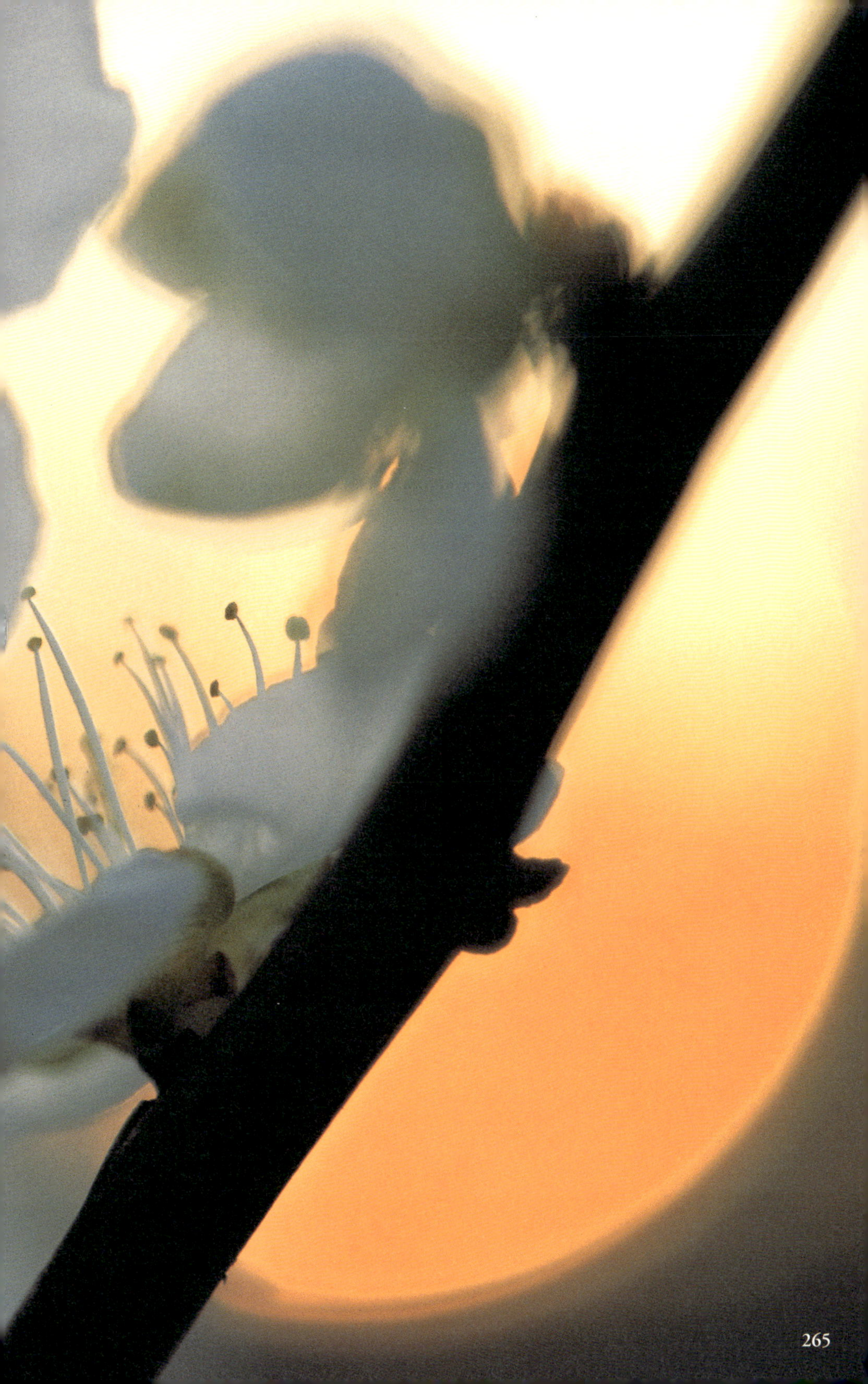

Plum blossoms fall
and scatter in my garden;
is this snow come streaming
from the distant heavens?

By the host, Ōtomo Tabito

822

八二二

わが園に梅の花散るひさかたの天(あめ)より雪の流れ来(く)るかも

主人(あるじ)(大伴旅人)

わが庭に梅の花が散る。天涯の果てから雪が流れ来るよ。

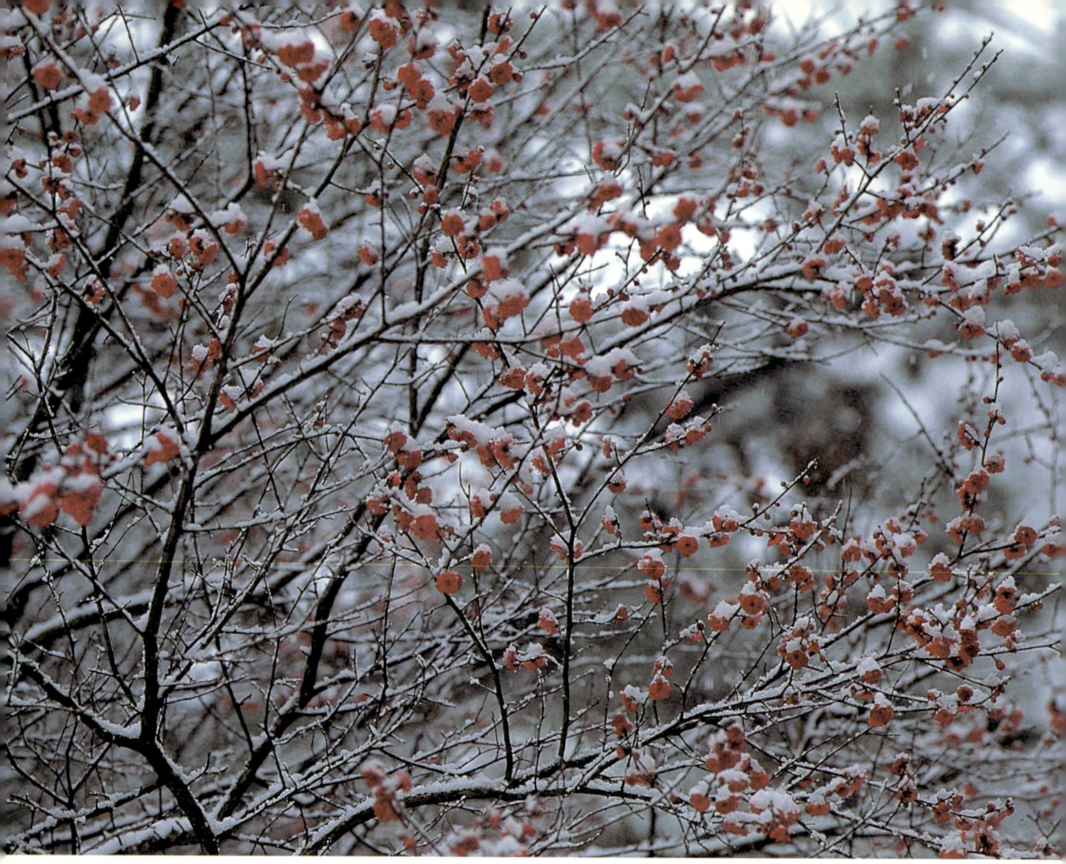

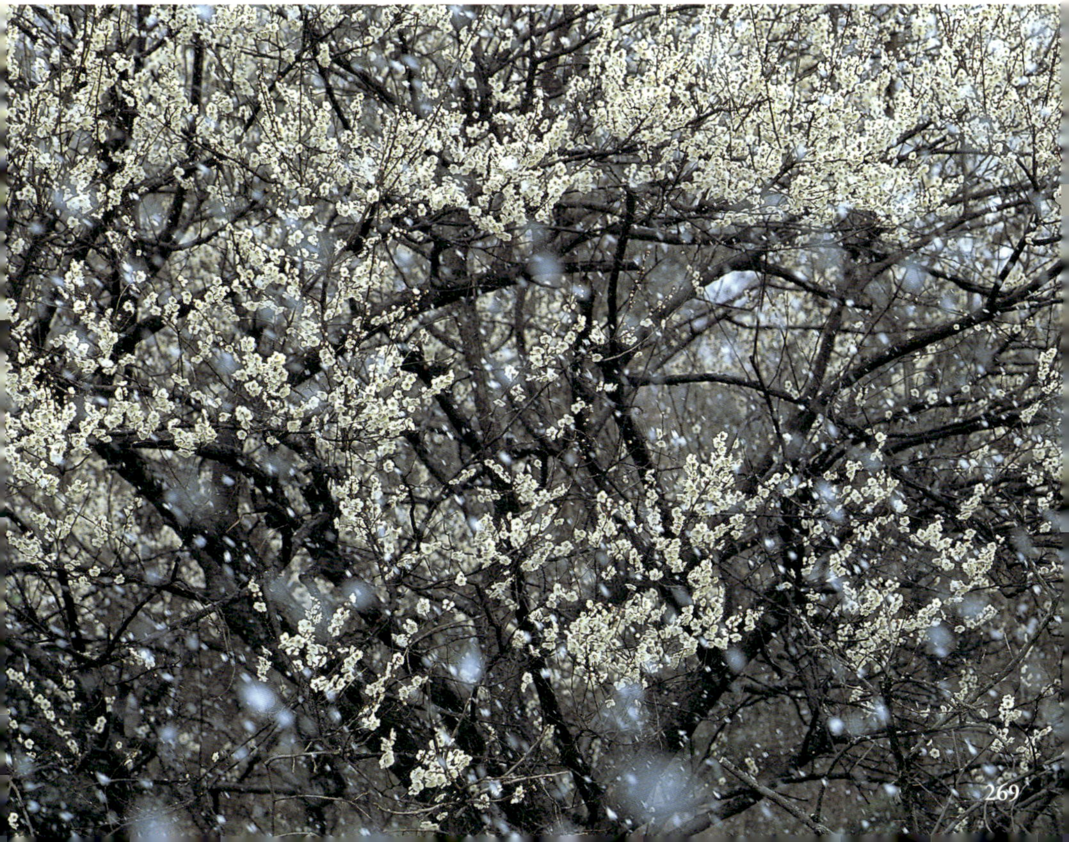

Mourning the plum blossoms' fall,
the nightingale cries
in the bamboo grove in my garden.

By Abe Okishima, Lieutenant of the Dazaifu

824

八二四

梅の花散らまく惜しみわが園の竹の林に鶯鳴くも

少監 阿氏奥島
（せうげん あしのおきしま）

梅の花の散ることを惜しんで、わが庭の竹林には鶯が鳴くことよ。

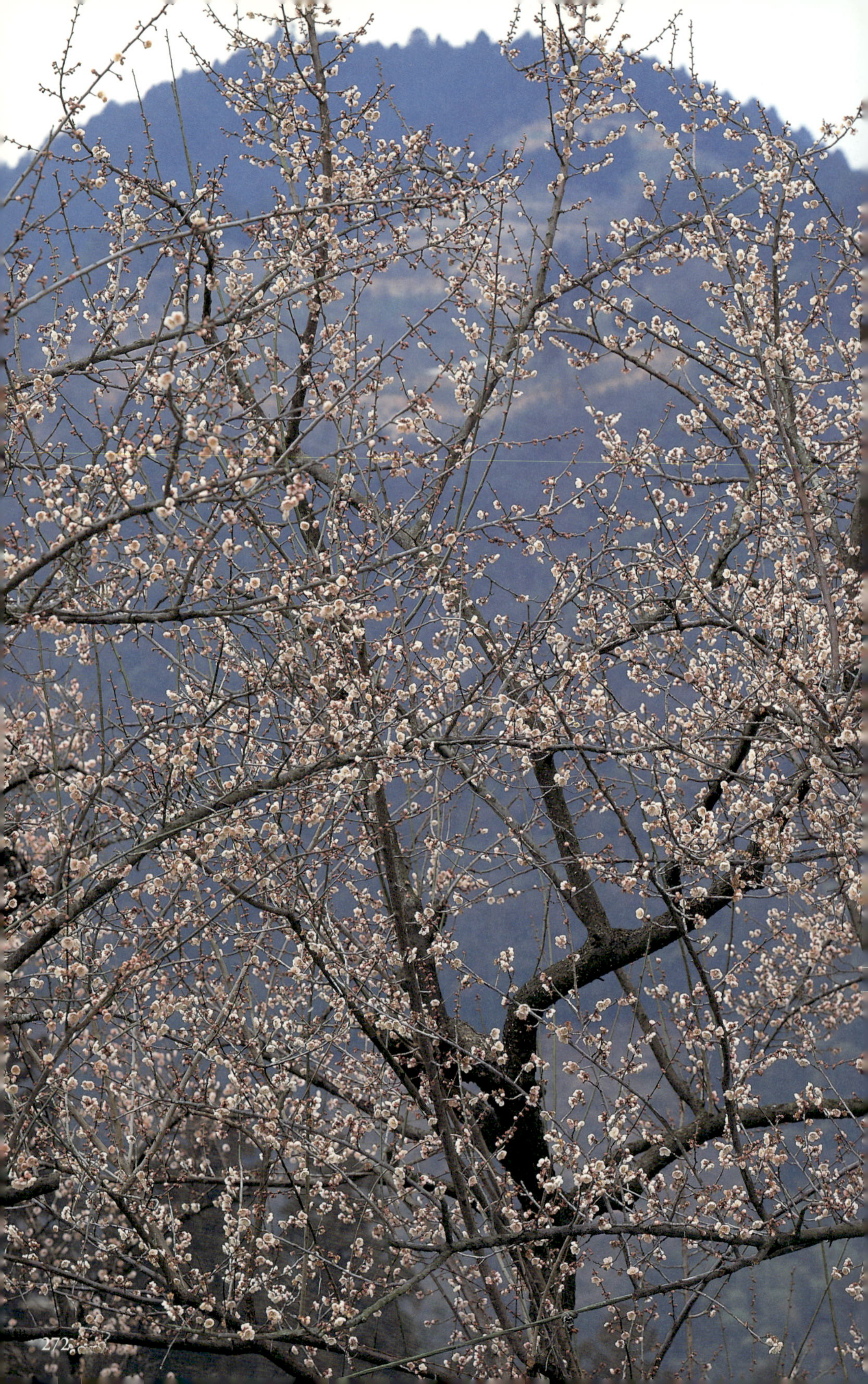

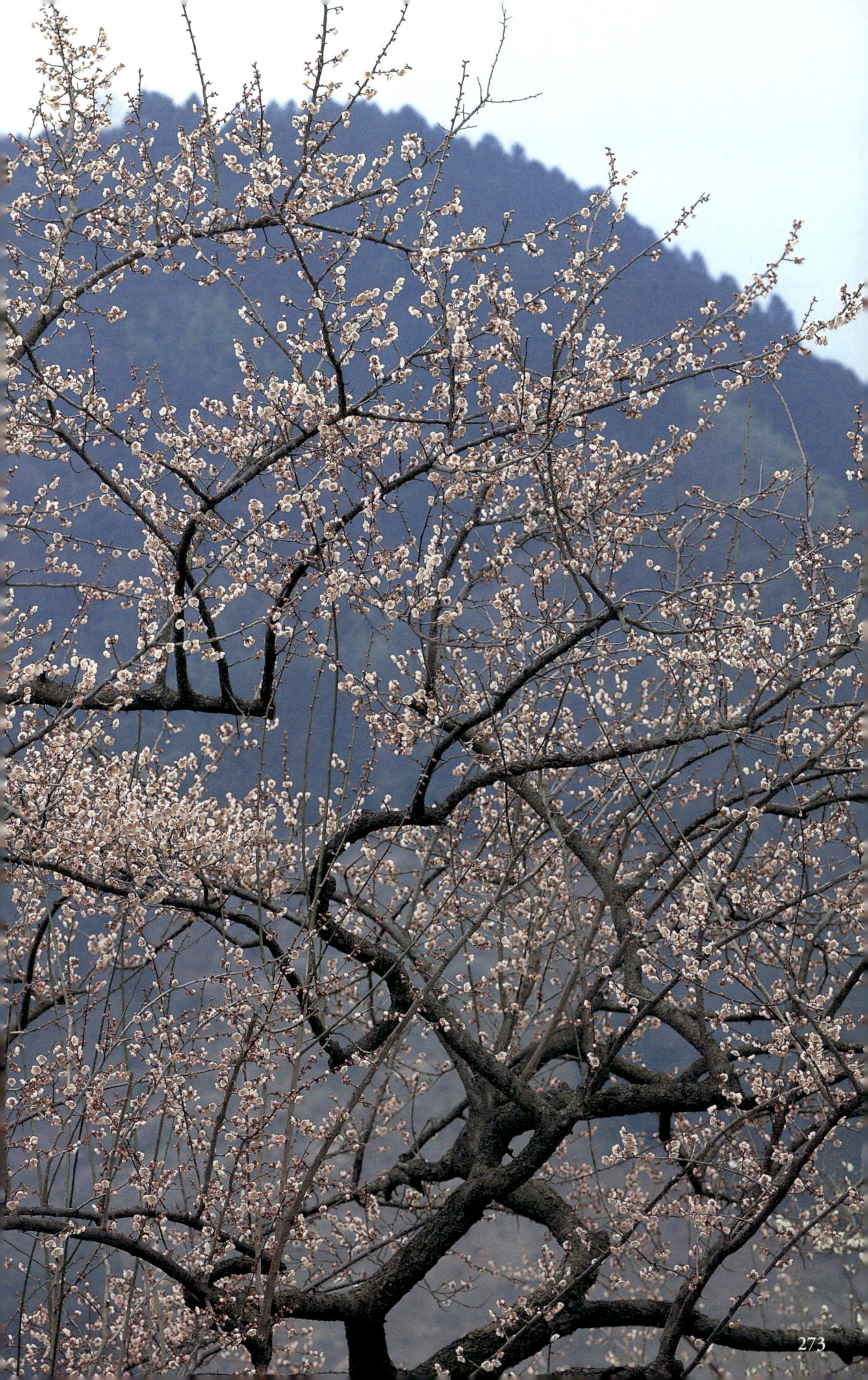

A poem, added later, responding to the plum blossom poems

The plum flourishes now,
its bloom is pillaging
the white from the snow.
Oh for someone to see it!

850

八五〇
後(のち)に追ひて梅の歌に和(こた)へたる四首（その一首）

雪の色を奪(うば)ひて咲ける梅の花今盛りなり見む人もがも

雪の白さを奪うかに咲く梅の花は今が盛りのことよ、見る人があってほしい。

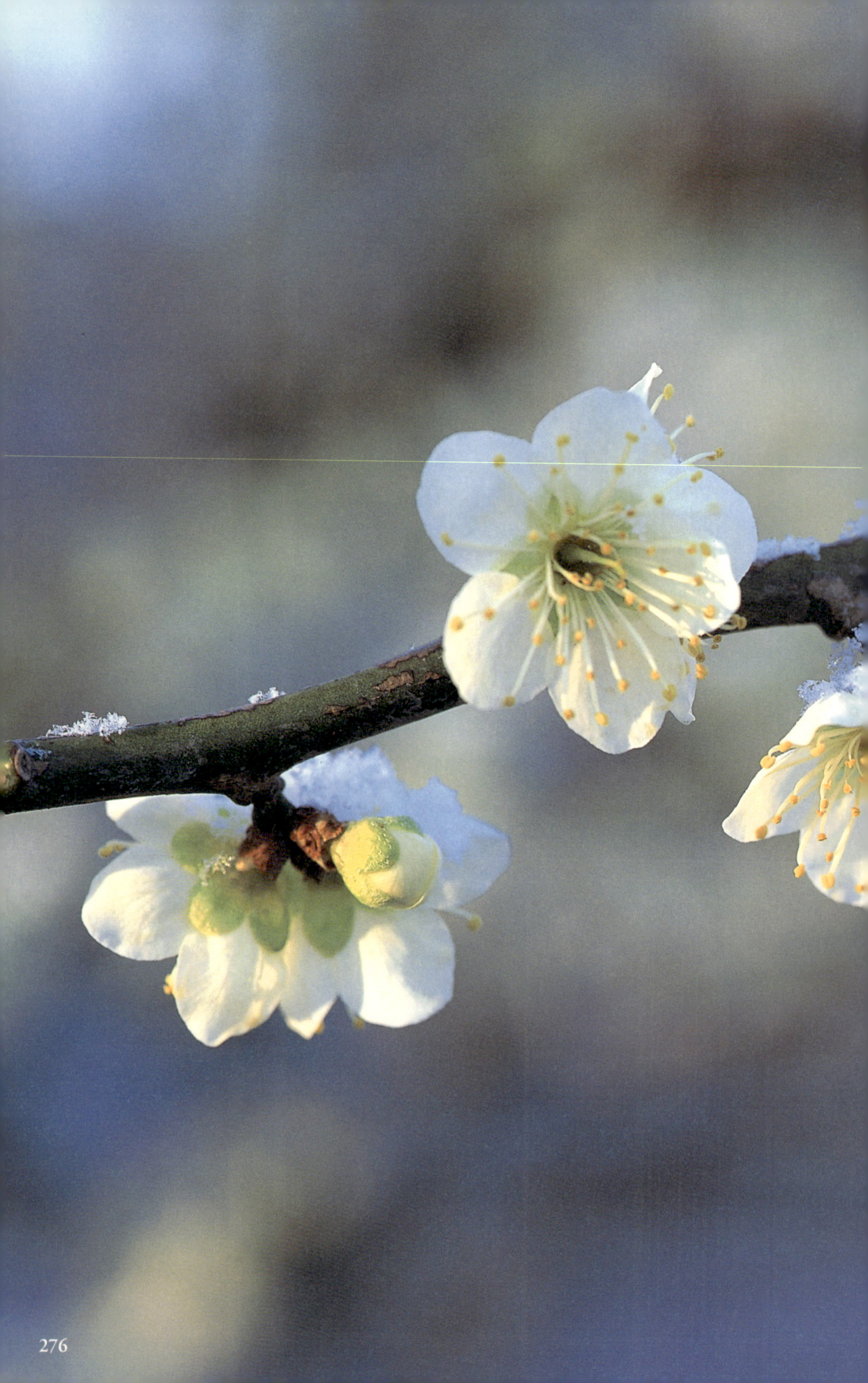

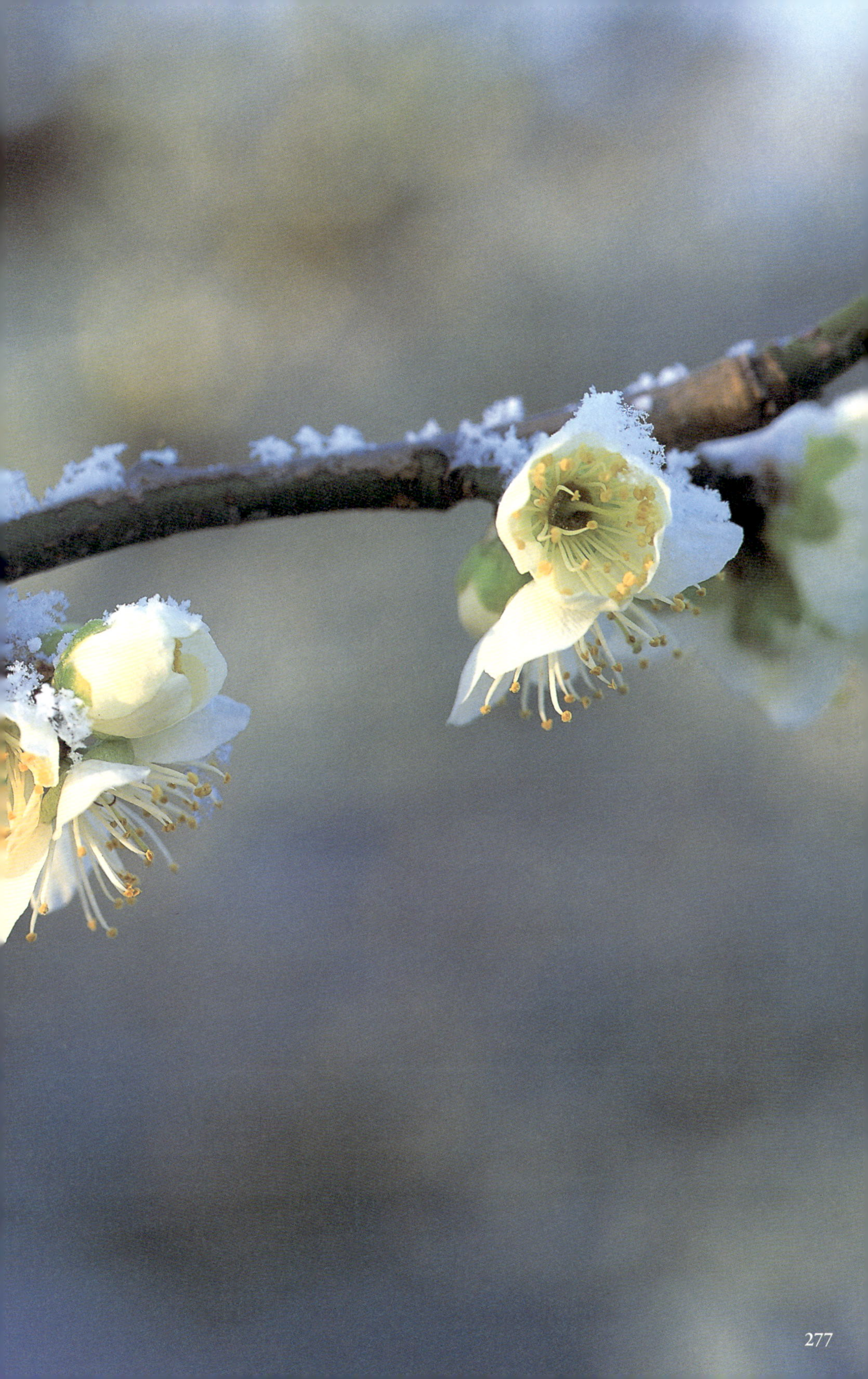

A poem expressing personal feelings

Have sympathy, O my master,
and when spring comes call me
to the capital at Nara.

882

八八二

敢(あ)へて私の懐(おもひ)を布(の)べたる歌三首（その一首）

吾(あ)が主(ぬし)の御霊(みたま)給ひて春さらば奈良の都に召(め)上(さ)げ給はね

あなたの御心をかけて下さって、春が来たら奈良の都に私を召し上げてくださいな。

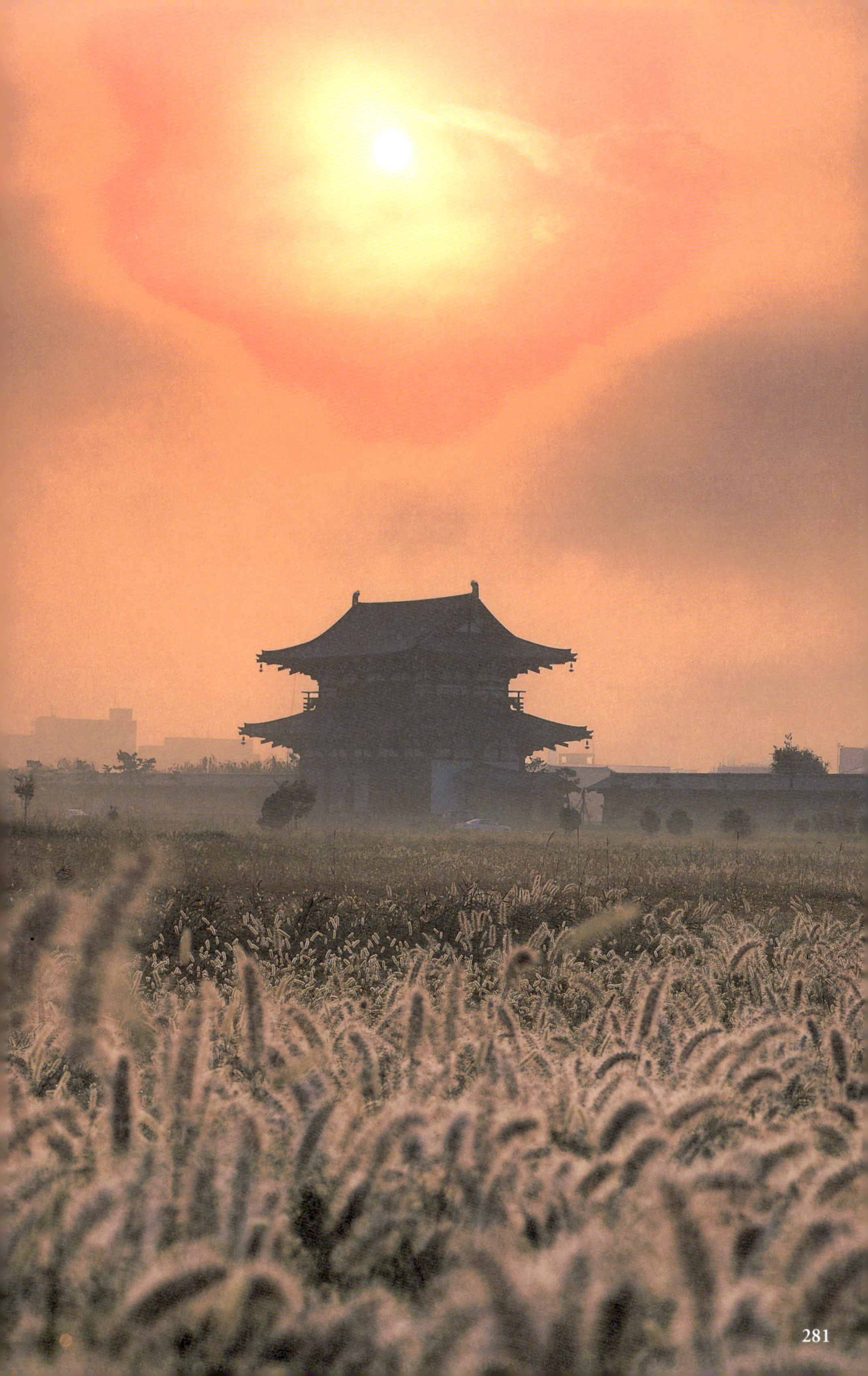

from
Dialog of the Destitute by Yamanoue Okura

"Wide, they say,
        are heaven and earth—
but have they shrunk for me?
Bright, they say,
        are the sun and moon—
but do they refuse to shine for me?
Is it thus for all men,
        or for me alone?
Above all, I was born human,
I too toil for my keep—
as much as the next man—
yet on my shoulders hangs
a cloth shirt
not even lined with cotton,
these tattered rags

thin as strips of seaweed.
In my groveling hut,
    my tilting hut,
sleeping on straw
cut and spread right on the ground,
with my father and mother
    huddled at my pillow
and my wife and children
    huddled at my feet,
I grieve and lament.
Not a spark rises in the stove,
and in the pot
a spider has drawn its web.
I have forgotten
what it is to cook rice!"

284

うち懸け　伏廬の　曲廬の内に　直土に　藁解き敷きて　父母
は　枕の方に　妻子どもは　足の方に　囲み居て　憂へ吟ひ
竈には　火気ふき立てず　甑には　蜘蛛の巣懸きて　飯炊く
事も忘れて

　天地は広大だというのに、私にとっては狭くなったのだろうか。太陽や月は明るいというのに、私のためにはお照りにならぬのだろうか。人は皆そうなのか。それとも自分だけそうなのか。とりわけ励んでいるのに、人並に自分も生業に励んでいるのに、綿も入っていない布肩衣の、海藻のようにばらばらと垂れ下がっているぼろばかりを肩にはおり、潰れたような、倒れかかったいおりの内に地面にじかに藁を解き敷いて、父母は頭の方に妻子は足の方に自分を囲んでいて、悲しみ歎息し、竈には火の気を立てることもなく、甑にはいつか蜘蛛の巣がかかって、飯をたくことも忘れて

八九二
（山上臣憶良の）貧窮問答の歌一首　より

天地は　広しといへど　吾が為は　狭くやなりぬる　日月は
明しといへど　吾が為は　照りや給はぬ　人皆か　吾のみや然
る　わくらばに　人とはあるを　人並に　吾も作れるを　綿も
無き　布肩衣の　海松の如　わわけさがれる　襤褸のみ　肩に

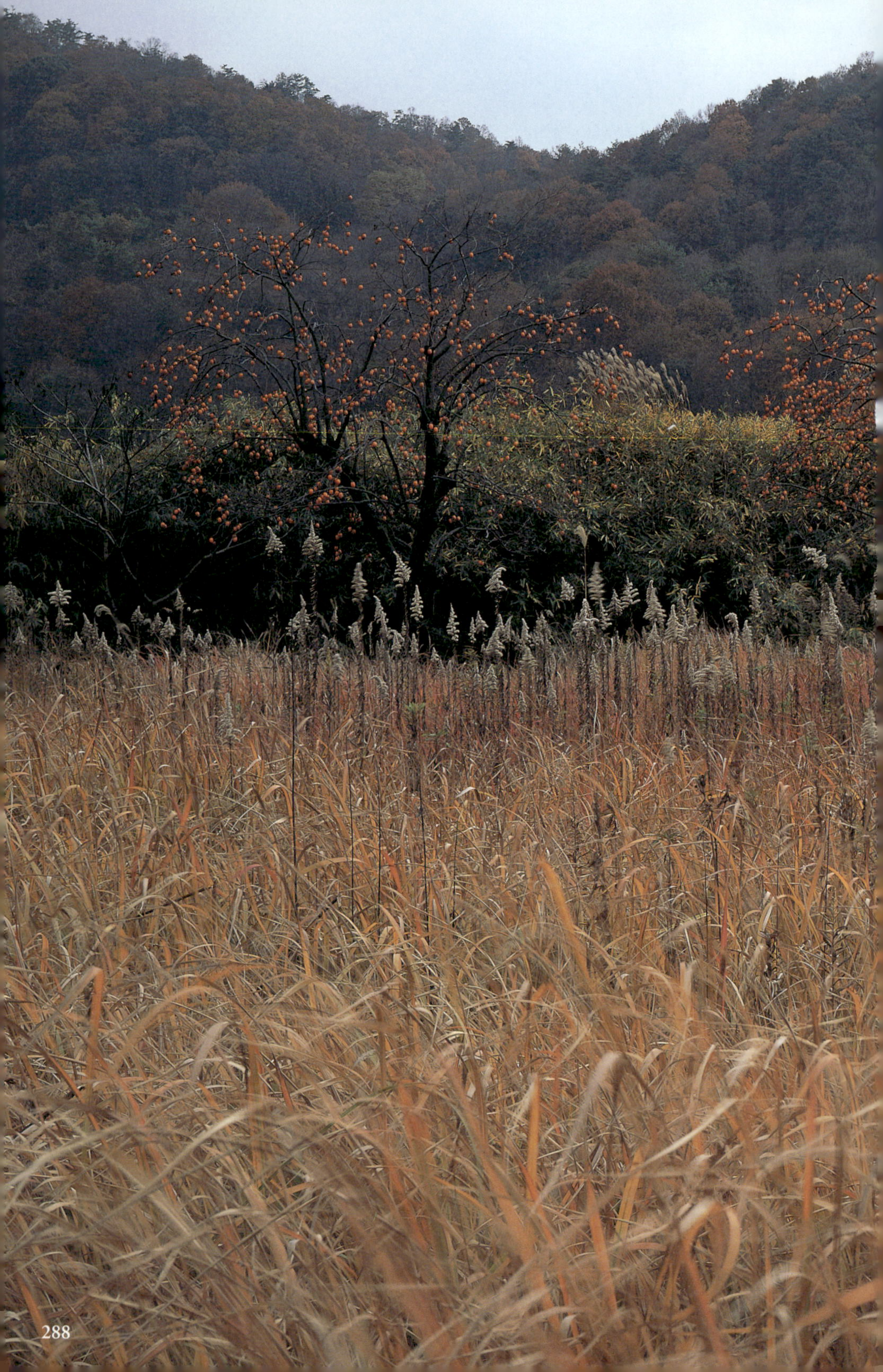

289

from
Poem wishing Godspeed to the Ambassador to China by Yamanoue Okura

It has been recounted
down through time
since the age of the gods:
that this land of Yamato
is a land of imperial deities'
                    stern majesty,
a land blessed by the spirit of words.

894

八九四

山上臣憶良の好去好来(かうきょかうらい)の歌一首　より

神代より　言(い)ひ伝(つ)て来らく　そらみつ　倭(やまと)の国は　皇神(すめがみ)の　巌(いつく)しき国　言霊(ことだま)の　幸(さき)はふ国と　語り継(つ)ぎ　言ひ継がひけり

神代から言い伝え来ることには、空に充ちる大和の国は、統治の神の厳しき国で、言霊の幸ある国と語りつぎ言いついで来ました。

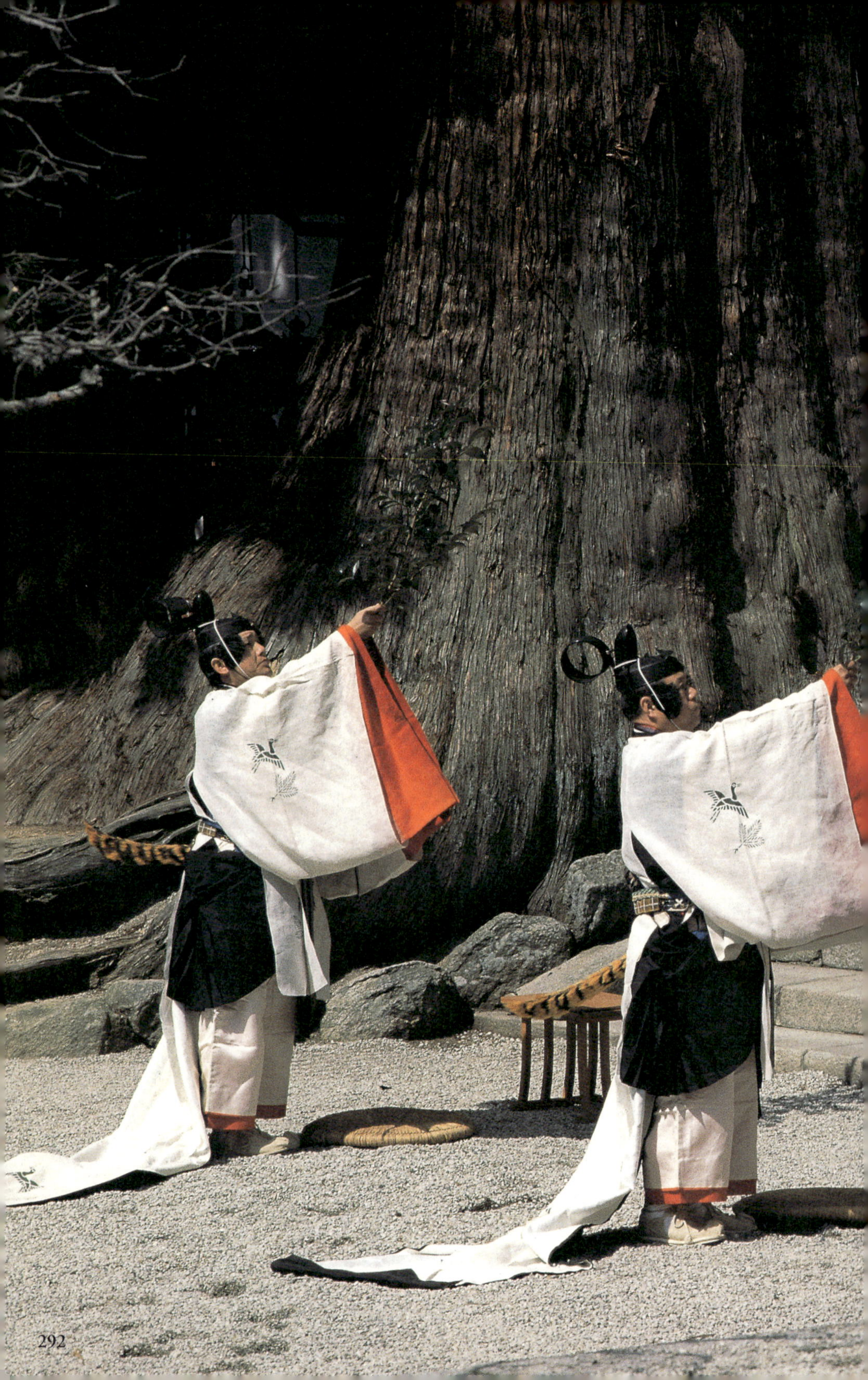

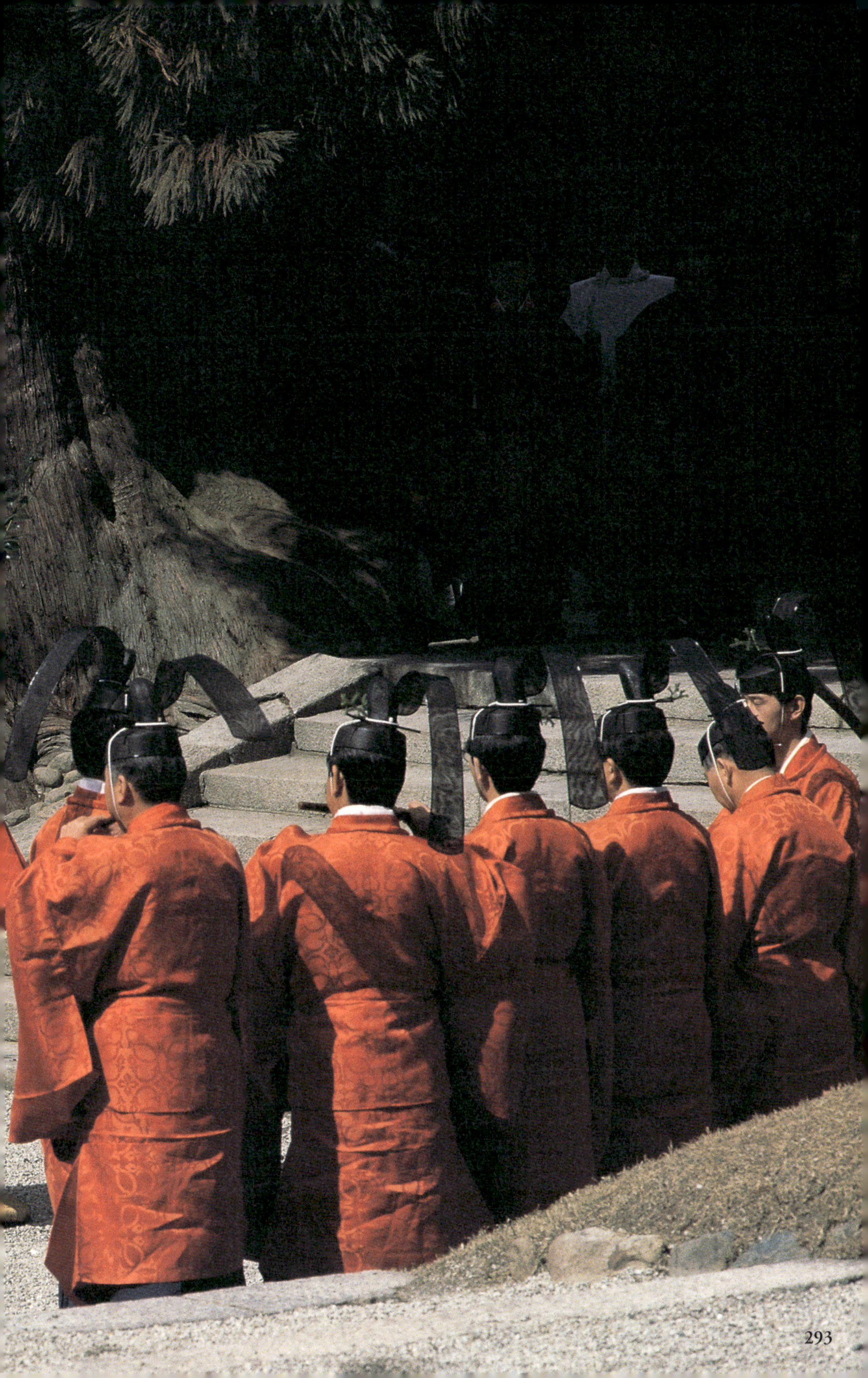

Envoy to seven poems about having disease added to my already aged body, the hardships of the years, and my longing for my children
by Yamanoue Okura

Oh cottons and silks of the rich,
more than can dress
their few children's bodies,
that they let rot and throw away!

900

九〇〇

（山上臣憶良の）老いたる身に病を重ね、年を経て辛苦(たしな)み、及(また)、児等(こら)を思(しの)へる歌七首（その反歌一首）

富人(とみひと)の家の児どもの着(き)る身無(みな)み腐(くた)し棄(す)つらむ絁綿(きぬわた)らはも

富裕な家の子らの、着る体がおいつかずに腐らせ棄ててしまっているだろう絁や綿よ。

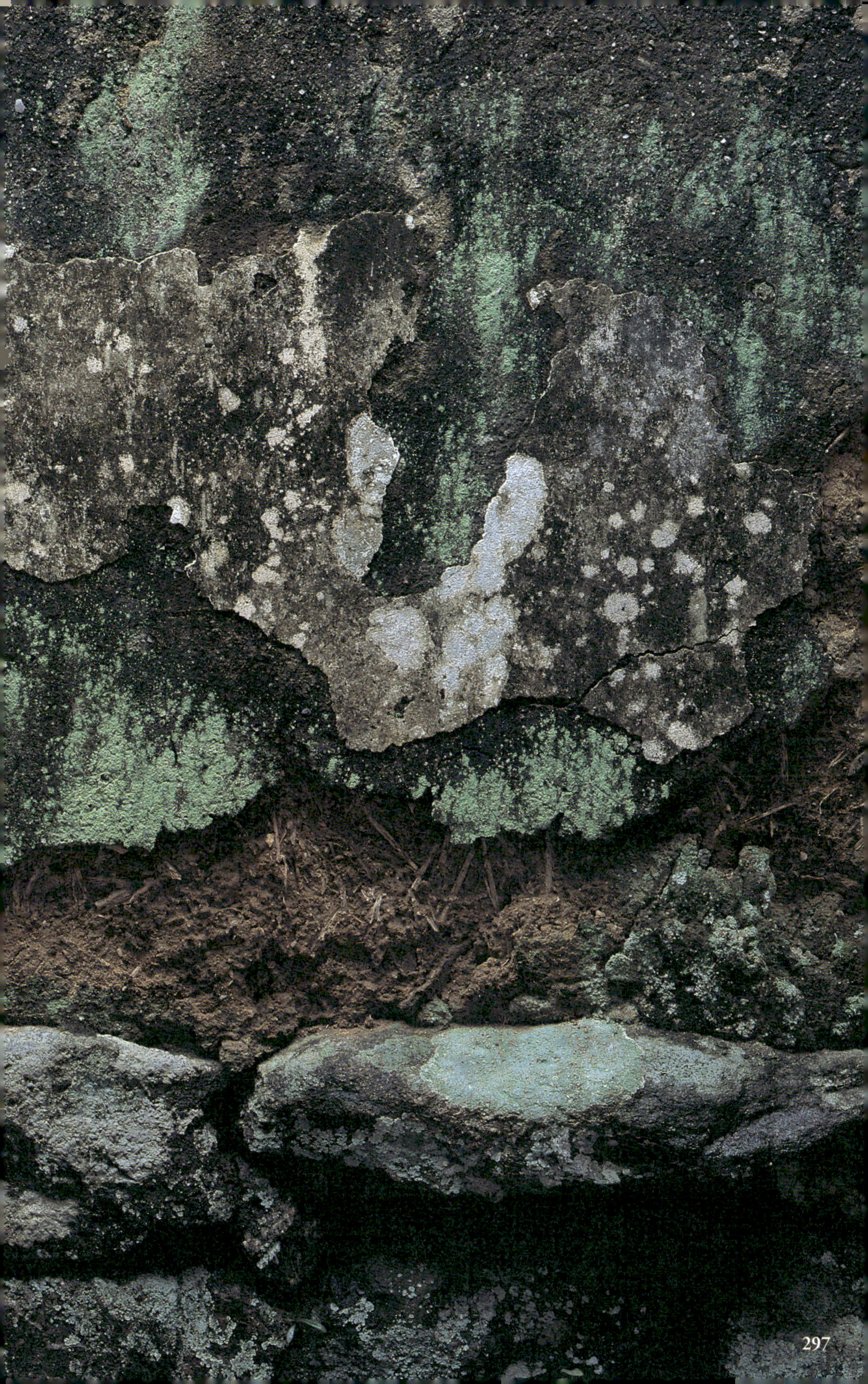

Envoys to poem by Yamanoue Okura,
longing for his dead son Furuhi

He is young,
and does not know the way.
O Angel of Hades,
I shall send you an offering.
Carry him there on your back.

905

九〇五

男子の、名は古日に恋ひたる歌三首（その反歌二首）

稚ければ道行き知らじ幣は為む黄泉の使負ひて通らせ

まだ稚いので死への道行きも知らないだろう。贈り物をしよう。あの世への使いの者よ、わが子を背負って通っていただきたい。

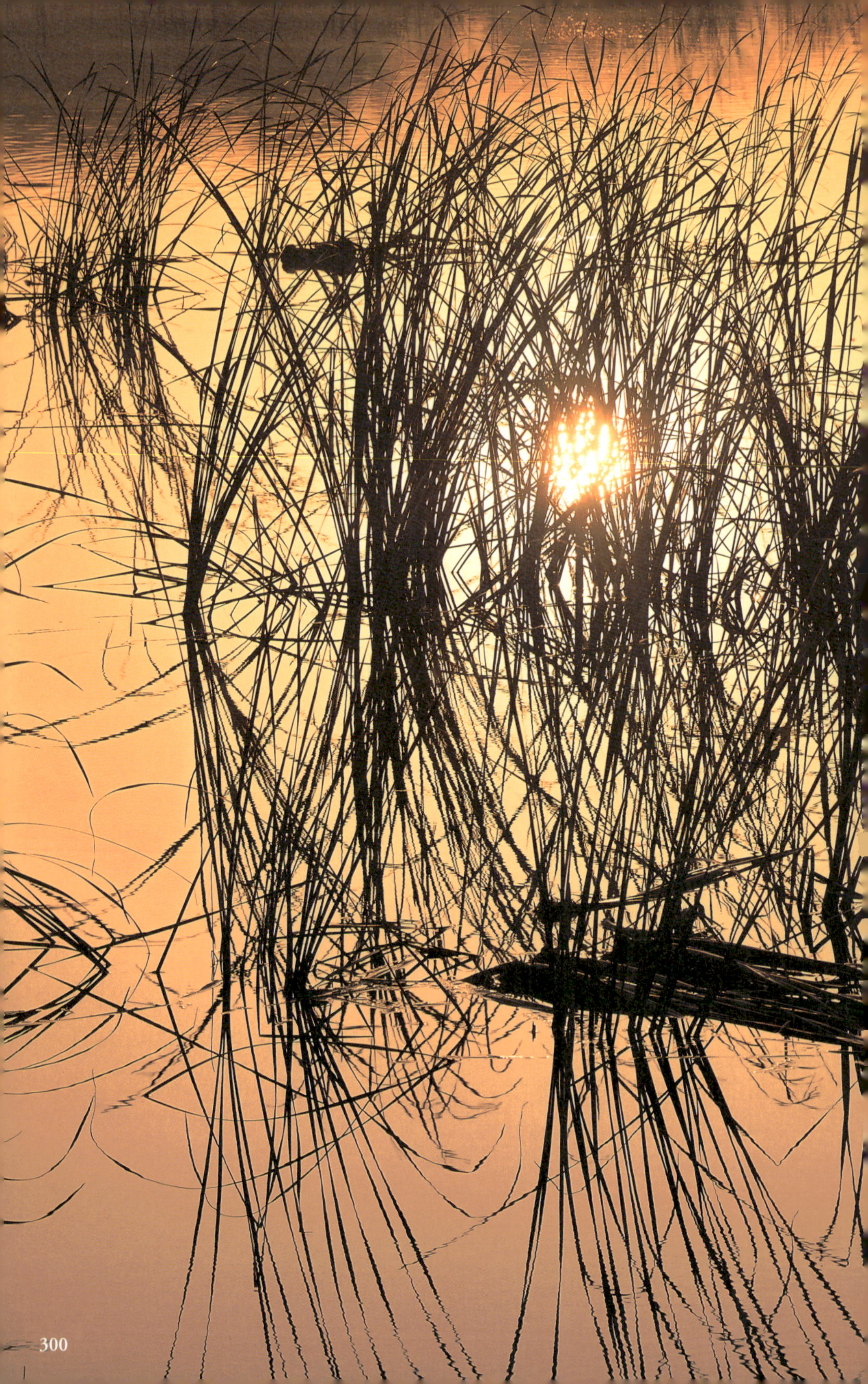

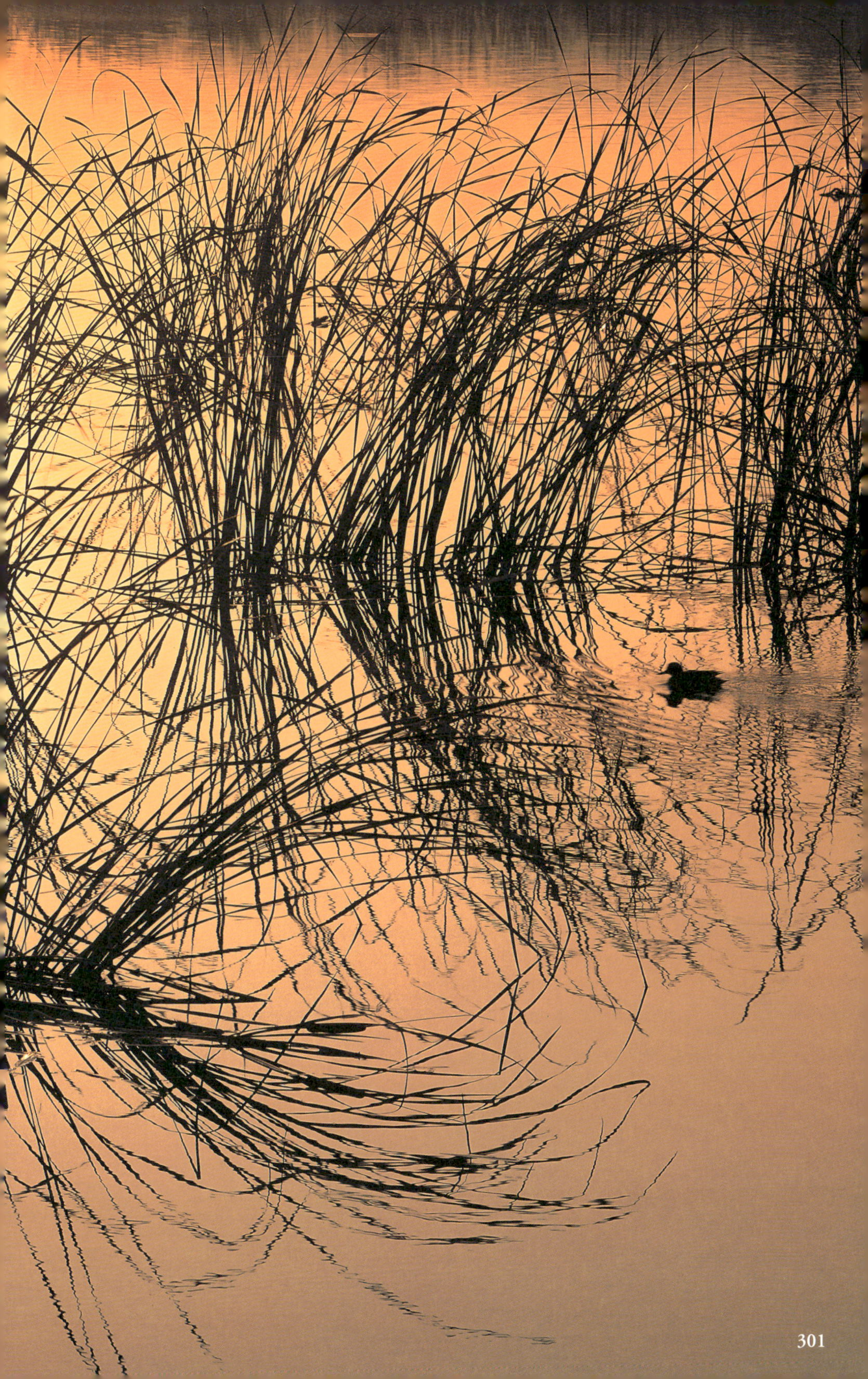

With offerings I implore you:
lead him directly
    without fail,
and show him the path
    to Heaven.

906

九〇六

布施置きてわれは乞ひ禱む欺かず直に率去きて天路知らしめ

布施をささげて私は乞い祈る。どうか欺くことなく、まっ直に連れていって天への道をおしえてほしい。

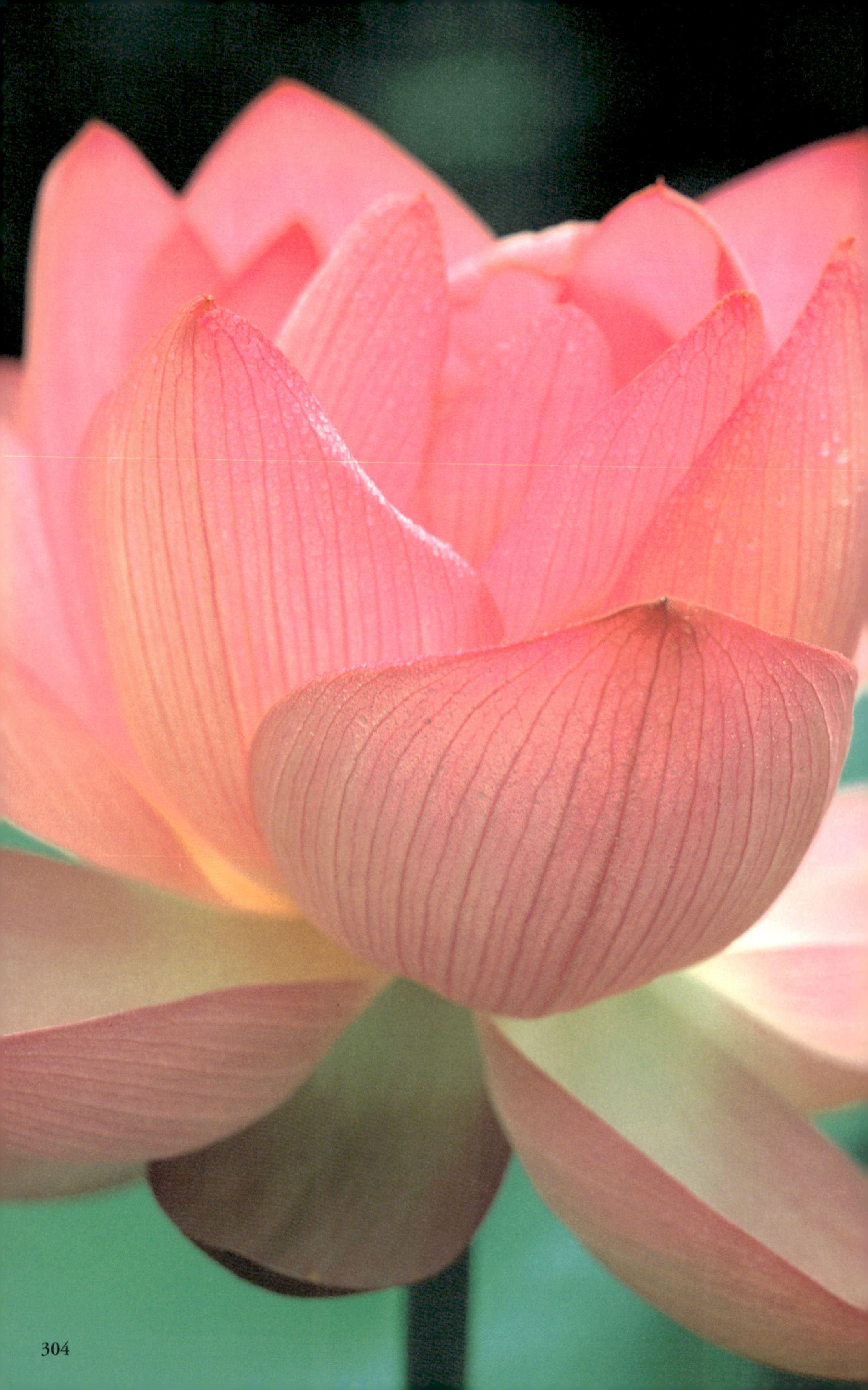

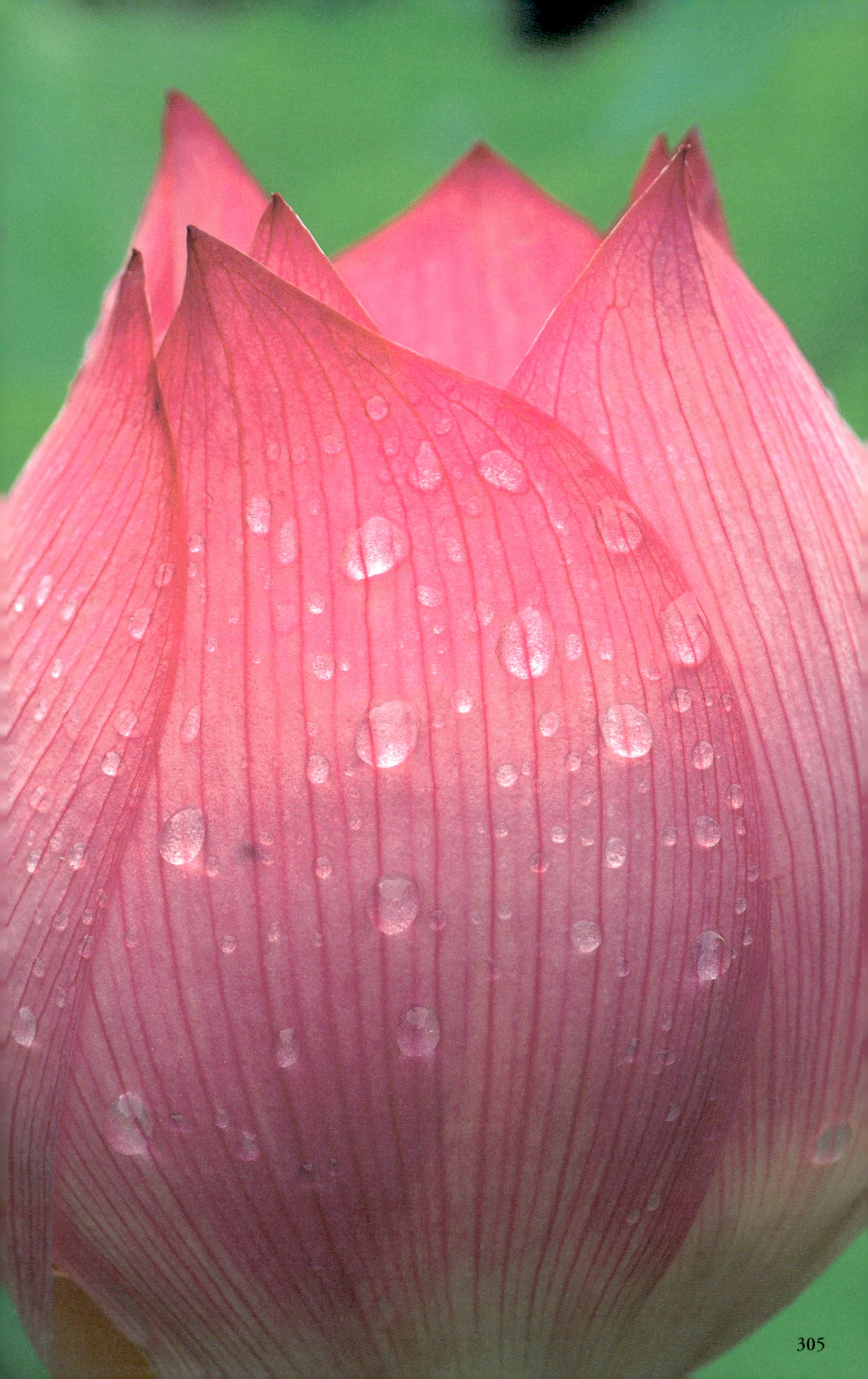

A poem on the crescent moon by Ōtomo Yakamochi

As I turn my gaze upward
and see the crescent moon,
I recall the trailing eyebrows
of the woman I saw but once.

994

九九四

大伴宿禰家持の初月(みかづき)の歌一首

振(ふ)り仰(さ)けて若月(みかづき)見れば一目見し人の眉引(まよびき)思ほゆるかも

空遠くふり仰いで三日月を見ると、一目だけ見た人の引き眉が思われることよ。

On the heavens

On the sea of heaven
the waves of clouds rise,
and I can see
the moon ship disappearing
as it is rowed into the forest of stars.

1068

一〇六八

天(あめ)を詠める

天(あめ)の海に雲の波立ち月の船星の林に漕(こ)ぎ隠る見ゆ

天上の海には雲の波が立ち月の船が星の林に漕ぎ隠れていくのが見える。

313

About a river

It seems this heart
that yearns for you
would be reconciled
only if the bubbles cease to rise
upon the streaming waters
of the Hatsuse River.

1382

一三八二

河に寄せたる

泊瀬川流る水沫の絶えばこそわが思ふ心逐げじと思はめ

泊瀬川を流れる水の泡が絶えるならこそ、私のこの恋心も折れると思えようが。

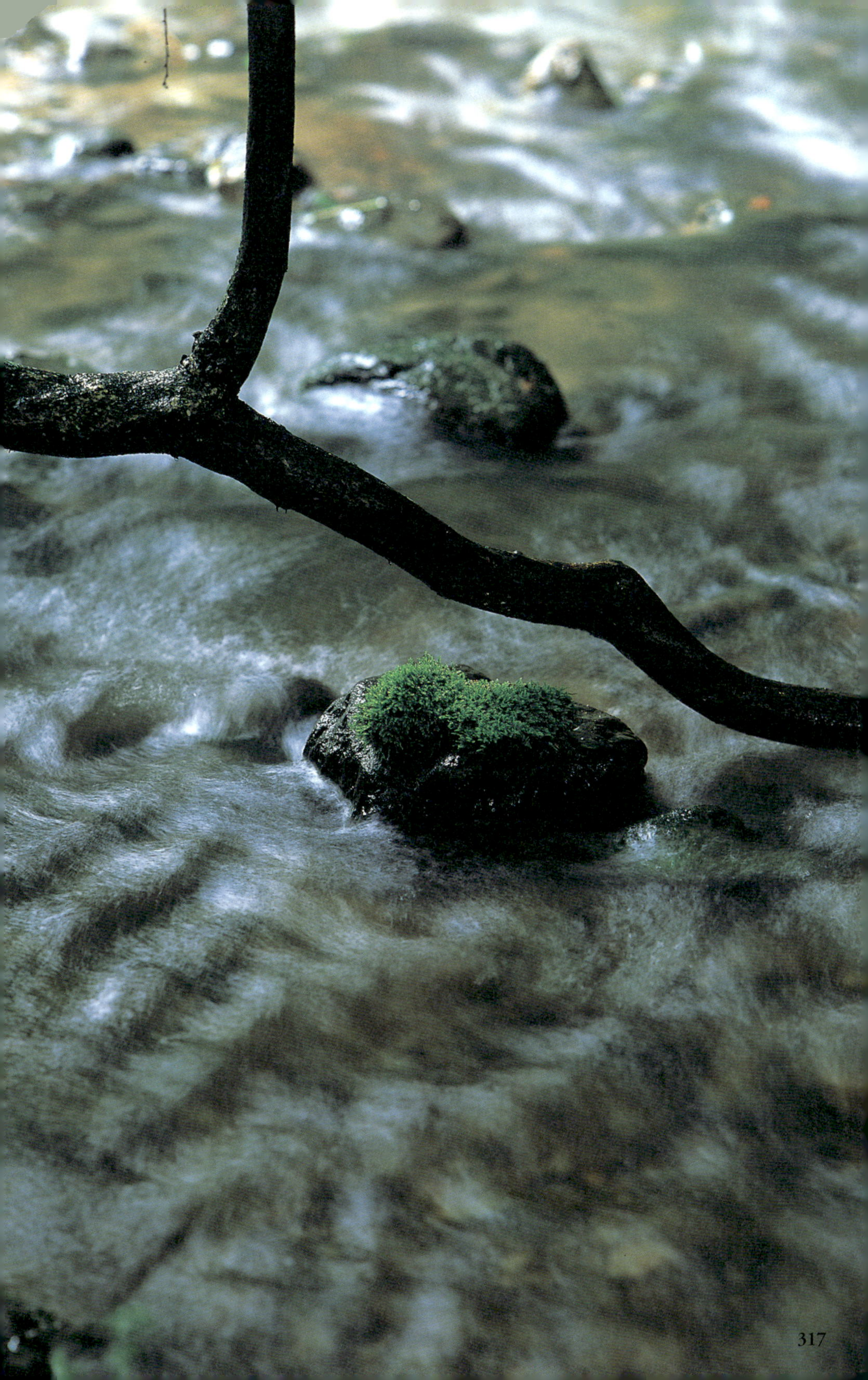

A poem by Yamabe Akahito

I who came to pluck the violets
on the fields of spring —
the fields were so dear to me
that I have passed the night
sleeping on them.

1424

一四二四
山部宿禰赤人の歌四首（その一首）
やまべのすくねあかひと

春の野にすみれ摘みにと来しわれそ野をなつかしみ一夜寝にける

春の野にすみれを摘もうとして来た私は、野があまりにもなつかしいので、一夜寝てしまったことだ。

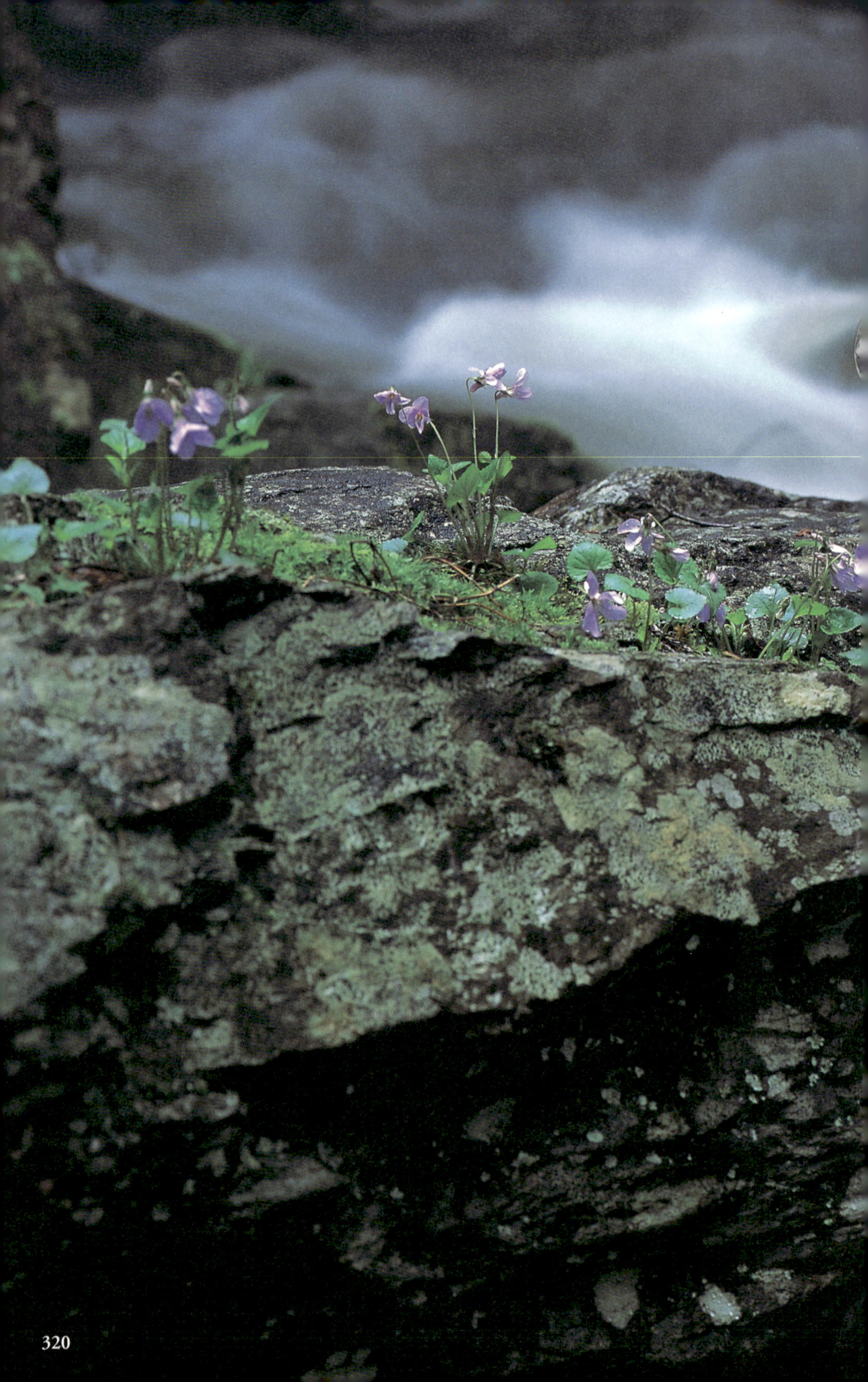

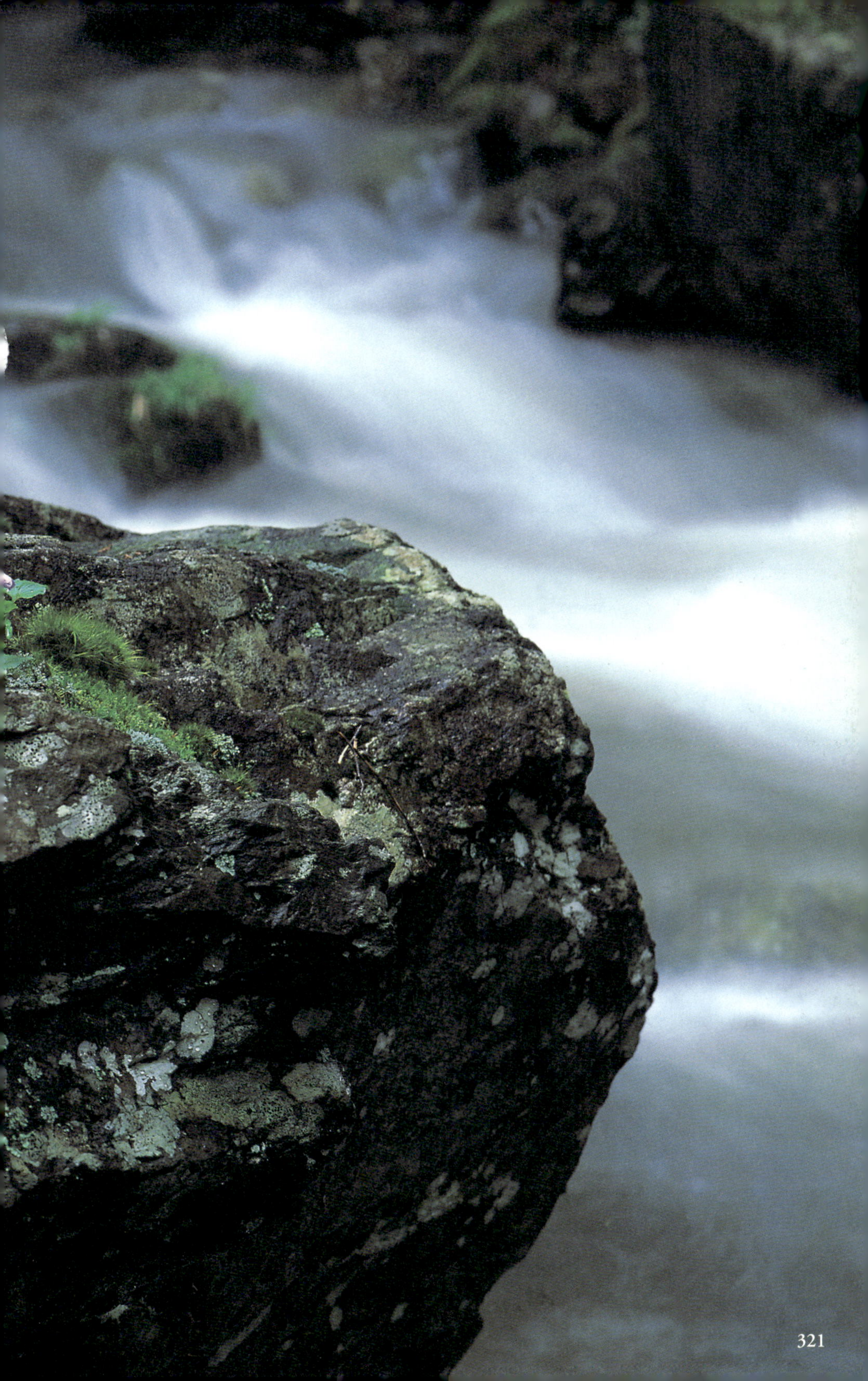

By Prince Hozumi

In this morning's dawn
I heard the cries of the wild geese;
the leaves must have yellowed
      on Kasuga Mountain.
The thought brings me pain.

1513

一五一三

穂積皇子の御歌二首(その一首)
はづみのみこ

今朝の朝明雁が音聞きつ春日山黄葉にけらしわが情痛し
けさ あさけ かりね かすが やま もみち こころ いた

今朝の夜明けに雁の声を聞いた。もう春日山は黄葉したことだろう。思うと心が切ない。

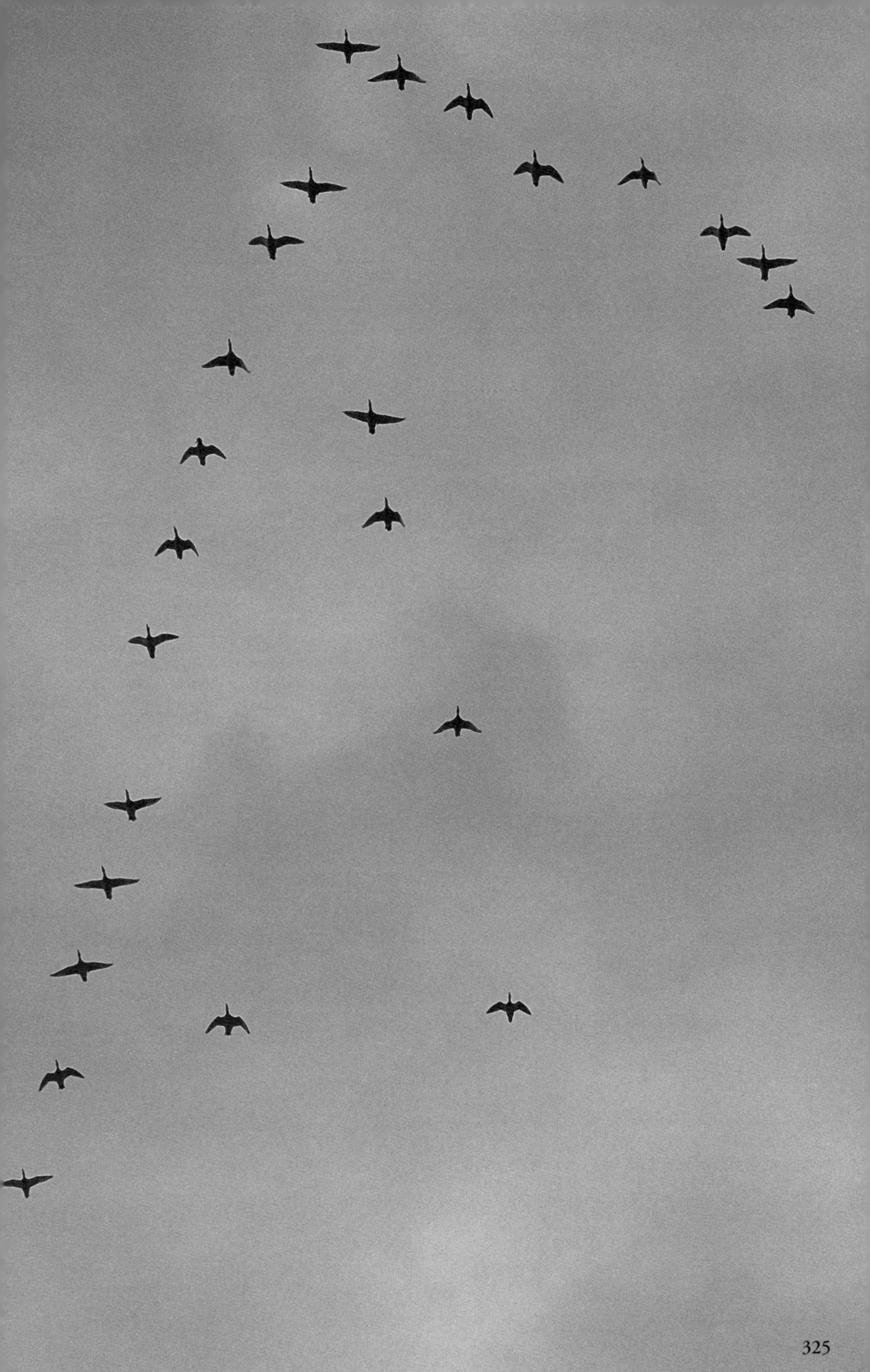

A poem by Prince Nagaya

How I regret the falling
of the yellowed leaves of autumn
that set to gleam
priestly Miwa Mountain,
      of the sweet wine.

1517

一五一七
長屋王の歌一首
ながやのおほきみ

味酒三輪の祝の山照らす秋の黄葉の散らまく惜しも
うまさけ　　はふり　　　　　　　　もみち

味酒三輪の神官がまもる山を輝かせる秋の黄葉の、散るのが惜しいよ。

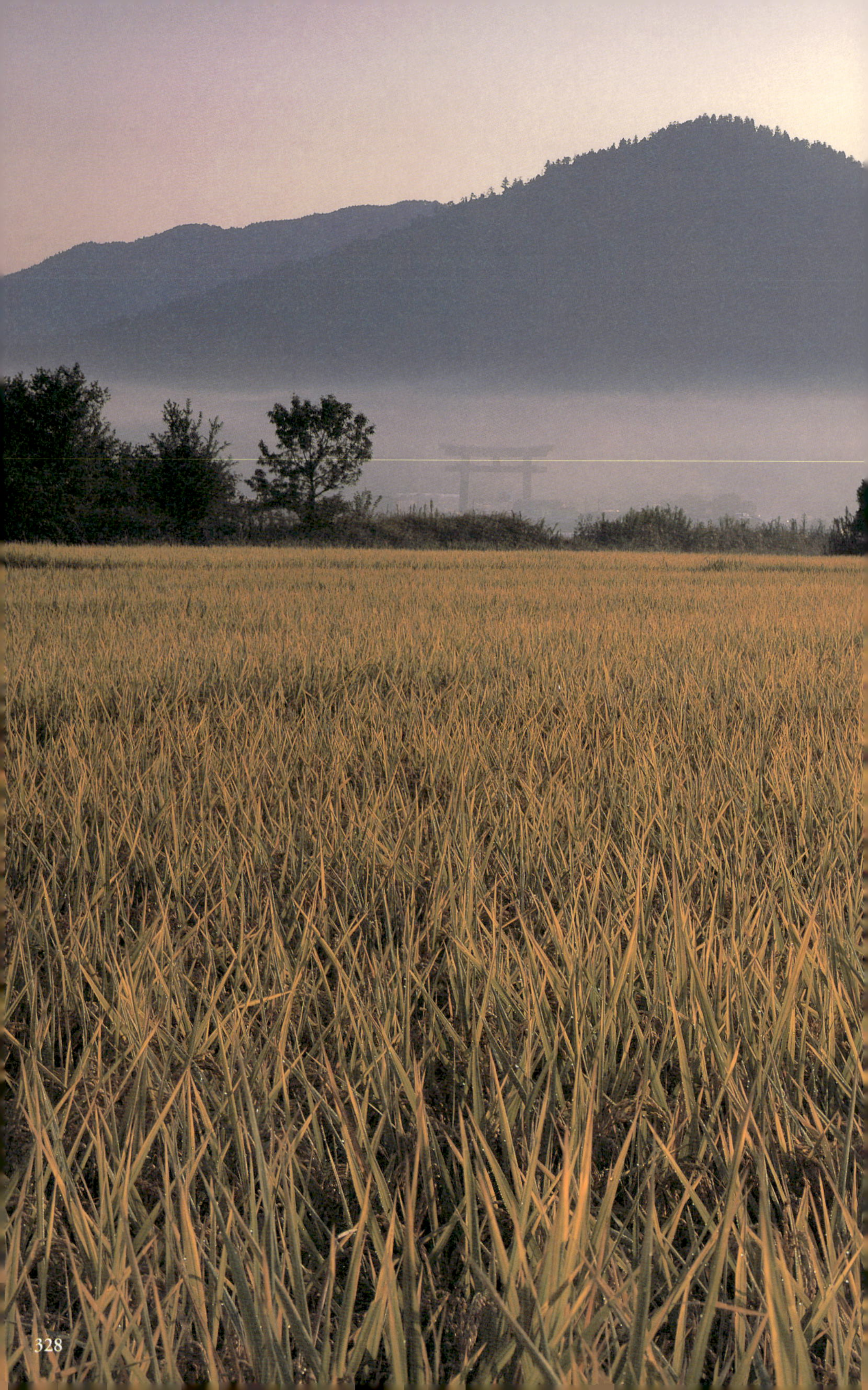

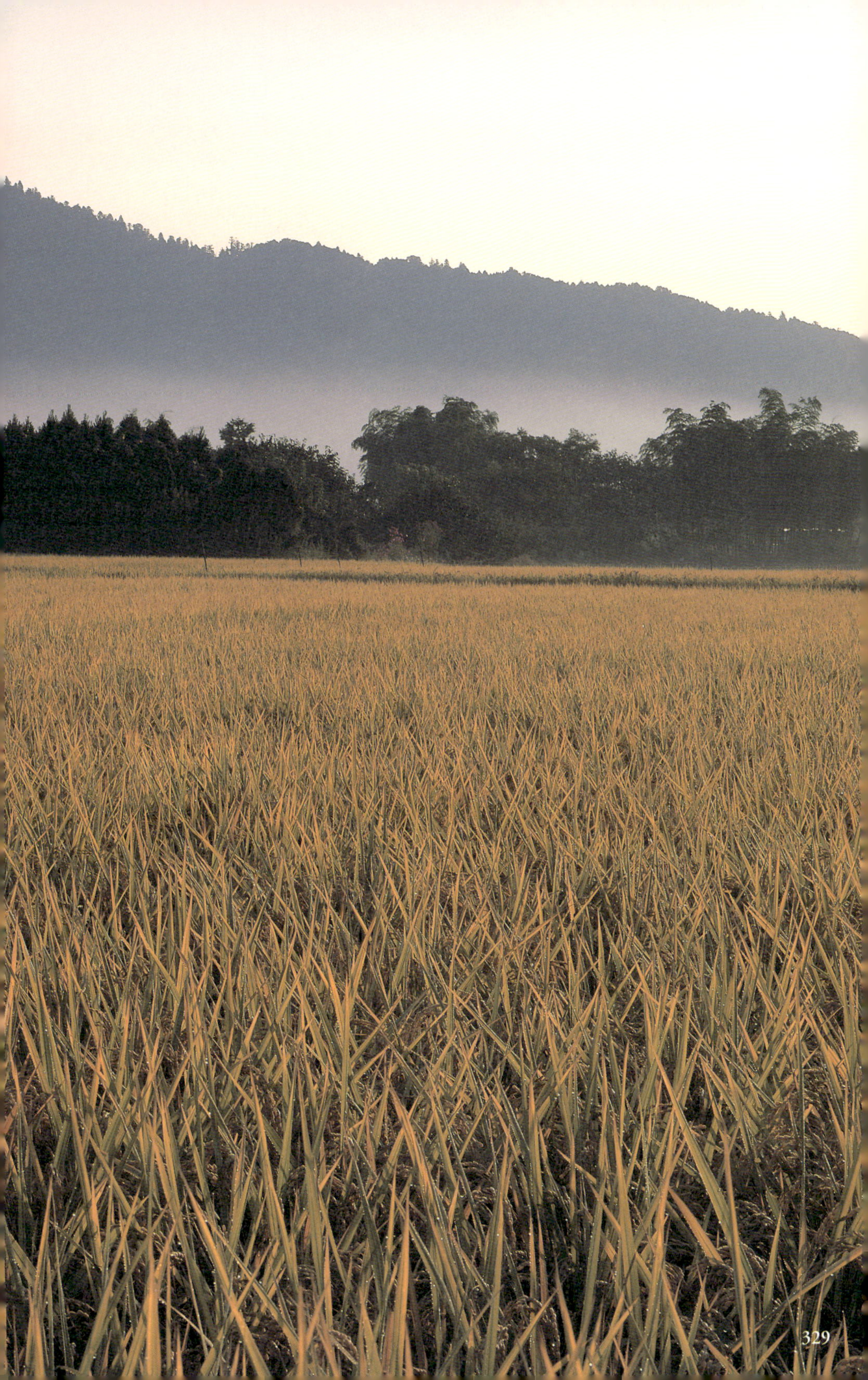

A Poem by Emperor Shōmu

How the cries of the wild geese
echo even in the darkness
as they cross, at day break,
over autumn fields,
over fields
where ears of rice have sprouted!

1539

一五三九
天皇の御製歌二首(その一首)
　　すめらみこと　おほみうた

秋の田の穂田を雁が音闇けくに夜のほどろにも鳴き渡るかも
　　　　ほだ　　かりねくら

秋の穂の出た田を、雁は
　まだ暗いのに夜明け方に
　も鳴き渡っていくよ。

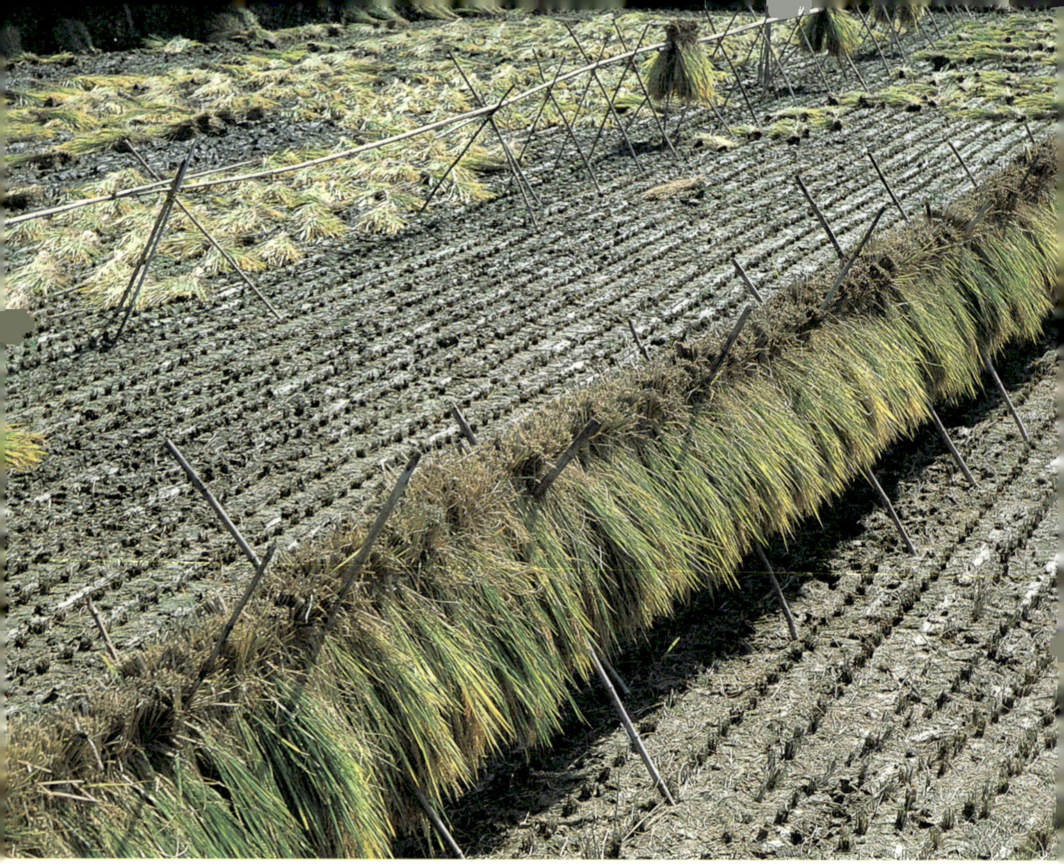

333

A poem by Lord Ōtomo Tabito, Commander of the Dazaifu, as he watched the snow falling on a winter day and remembered the capital

As the light snow
continues to pour,
streak by streak,
my thoughts turn
to the capital at Nara.

1639

一六三九

大宰帥大伴卿の冬の日に雪を見て京を憶へる歌一首

沫雪のほどろほどろに降り敷けば平城の京し思ほゆるかも

沫雪がまだらに降りつづくと、平城の京が思われることよ。

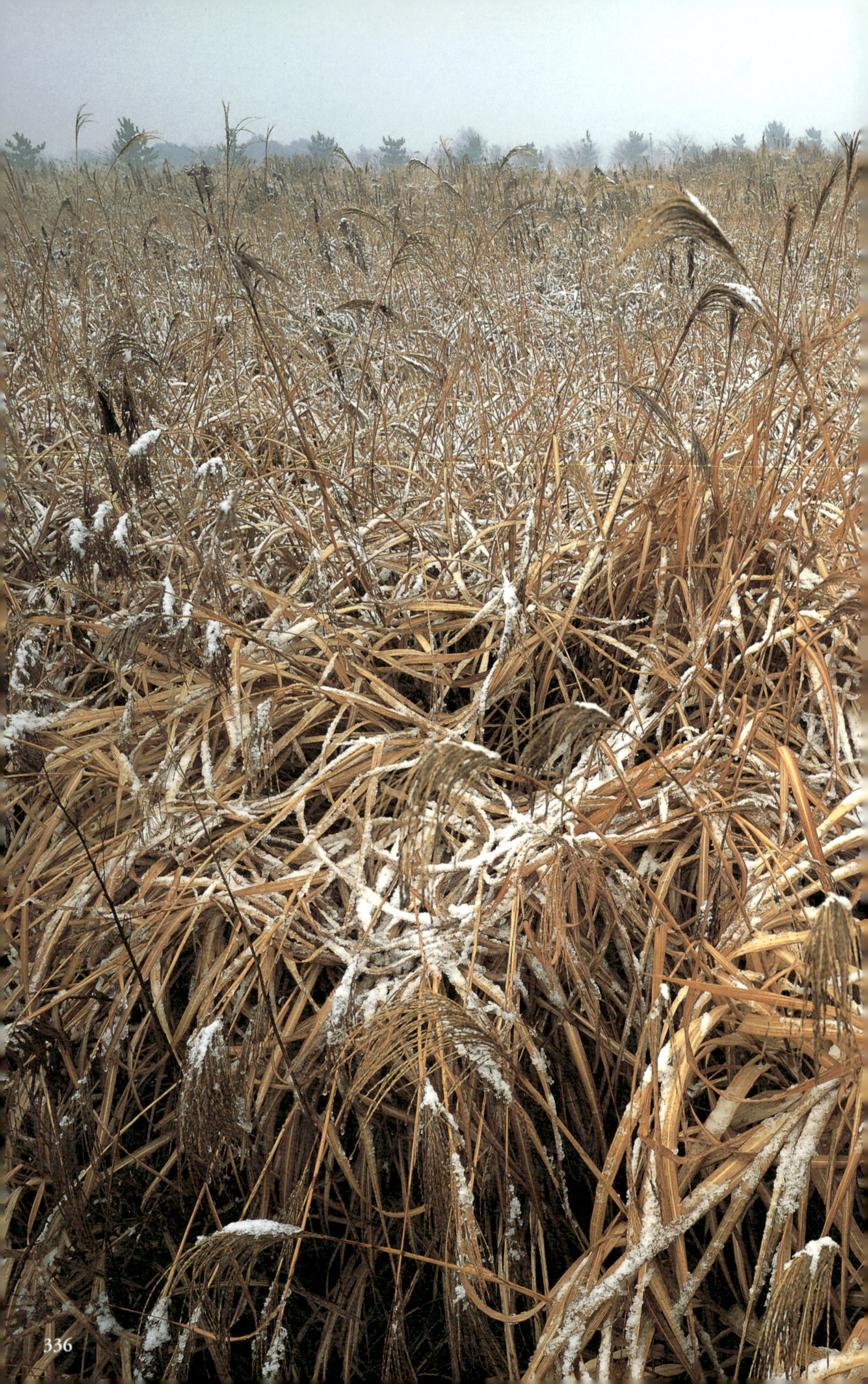

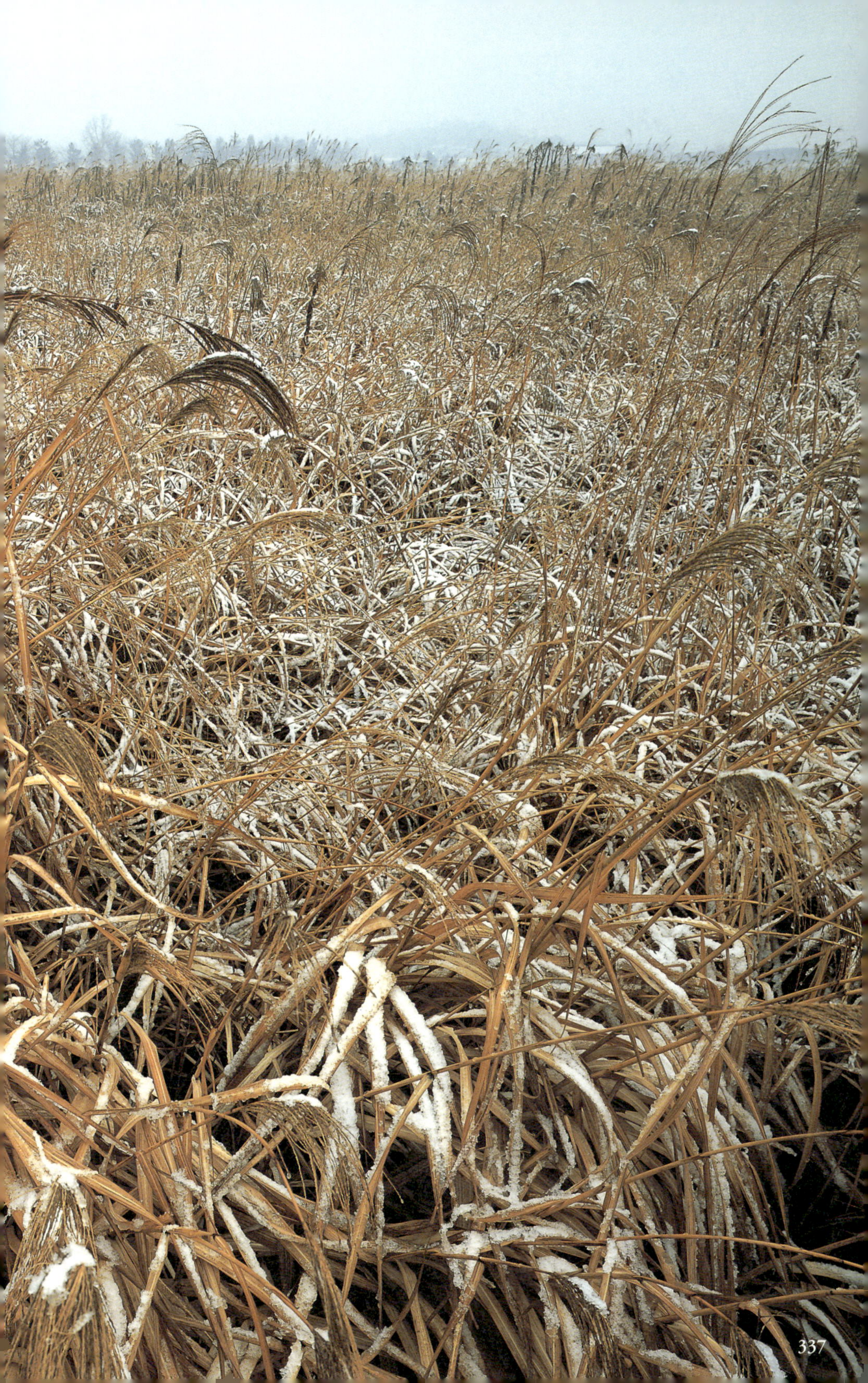

A Poem by Lady Ōtomo Sakanoue

These days the light snow
continues to fall unabated;
will the first blossoms of the plum
                all scatter away?

1651

一六五一

大伴坂上郎女の歌一首

沫雪のこの頃続ぎてかく降れば梅の初花散りか過ぎなむ

沫雪がこの頃は毎日このように降るので、梅の初花は散り果ててしまうだろうか。

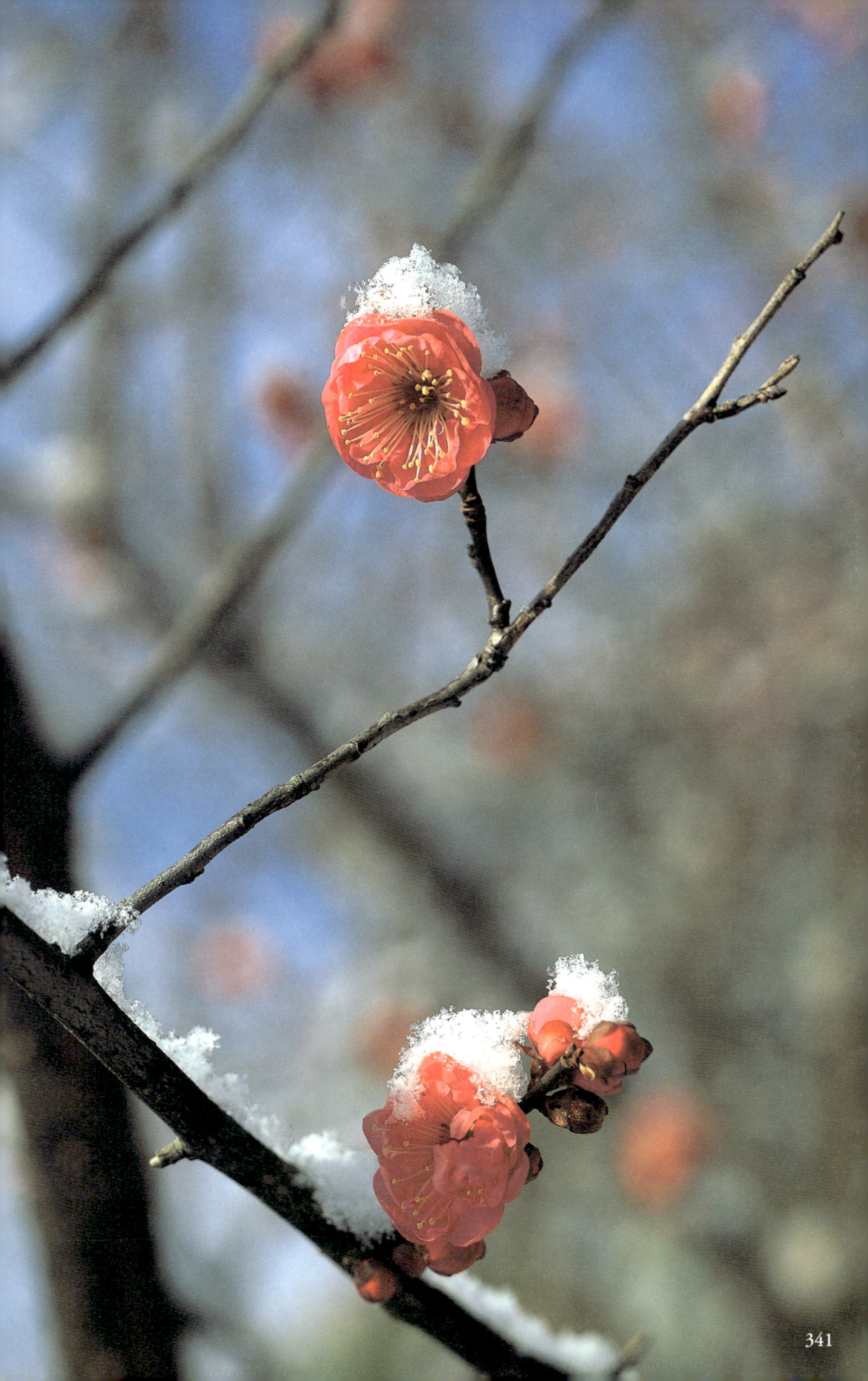

Disporting on the Fields

Is it in their leisure
that the courtiers of the great palace,
 its ramparts thick with stone,
assemble here with garlands
of plum blossoms in their hair?

1883

一八八三

野遊（のあそび）

ももしきの大宮人（おほみやびと）は暇（いとま）あれや梅を插頭（かざ）してここに集（つど）へる

ももしきの大宮人は暇があるからか、梅を髪に挿してここに集っているなあ。

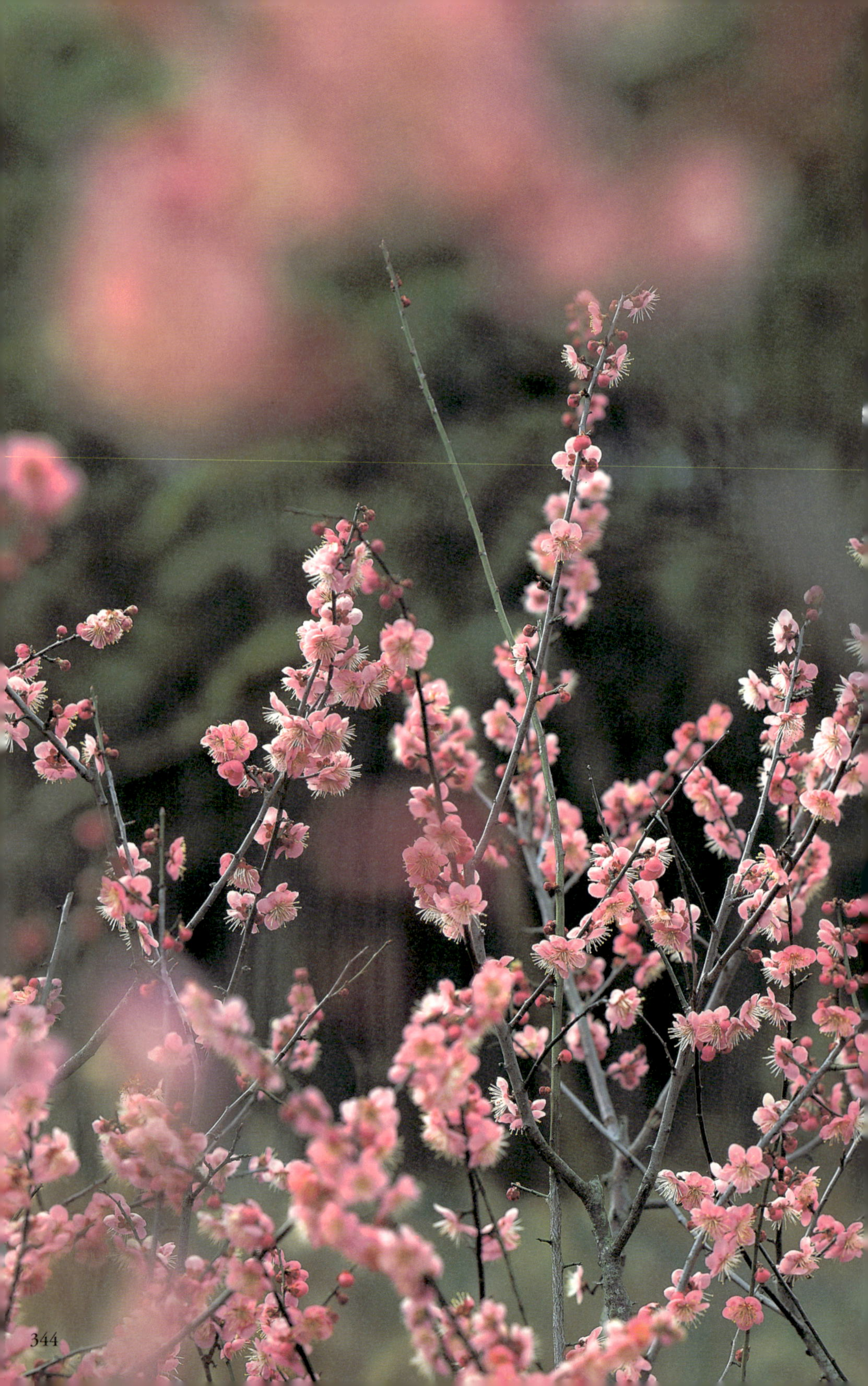

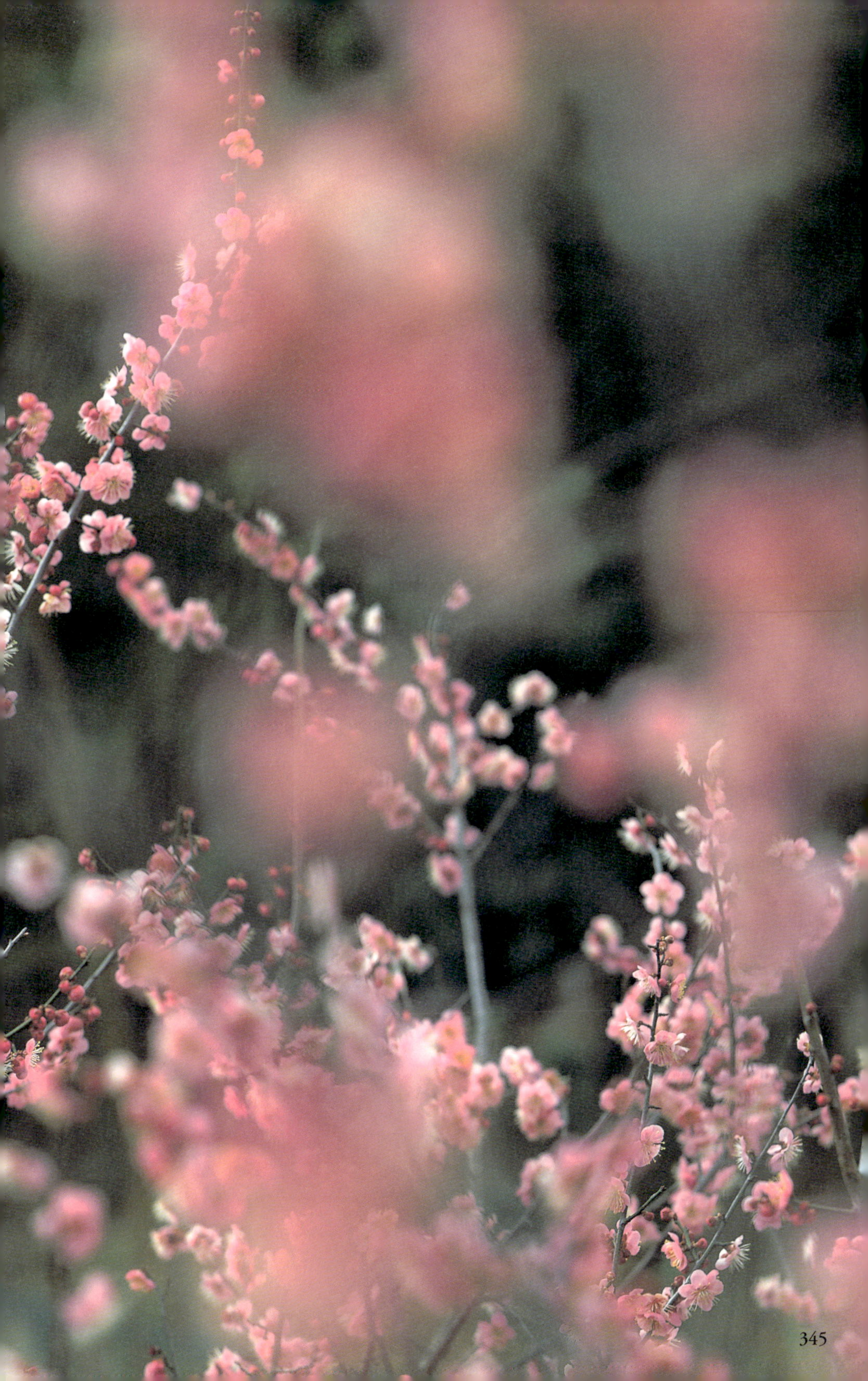

from
Poems expressing feelings through things

Not a single day passes
when I fail to pray
at the shrine of the awesome gods:
O let my lord come to me
      night after night!

2660

二六六〇

物に寄せて思を陳べたる歌三百二首（その二首）

夜並べて君を来ませとちはやぶる神の社を祈まぬ日は無し

毎夜続けてあの方よいらっしゃいと、神威ある神の社に祈らない日はない。

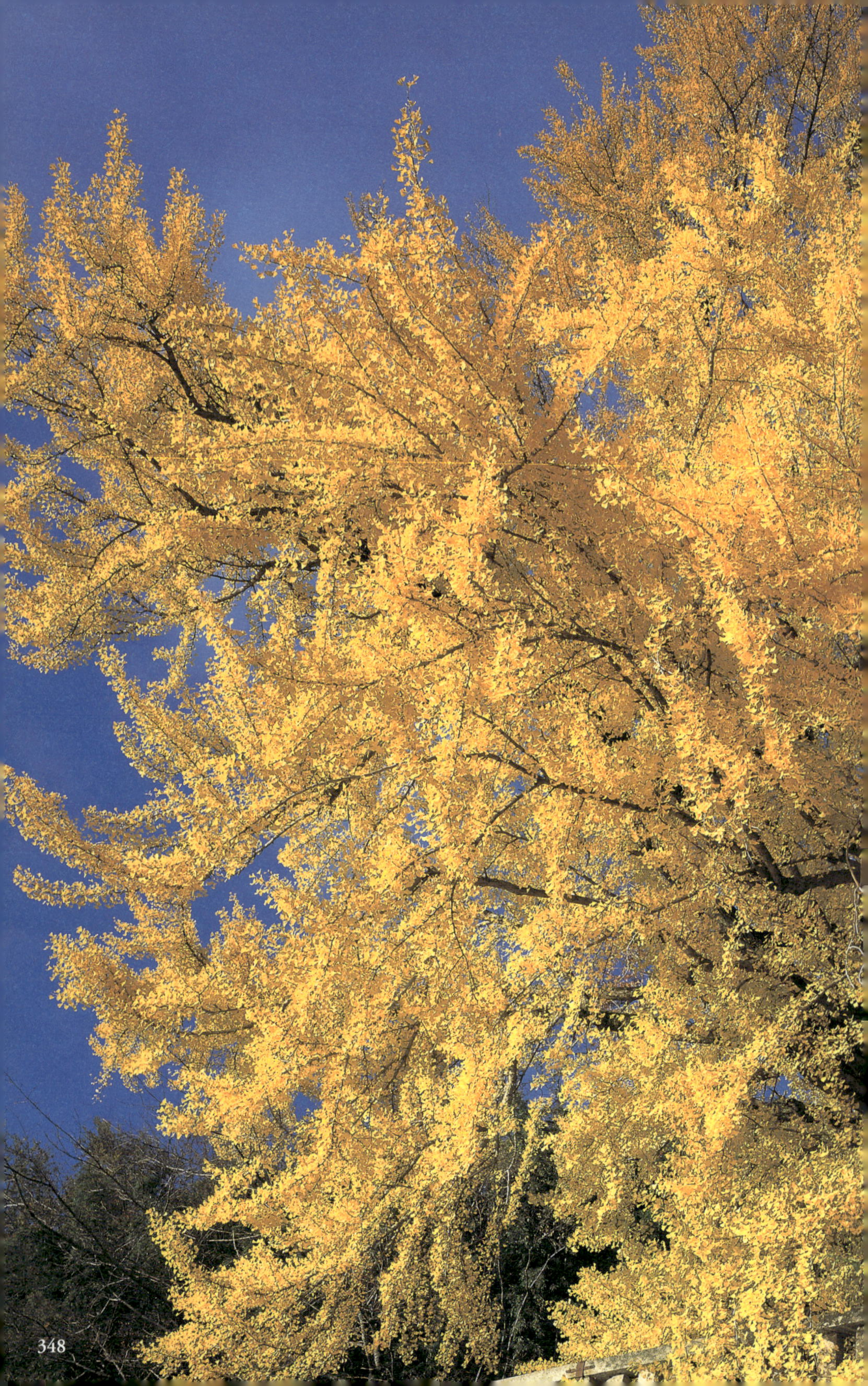

149

These days when I have come away,
                far from my wife,
though I regret it
as I do the moon's concealment
             behind Futakami Mountain.

2668

二六六八

二上(ふたがみ)に隠(かく)らふ月の惜(を)しけれども妹が手本(たもと)を離(か)るるこのころ

西空の二上山に隠れてしまう月のように惜しいのだが、妻の手本を離れているこのごろよ。

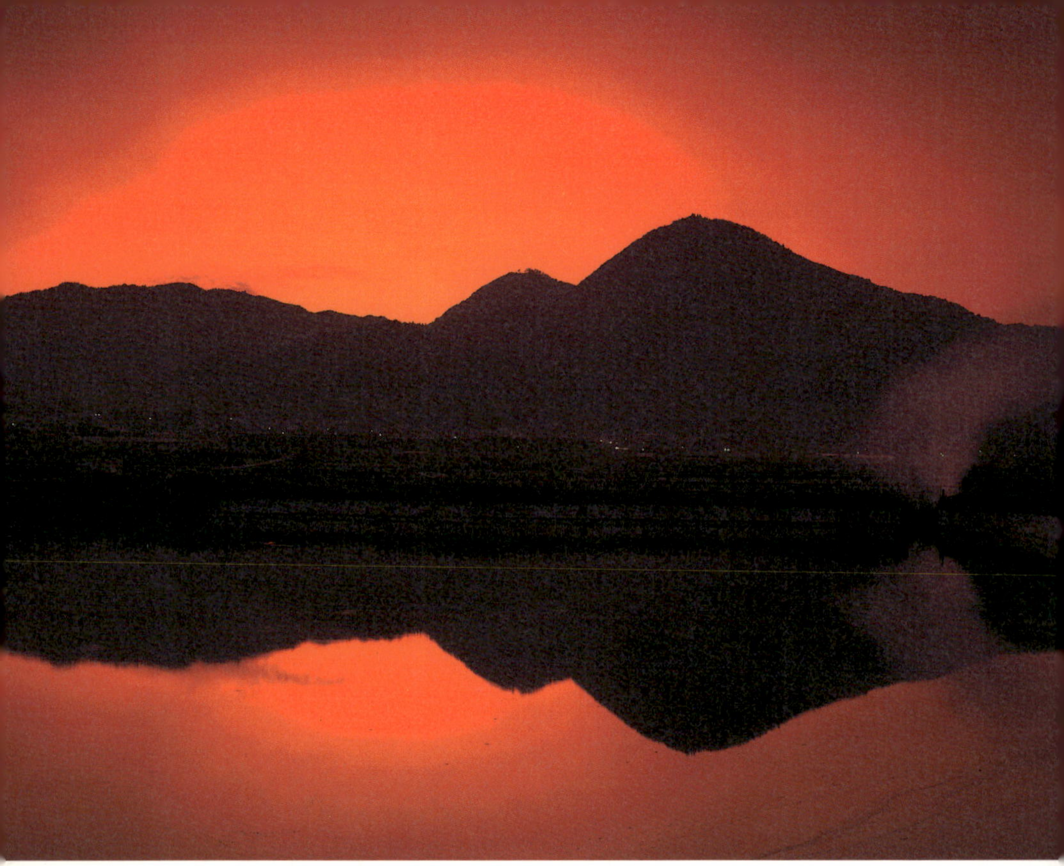

353

from
Personal exchanges on thinking of one's native land

It is good to pass by the gate
of that girl's house
even though she remains inside,
unseen to me,
as the deer crouches hidden in the grass.

3530

三五三〇

いまだ国を勘へぬ相聞往来の歌百十二首（その一首）

さを鹿の伏すや草群見えずとも児ろが金門よ行かくし良しも

鹿が草群に隠れ伏すように、あの子の姿は見えずとも、あの子の家の門の前を通って行くのは、よいものよ。

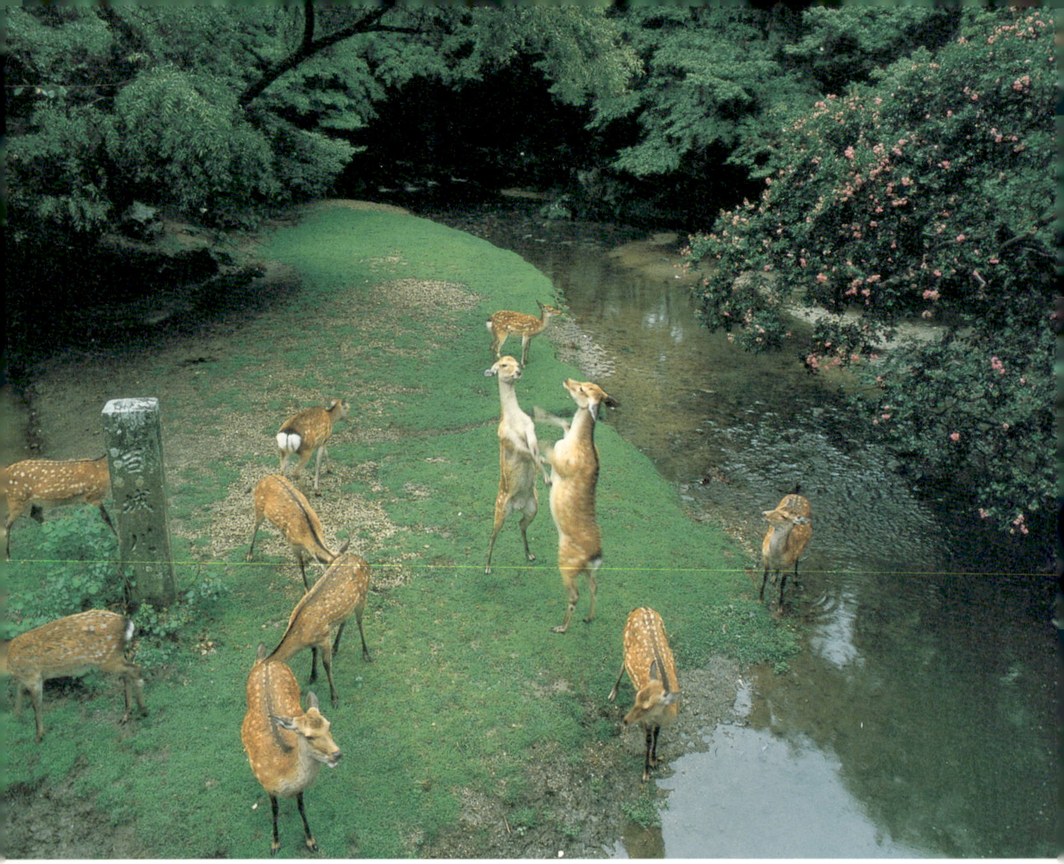

357

A poem abhorring the impermanence of life in this world

I loathe the two seas
        of life and death,
and so I long for the mountains
        where tides never rise.

3849

三八四九
世間(よのなか)の無常を厭(いと)へる歌二首（その一首）

生死(いきしに)の二つの海を厭(いと)はしみ潮干(しほひ)の山をしのひつるかも

生と死との二つの海がいとわしいので、潮のない山が慕わしいことよ。

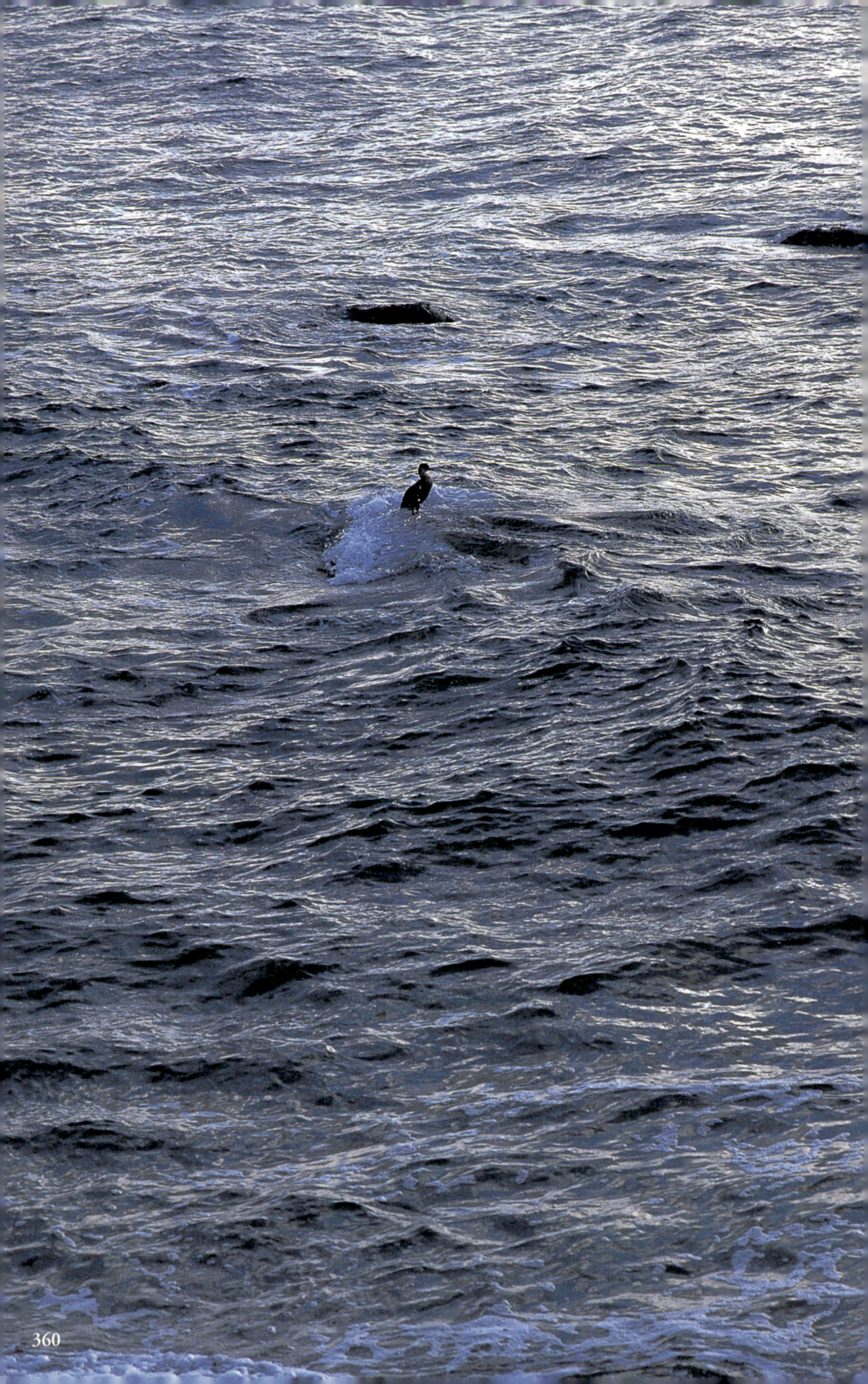

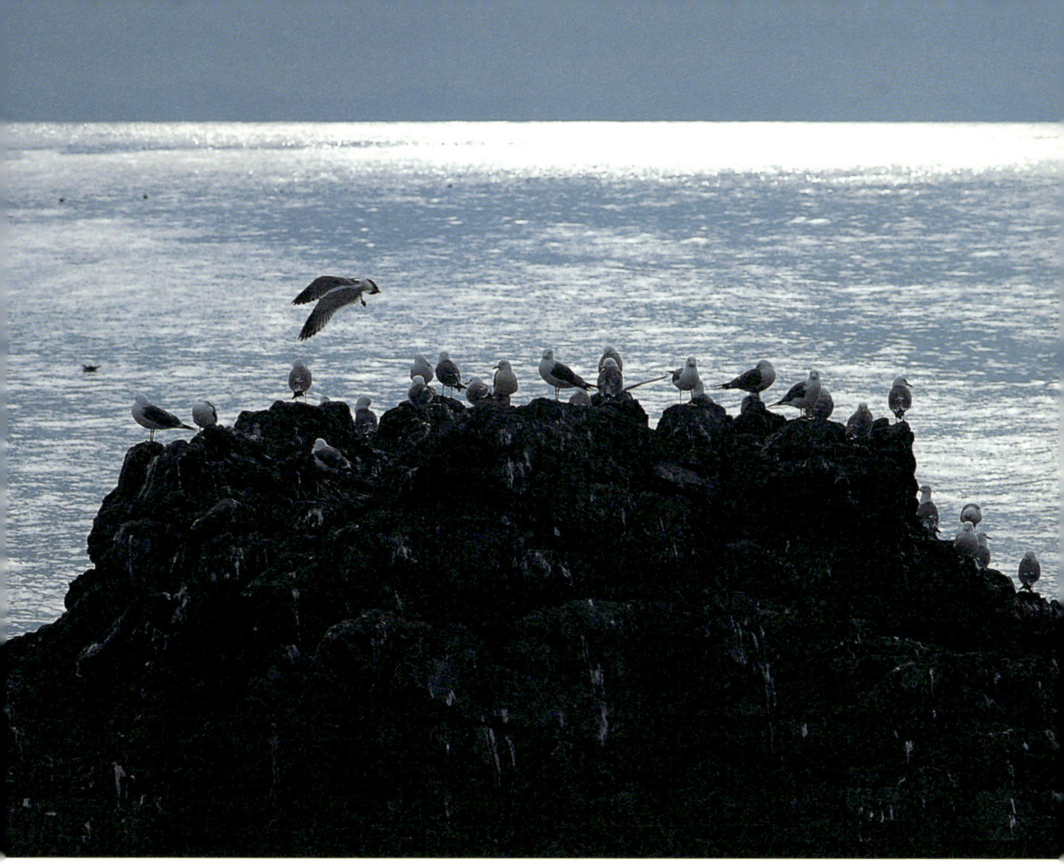

Upon departing from Kashima harbor and sailing for Kumaki Village

I think of the capital
without a moment's rest,
like the unresting oars
of the ship that heads
from Kashima to Kumaki.

4027

四〇二七

能登郡の香島の津より発船して、
熊来村を指して往きし時に作れる歌二首(その一首)

香島(かしま)より熊来(くまき)を指して漕ぐ船の梶(かぢ)取る間(ま)なく都(みやこ)し思ほゆ

香島から熊来に向けて漕ぐ船の、梶の手を休めることのないように、都が絶えず思われるよ。

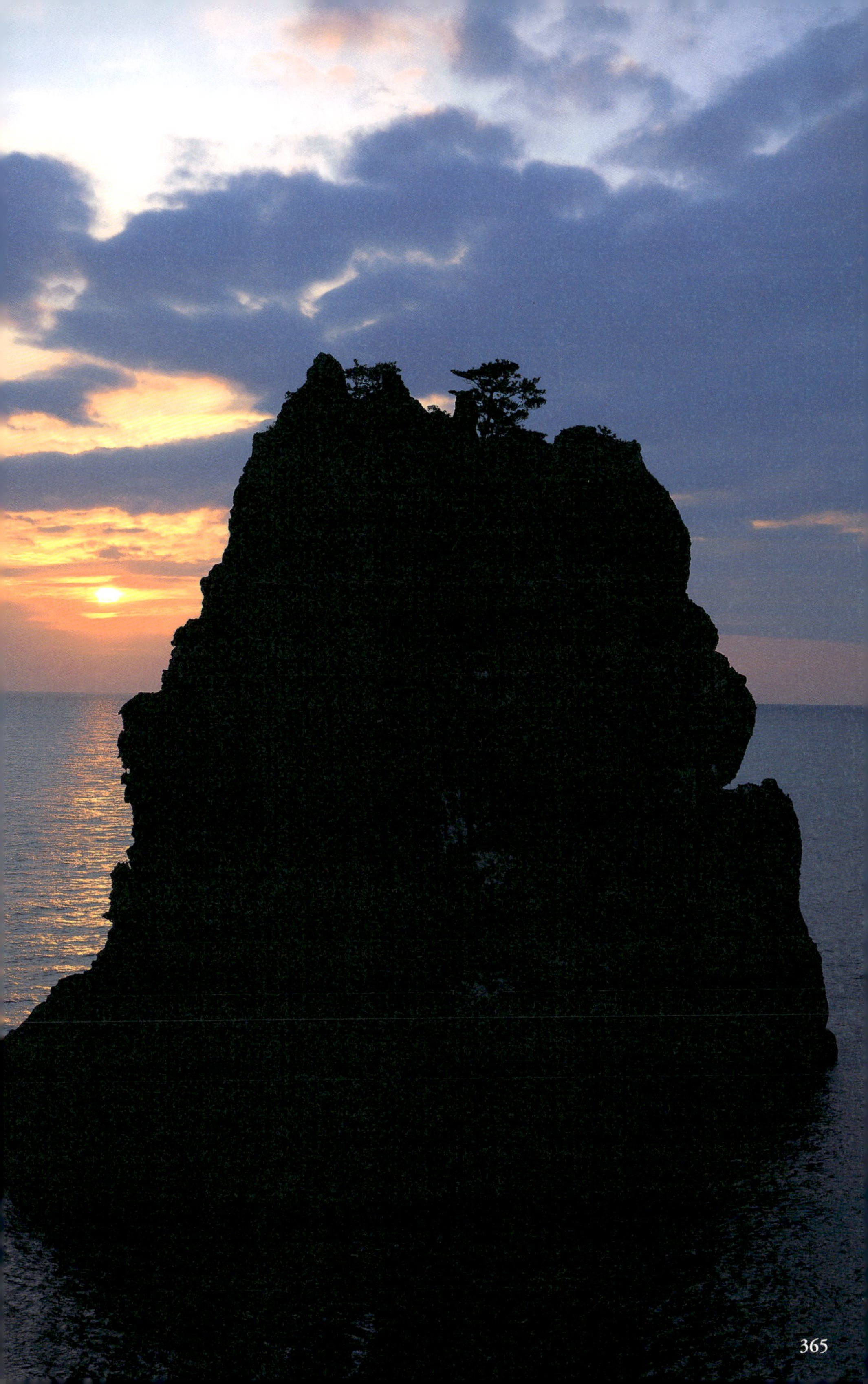

Composed upon viewing the peach and damson plum blossoms in the spring garden in the twilight of the first day of the third month, the second year of Tempyō Shōhō (750)

The spring garden,
the lustrous crimson:
girl who appears
standing on the path
beneath the gleam of peach blossoms.

4139

四一三九

天平勝宝(しょうほう)二年三月一日の暮(ゆふへ)に、春の苑(その)の桃李(ももすもも)の花を眺矚(なが)めて作れる二首（その一首）

春の苑(そのくれなひ)紅にほふ桃の花下(した)照(で)る道に出で立つ少女(をとめ)

春の苑に紅がてりはえる。
桃の花の輝く下の道に、
立ち現われる少女。

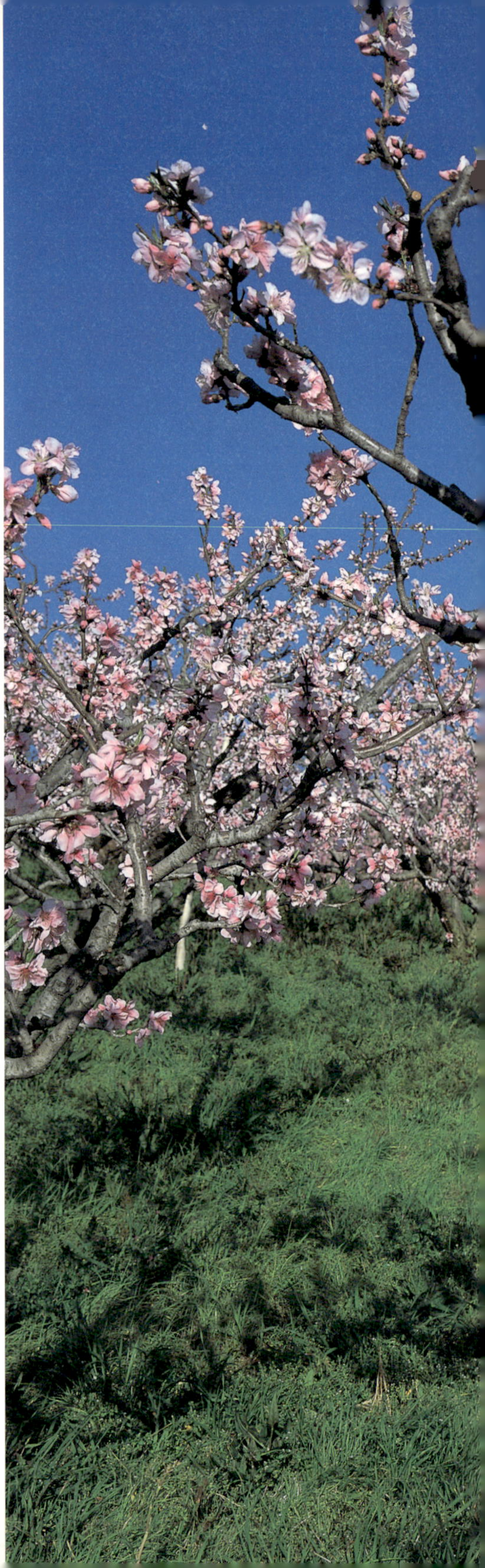

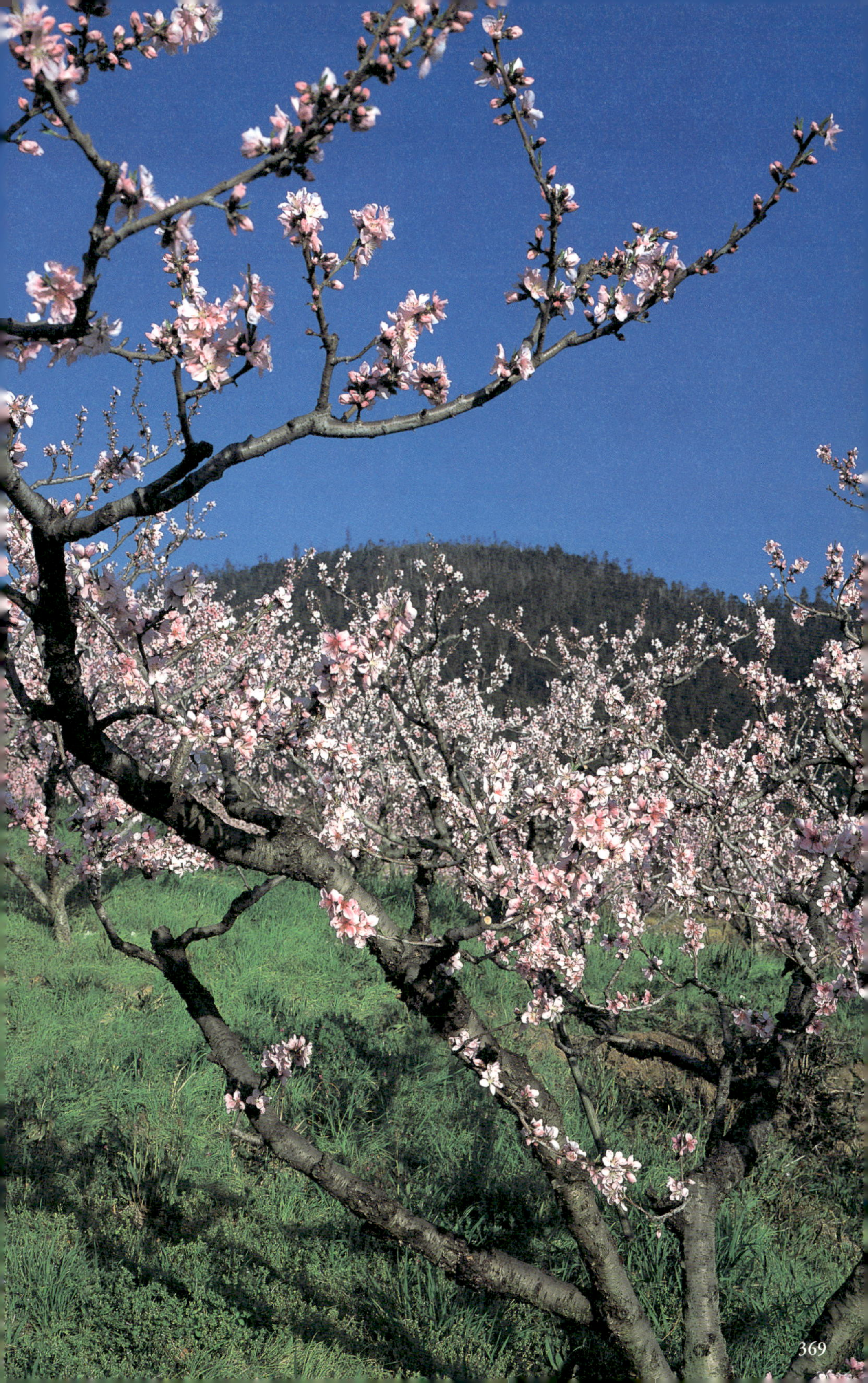

A poem composed on the second day of the third month, as the poet broke off a branch of wisteria, beautiful like a woman's eyebrows, and recalled the capital

As I break off and admire
a branch of the wisteria
swelling large on a spring day,
my mind turns
to the broad avenues of the capital.

4142

四一四二

二日に、柳黛を攀ぢて京師を思へる歌一首

春の日に張れる柳を取り持ちて見れば都の大路思ほゆ

春日にふくらんだ柳を折りとって見ると、都の大路がしのばれるよ。

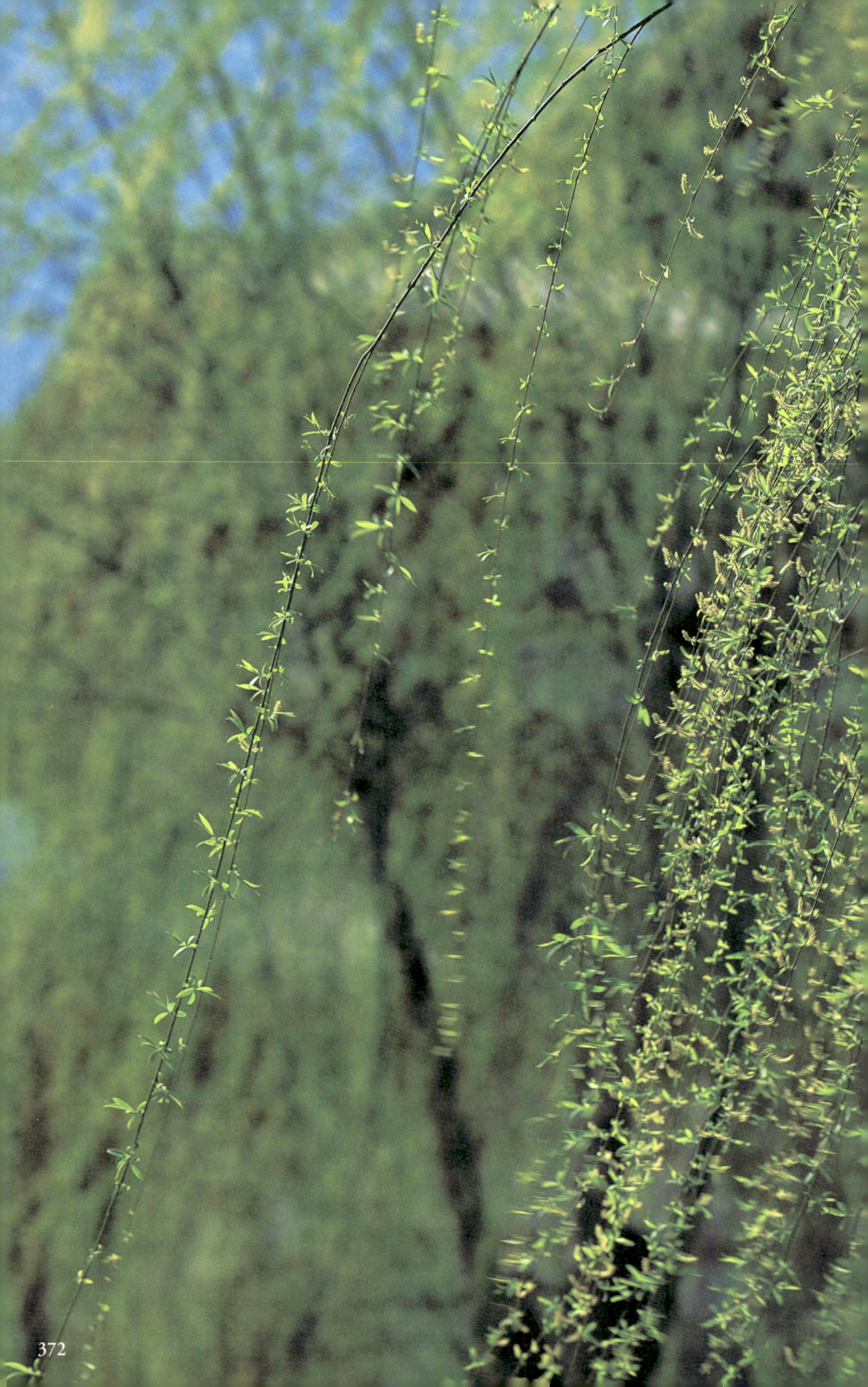

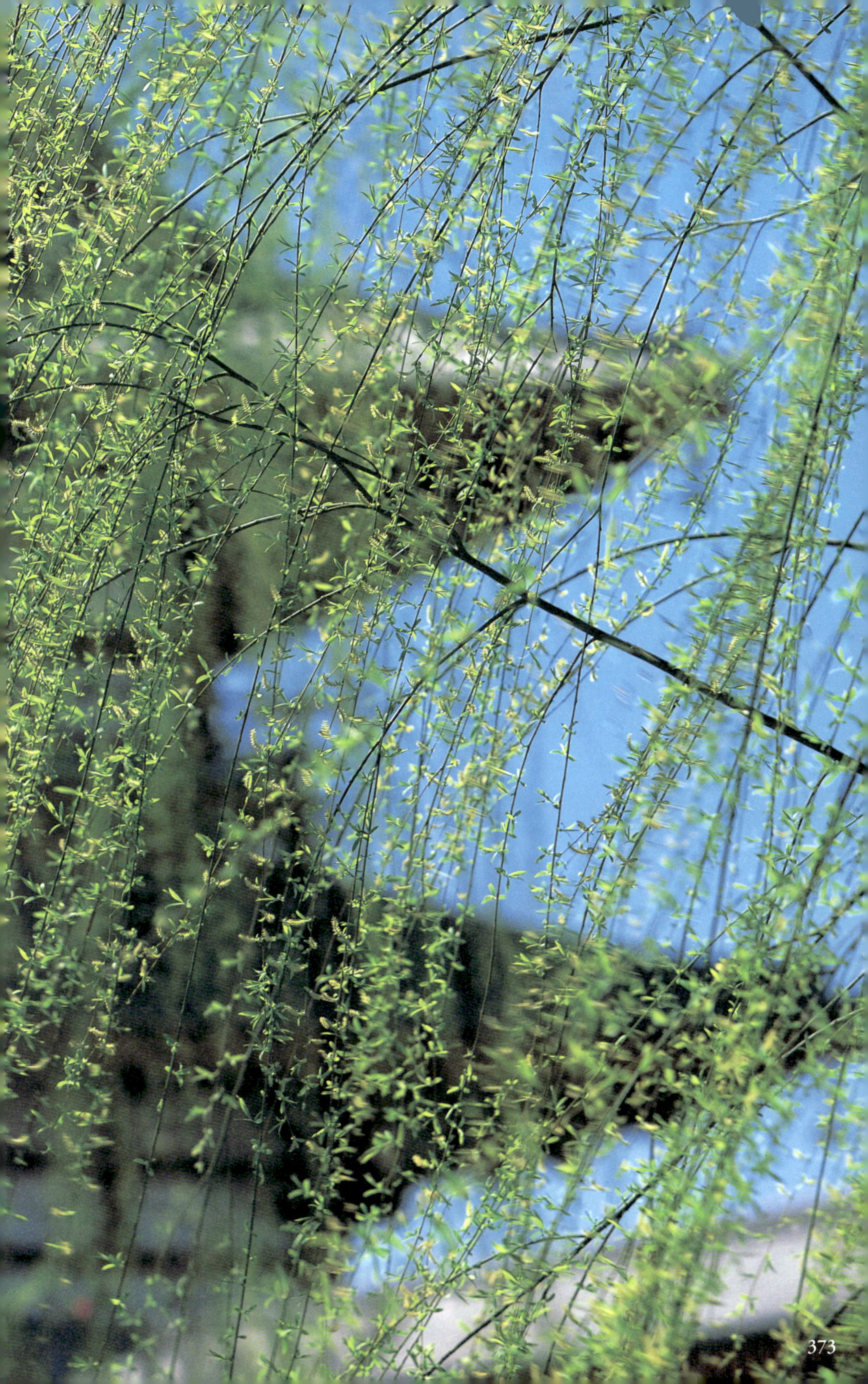

A poem composed by the Fujiwara Empress, on a day when a ritual to the gods was held on the fields of Kasuga. The poem was then sent to Fujiwara Kiyokawa, who had been appointed the Ambassador to China.

On a great ship,
its broadsides pierced
with oars from stern to bow,
we send our lad to China.
Give him your blessings, o gods!

4240

四二四〇

春日に神を祭りし日に、藤原太后の作りませる歌一首。
即ち入唐大使藤原朝臣清河に賜へり。

大船に真楫繁貫きこの吾子を韓国へ遣る斎へ神たち

大船に左右の楫を一面に通して、この子を唐へ遣わす。祝福を与えよ。神々たちよ。

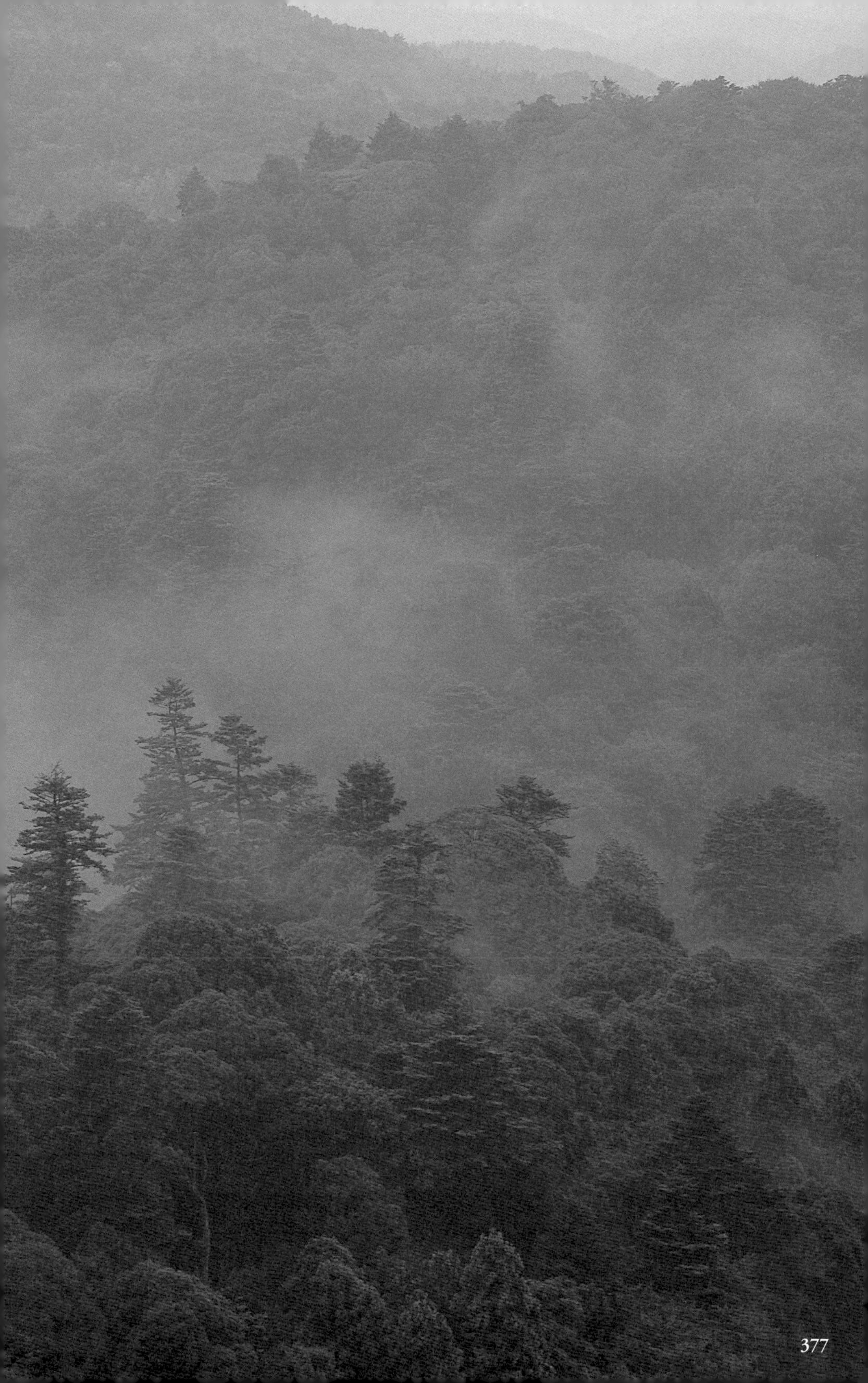

A banquet poem given to the local officials during celebrations at the provincial government office in the land of Inaba, on New Year's day in the third year (of Tempyō Hōji, 759)

Let good fortune
accumulate even more
like the snow that falls this day,
    this first day,
at the beginning of a new year.

4516

四五一六

三年の春正月一日に、因幡国の庁にして、饗を国郡の司等に賜へる宴の歌一首

新しき年の始の初春の今日降る雪のいや重け吉事

新しい年のはじめの、新春の今日を降りしきる雪のように、いっそう重なれ、吉き事よ。

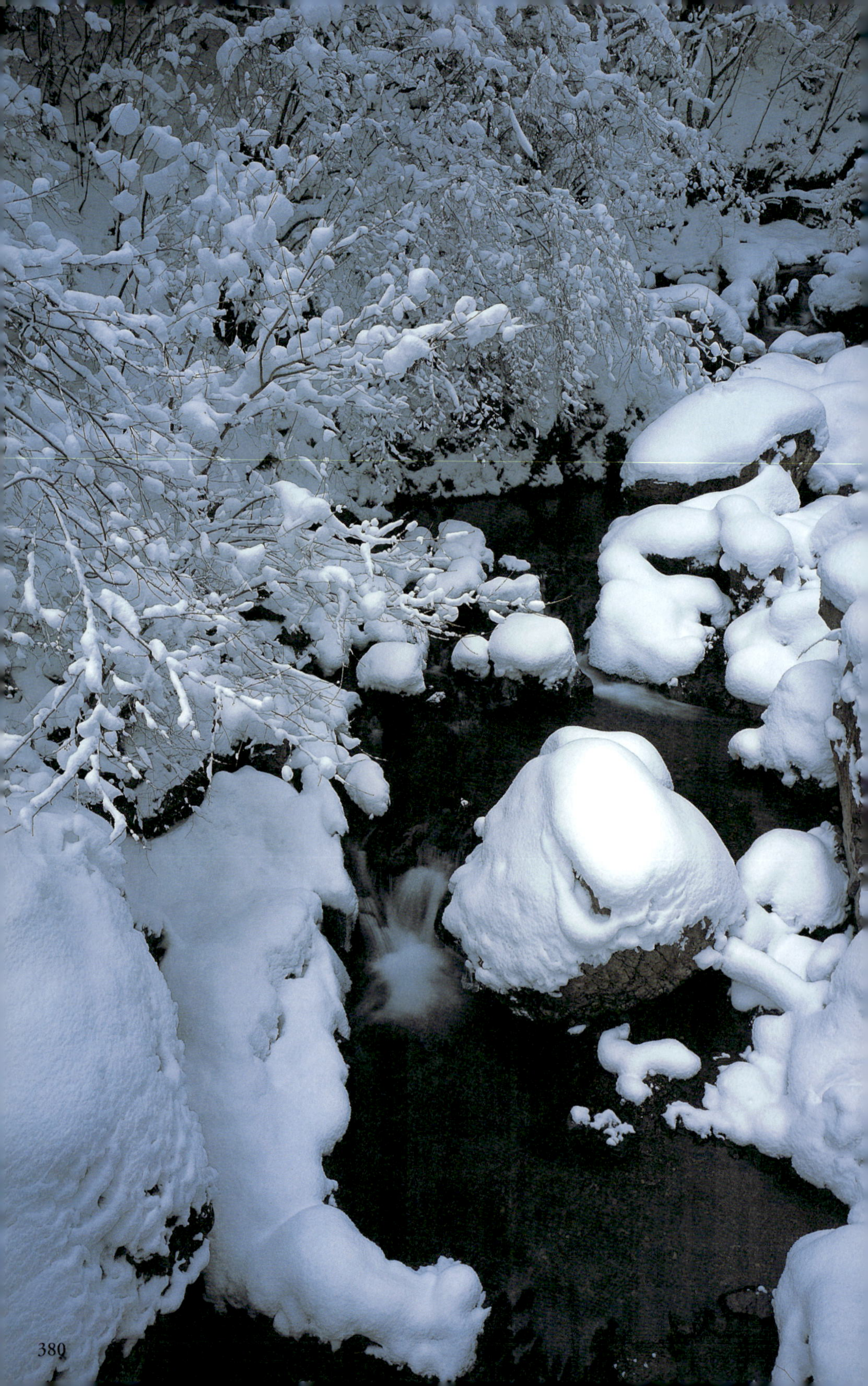

008	Image of Buddha at Asuka-dera Temple
	Asuka, Asukamura, Nara
012	Tamonten (One of the Four Deva Kings) at Kaidan'in Hall
	Todai-ji Temple, Nara
016	Gurdian Deity at Shinyakushi-ji Temple, Takabatake-cho, Nara
020-021	Inabuchi, Asukamura, Nara
024-025	Kawakami-cho, Nara
028-029	Fujie, Akashi-shi, Hyogo
033	Yatakyuryo, Nara
036-037	View from Kamisenbon, Yoshino-cho, Nara
040-041	Lake Biwa
	Onoe, Kozuki-cho, Shiga
044-045	Yoshino River
	Miyataki, Yoshino-cho, Nara
049	Yoshino River
	Miyataki, Yoshino-cho, Nara
052-053	Kagiroi-no-oka
	Sakoma, Ouda-cho, Uda-gun, Nara
056-057	Sakoma, Ouda-cho, Uda-gun, Nara
060-061	Hihara-no-sato, Chihara, Sakurai-shi, Nara
065	Kokuzo-bosatsu statue at Horin-ji Temple
	Mii, Ikaruga-cho, Ikoma-gun, Nara
068-069	Minakami-ike, Saki-cho, Nara
072-073	Yoshino Mountains, Yoshino-cho, Nara
076-077	Shosoin, Zoushi-cho, Nara
080-081	Tomb of Iwanohimenomikoto at Saki-cho, Nara
084-085	Otabisho Detached Shrine of Kasuga Wakamiya Deity, Nara
088-089	Hosokawa, Asukamura, Nara
092-093	Miho-no-Matsubara, Shimizu-shi, Shizuoka
096-097	Lake Biwa, Onoe, Kozuki-cho, Shiga
100-101	Oso, Asukamura, Nara
105	Nijo Mountain, Taima-cho, Nara
108-109	Jogo, Asukamura, Nara
112-113	Sakoma, Ouda-cho, Nara
116-117	Inabuchi, Asukamura, Nara
120	Akino, Sakoma, Ouda-cho, Nara
124-125	Primeval forest in Kasuga, Nara
128-129	Iimori Mountain, Kawakami-cho, Nara

132-133	Senjyojiki, Shirahama-cho, Wakayama
136-137	Fire of Shunie at Nigatsudo in Todaiji Temple, Nara
140-141	Echizen Beach, Fukui
145	Fujie, Akashi-shi, Hyogo
148-149	Lake Biwa, Onoe, Kozuki-cho, Shiga
152-153	Stream of Kisa, Kisadani, Yoshino-cho, Nara
156-157	Mt. Fuji, Narusawamura, Minami-Tsuru-gun, Yamanashi
161	Mt. Fuji, Narusawamura, Minami-Tsuru-gun, Yamanashi
164-165	View of Mt. Fuji from the shores of the Okitsugawa River estuary
168-169	Mt. Fuji, Gotenba-shi, Shizuoka
172-173	Mt. Fuji, Narusawamura, Minami-Tsuru-gun, Yamanashi
176-177	View from Nara Okuyama Drive way, Kawakami-cho, Nara
180-181	Wakamiya Shrine, Kasuga Taisha, Nara
185	Suzaku Gate at Site of Heijo-kyu, Nara
188	Ridge-end Ornamental Tile, at Site of Heijo-kyu, Nara
189	Cherry Blossom at Kiko Temple, Nara
192-193	Bugaku play at the Garden, Kasuga Taisha, Nara
196-197	Gulf of Hakata, Fukuoka
200-201	Lake Biwa, Chinaihama, Makino-cho, Shiga
204-205	Asuka River, Inabuchi, Asukamura, Nara
208-209	Sky from Site of Heijo-kyu, Nara
212-213	Kasugaokuyama, Nara
216-217	Tomb of Azumishinno at Shirasu, Watsuka-cho, Soraku-gun, Kyoto
221	Saho River, Kawakami-cho, Nara
225	Mifune fall, Ikari River, Ikari, Kawakamimura, Yoshino-gun, Nara
228-229	Buddhist Painting at Chisoku-in Temple, Todai-ji Temple, Nara
232-233	Asuka River, Inabuchi, Asukamura, Nara
237	Lily at Miwa Shrine, Sakurai-shi, Nara
240-241	Saho River, Funahashi cho, Nara
244-245	Ikari River, Ikari, Kawakamimura, Yoshino-gun, Nara
248	Tenjukoku Shuchozanketsu, Chugu-ji Temple, Ikaruga-cho, Ikoma-gun, Nara
249	Iimori, Kawakami-cho, Nara
252-253	Sekibutsugan Shakanyorai at Jurin-in Temple, Jurinin-cho, Nara
257	Mask of Gigaku, Todai-ji Temple, Nara

260	Lake Yamanaka, Yamanakakomura, Yamanashi
261	Soul Consolation Ritual at Isonokami Shrine, Tenri-shi, Nara
264-265	Iimori, Kawakami-cho, Nara
268	Mii, Ikaruga-cho, Ikoma-gun, Nara
269	Odanaka-cho, Tenri-shi, Nara
272-273	Anou, Nishi-Yoshinomura, Yoshino-gun, Nara
276-277	Rokuyaon-cho, Nara
281	Suzaku Gate at Site of Heijo-kyu, Nara
284-285	Part of Lotus Shaped Pedestal for Buddha Image at Todai-ji Temple, Nara
288-289	Iimori, Kawakami-cho, Nara
292-293	Yamato-mai for Kasuga Festival at Kasuga-Taisha, Nara
296-297	Byakugoji-cho, Nara
300-301	Minakami-ike, Hokkeji-cho, Nara
304-305	Lotus Flowers
309	Nishi-no-kyo, Hichijo Oike, Nara
312-313	Site of Daikandai-ji, Asukamura, Nara
317	Hosotani River, Kasugano-cho, Nara
320-321	Stream of Kisa, Kisadani River, Yoshinoyama, Yoshino-cho, Nara
325	Site of Heijo-kyu, Nara
328-329	Miwa Mountain, Kaminosho, Sakurai-shi, Nara
332	Hosokawa, Asukamura, Nara
333	Nishi-Kitakubo, Gose-shi, Nara
336-337	Site of Heijo-kyu, Nara
341	Okamoto, Ikaruga-cho, Ikoma-gun, Nara
344-345	Yashima-cho, Nara
348-349	Hitokotonushi Shrine, Moriwaki, Gose-shi, Nara
352-353	Nijo Mountain, Ryofuku-ji, Kashiba-shi, Nara
356	Yoshiki River, Nara-koen, Nara
357	Daibutsu Pond, Zoushi-cho, Nara
360	Shikanoshima, Fukuoka-shi, Fukuoka
361	Echizen Beach, Tsuruga-shi, Fukui
365	Echizen Beach, Fukui
368-369	Hibara-no-sato, Chihara, Sakurai-shi, Nara
372-373	Suzaku Gate at Site of Heijo-kyu, Nara
376-377	Primeval forest in Kasuga, Nara
380	Takahara River, Kawakamimura, Yoshino-gun, Nara

008	釈迦如来像 飛鳥寺
	奈良県明日香村飛鳥
012	四天王 多聞天 東大寺戒壇院
	奈良市東大寺
016	十二神将迷企羅大将
	奈良市高畑町新薬師寺
020-021	奈良県明日香村稲渕
024-025	奈良市川上町
028-029	兵庫県明石市藤江
033	奈良市矢田丘陵
036-037	奈良県吉野町上千本より
040-041	滋賀県高月町尾上（琵琶湖）
044-045	奈良県吉野町宮滝
	吉野川
049	奈良県吉野町宮滝
	吉野川
052-053	奈良県宇陀郡大宇陀町迫間
	かぎろいの丘
056-057	奈良県宇陀郡大宇陀町迫間
060-061	奈良県桜井市茅原　桧原の里
065	虚空蔵菩薩像 法輪寺
	奈良県生駒郡斑鳩町三井
068-069	奈良市佐紀町水上池
072-073	奈良県吉野町吉野山
076-077	奈良市雑司町正倉院
080-081	奈良市佐紀町　磐之媛命陵
084-085	奈良市春日大社　春日若宮おん祭　お旅所
089	奈良県明日香村細川
092-093	静岡県清水市　三保の松原
096-097	滋賀県高月町尾上（琵琶湖）
100-101	奈良県明日香村尾曽
105	奈良県当麻町　二上山
108-109	奈良県明日香村上居
112-113	奈良県大宇陀町迫間
116-117	奈良県明日香村稲渕
120	奈良県大宇陀町迫間（通称 阿紀野）

124-125	奈良市春日山原始林
128-129	奈良市川上町飯守山
132-133	和歌山県白浜町千畳敷
136-137	奈良市東大寺二月堂　修二会の火
140-141	福井県越前海岸
145	兵庫県明石市藤江
148-149	滋賀県高月町尾上（琵琶湖）
152-153	奈良県吉野町喜佐谷（象の小川）（喜佐川）
156-157	山梨県南都留郡鳴沢村　富士山五合目より
161	山梨県南都留郡鳴沢村　富士山
164-165	興津川河口沖より富士山を眺める
168-169	静岡県御殿場市より　富士山
172-173	山梨県南都留郡鳴沢村　富士山
176-177	奈良市川上町奈良奥山ドライブウェイより
180-181	奈良市春日大社　若宮神社
184-185	奈良市平城宮跡朱雀門
188	奈良市平城宮跡出土鬼瓦
189	奈良市喜光寺山桜
192-193	奈良市春日大社　神苑での舞楽
196-197	福岡市博多湾
200-201	滋賀県マキノ町知内浜（琵琶湖）
204-205	奈良県明日香村稲渕（飛鳥川）
208-209	奈良市平城宮跡の空
212-213	奈良春日奥山
216-217	京都府相楽郡和束町白栖（聖武天皇の皇子　安積親王の墓）
221	奈良市川上町佐保川
225	奈良県吉野郡川上村　井光川上流　御船の滝
228-229	奈良市東大寺知足院　六道絵
232-233	奈良県明日香村稲渕（飛鳥川）
237	奈良県桜井市大神神社　笹ゆり
240-241	奈良市船橋町佐保川
244-245	奈良県吉野郡川上村井光　井光川
248	奈良県生駒郡斑鳩町中宮寺　天寿国繍帳残欠
249	奈良市川上町飯守
252-253	奈良市十輪院町十輪院　石仏龕釈迦如来
257	奈良市東大寺　伎楽面　行道

260	山梨県山中湖村　山中湖
261	奈良県天理市石上神宮（鎮魂祭灯火）
264-265	奈良市川上町飯守
268	奈良県生駒郡斑鳩町三井
269	奈良県天理市小田中町
272-273	奈良県吉野郡西吉野村賀名生
276-277	奈良市鹿野園町
281	奈良市平城宮跡朱雀門
284-285	奈良市東大寺大仏殿　蓮辨
288-289	奈良市川上町飯守
292-293	奈良市春日大社　春日祭　和舞
296-297	奈良市白毫寺町
300-301	奈良市法華寺町水上池
304-305	蓮の花
309	奈良市七条大池（西の京）
312-313	奈良市明日香村大官大寺跡付近
317	奈良市春日野町細谷川
320-321	奈良県吉野町吉野山喜佐谷川（象の小川）
325	奈良市平城宮跡
328-329	奈良県桜井市上之庄　三輪山
332	奈良県明日香村細川
333	奈良県御所市西北窪
336-337	奈良市平城宮跡
341	奈良県生駒郡斑鳩町岡本
344-345	奈良市八島町
348-349	奈良県御所市森脇　一言主神社
352-353	奈良県香芝市良福寺　千股池より二上山
356	奈良市奈良公園吉城川
357	奈良市雑司町大仏池
360	福岡県福岡市志賀島
361	福井県敦賀市越前海岸
365	福井県越前海岸
368-369	奈良県桜井市茅原（桧原の里）
372-373	奈良市平城宮跡朱雀門
376-377	奈良市春日山原始林
380	奈良県吉野郡川上村高原川

リービ英雄（リービ・ひでお）　1950年、アメリカ生まれ。　1967年にはじめて日本に移り住み、以降、日米往環をくり返し、その間プリンストン大学、スタンフォード大学で日本文学の教授をつとめ、1982年、『万葉集』の英訳により全米図書賞を受賞。　処女作『星条旗の聞こえない部屋』（講談社）は、西洋出身者が日本語で書いたはじめての現代文学として高い評価を獲得し、第14回野間文芸新人賞を受賞。　主な著書に、『日本語の勝利』『アイデンティティーズ』『国民のうた』（講談社）、『新宿の万葉集』（朝日新聞社）、『日本語を書く部屋』（岩波書店）。

井上博道（いのうえはくどう）　1931年、兵庫県生まれ。　産経新聞大阪本社編集局写真部を経てフリーの写真家となる。　1983年から1997年まで大阪芸術大学写真学科勤務。　主な著書に『東大寺』(中央公論社)、『やまとのかたち』、『やまとのこころ』、『日本の庭園』(講談社)、『隠れた仏たち』(営生社)、『奈良万葉』(光村推古書院)、『日本の壁』(駸々堂)、『隠れた仏たち』(学生社)、『室生寺』(淡交社)。　龍谷大学より龍谷賞授与、他。　日本写真家協会会員。

高岡一弥（たかおかかずや）　1945年、京都府生まれ。　アートディレクター。　主な著書に『千年』(毎日新聞社)、『野菜から見た肉』(パルコ出版)、『春・観る』(時事通信社)、『女性とエイズ』『Quality of Life』(日本財団)、『katachi』(ピエ・ブックス)、雑誌『活人』少女光線、日本未少年(毎日新聞社)。　『彼方へ』『東京LIVING WITH AIDS & HIV』等、展覧会イベントを主催。　日宣美展特選、日本グラフィックデザイン展金賞、講談社出版文化賞受賞、他。

本書は『万葉集』についての学術的な専門書ではありません。
歌のページに記載された数字はそれぞれの歌番号を示しています。
また、歌が収められている巻数は省略しました。
長歌は一部抜粋して掲載しているものがあります。
本書に収録した歌の読み下し文および口訳は、
中西 進『万葉集 全訳注原文付』
全四巻別巻一巻（講談社文庫）を底本にしました。

The numbers at the bottom of each page
correspond to the numbers
assigned to each poem in the original text;
the volume numbers are not given.
Some of the longer poems appear as excerpts.

Man'yō Luster 万葉集

2002年2月5日　第1刷発行
2003年8月2日　第4刷発行

英訳　リービ英雄
写真　井上博道
アートディレクション　高岡一弥

デザイン　伊藤修一　淡海季史子
制作進行　岸田麻矢

編集　高岡一弥

発行者　三芳伸吾
発行所　ピエ・ブックス
〒170-0005 東京都豊島区南大塚2-32-4
編集　Tel: 03-5395-4820　Fax: 03-5395-4821
　　　　E-mail: editor@piebooks.com
営業　Tel: 03-5395-4811　Fax: 03-5395-4812
　　　　E-mail: sales@piebooks.com
http://www.piebooks.com

印刷・製本　株式会社サンニチ印刷

Photographs copyright ©2002 Hakudo Inoue
English Text copyright ©2002 Ian Hideo Levy
Text copyright ©2002 Susumu Nakanishi
Book and cover design ©2002 Kazuya Takaoka
Published by PIE BOOKS

ISBN4-89444-186-1 C0072
Printed in Japan

本書の収録内容の無断転載、複写、引用等を禁じます。
落丁・乱丁はお取り替えいたします。